Playing Ourselves

Playing Ourselves

Interpreting Native Histories at Historic Reconstructions

Laura Peers

ALTAMIRA
PRESS

ROWMAN & LITTLEFIELD PUBLISHERS, INC.
Lanham • New York • Toronto • Plymouth, UK

ALTAMIRA PRESS
A division of Rowman & Littlefield Publishers, Inc.
A wholly owned subsidary of The Rowman & Littlefield Publishing Group, Inc.
4501 Forbes Boulevard, Suite 200
Lanham, MD 20706
www.altamirapress.com

Estover Road
Plymouth PL6 7PY
United Kingdom

Some material drawn from "Playing Ourselves: First Nations/Native American
Interpreters at Living History Sites," by Laura Peers, in *The Public Historian* 21.4,
and "Fur Trade History, Native History, Public History: Communication and
Miscommunication," by Laura Peers, in *New Faces of the Fur Trade*, eds. Jo-Anne
Diske, Susan Sleeper Smith, and William Wicken, Michigan State University Press,
1998.

British Library Cataloguing in Publication Information Available

Library of Congress Cataloguing-in-Publication Data

Peers, Laura L. (Laura Lynn)
   Playing ourselves : interpreting Native histories at historic reconstructions / Laura
Peers.
      p. cm.—(American Association for State and Local History book series)
   Includes bibliographical references and index.
   ISBN-13: 978-0-7591-1061-8 (cloth : alk. paper)
   ISBN-10: 0-7591-1061-1 (cloth : alk. paper)
   ISBN-13: 978-0-7591-1062-5 (pbk. : alk. paper)
   ISBN-10: 0-7591-1062-X (pbk. : alk. paper)
   1. Indians of North America—Museums. 2. Historic sites—Interpretive programs—
North America. 3. Intercultural communication. 4. Museum techniques. 5. Indians in
popular culture. 6. Indians of North America—Public opinion. I. Title.

E76.85.P44 2007
970.004'970075—dc22   2006101547

Printed in the United States of America

∞™ The paper used in this publication meets the minimum requirements of American
National Standard for Information Sciences—Permanence of Paper for Printed Library
Materials, ANSI/NISO Z39.48-1992.

Contents

List of Figures

LANDSCAPES

COSMOLOGIES

ANISHINAABEG

AUTHENTICITIES AND MATERIALITIES

VISITORS

Acknowledgments

This research could not have been undertaken without the permission and generous assistance of administrative and interpretive staff at the historic sites where I worked for several periods across a decade. Some of these individuals have since moved on from working at historic sites and others preferred not to have their names recorded, but I would especially like to thank: at Lower Fort Garry National Historic Site, Robert Andrews, Ruth Christie, Gisele Gauthier, Ken Green, Tom Kynman, Dave McVetty, Leah Still, Steve Greyeyes, and Elena Vandale. At Parks Canada, Bob Coutts and Kathleen Dahlin. At Fort William Historical Park, Sheena Albanese, Peter Boyle, Cecilia Littlewolf-Walker, Freda McDonald, Ann Magiskan, Paul Ruebsam, and Arla Singleton. At the North West Company Fur Post, Della Baker, Sandy Gimple, Robert Gimple, Carolyn Maack, Patrick Schifferdecker, Mary Ann Vanderpoel, and Audrey Wyman. At Colonial Michilimackinac, David Armour, Steve Brisson, Keith Knecht, Annette Naganash, and Phil Porter. At Sainte-Marie among the Hurons, Yvonne and Marie Brunelle, Pierre Lefaive, Del Taylor, and Rosemary Vyvyan. At Colonial Williamsburg, Rex Ellis, Travis Henline, Robin Reed, and Bill Weldon. To these individuals, and the many others at these places who struggle each day with the past, I offer my sincere admiration and thanks.

When I first began researching First Nations histories, I did so because I had met strong tribal survivors who were nowhere to be found in the existing academic literature. I also found such people working at historic sites, struggling to tell their own and their peoples' stories in their own voices, and I thank them for letting me see their inspiring courage, determination, strength, anger, and joy.

On two separate research trips to Winnipeg, Maureen Matthews and Jennifer S. H. Brown and her husband Wilson Brown not only hosted me and drove me about, but also lent their perspectives and photographic expertise. Their support has made much of this work possible.

Within the community of public historians, I must single out David Neufeld, Bob Coutts, and Michael Payne for stimulating and tolerant companionship over the years. Since moving to Oxford, colleagues in the School of Anthropology have provided opportunities to try out new ideas, and I would especially like to thank Elizabeth Edwards, Marcus Banks, and Clare Harris. Nick Stanley of the Birmingham Institute of Art and Design and Joy Hendry of Oxford Brookes University helped me to clarify my thoughts and encouraged me at crucial moments. Several of my students have contributed significantly to the volume: Meghan O'Brien, whose work on English reenactors and issues of identity has been fun to think with, Noel Lobley who helped to retrieve relevant literature, and Cat Roberts who was invaluable in sorting the references and smoothing the manuscript.

Crucial funding for initial fieldwork in 1994 was provided by the School of Graduate Studies, McMaster University, and by a Social Sciences and Humanities Research Council of Canada Doctoral Fellowship, and for the 2005 revisits and updates by the British Academy. The Institute of Social and Cultural Anthropology at Oxford also generously contributed funds for equipment and student assistance in 2005.

This work began as my Ph.D. dissertation. My supervisor, Trudy Nicks, and the members of my committee, Bill Rodman, Wayne Warry (all of McMaster University), and Tom Hill (then Director of the Woodland Cultural Centre), were supportive, enthusiastic, and constructively critical of this project from proposal to defense. They made the dissertation an unusually enjoyable experience.

Earlier versions of portions of the material in this book were published in *The Public Historian* (1999) and in *New Faces of the Fur Trade* (eds. Jo-Anne Fiske, Susan Sleeper Smith, and William Wicken, Michigan State University, 1998).

Drew Davey, husband extraordinaire, contributed vital photographic skills and theoretical perspectives, warded off overenthusiastic voyageurs, drove me about, and learned to throw a tomahawk much better than I did. I would like to thank him for being there, then and always.

Vignette: Ruth Christie, Lower Fort Garry National Historic Site

Ruth Christie, an interpreter at this 1850s fur trade site, is a grandmother and Elder who is descended from local Aboriginal and Métis families. She has a formidable command of northern Cree and Ojibwa cultures, and has read every scholarly publication on local Aboriginal history she could find: she is a highly knowledgeable historian, well versed in nineteenth-century material culture and social relations, able to recite a Standard of Trade, and well aware of who married whom around Lower Fort Garry in the 1850s. This morning she is walking across the site from the staff changing area in one of the historic buildings inside the fort's stone walls, to the Native encampment area. She is wearing replica clothing appropriate to one of the local northern Cree women who lived near the fort: moccasins, leggings, trade cloth dress, trade blanket coat, necklaces of trade beads. She looks every bit the part of her great-grandmother, whom she likes to portray.

As she approaches the tipis and fishing nets in the Native encampment, she waves hello to a group of schoolchildren who are coming onsite with their teacher for the first educational program of the day. One of the children—a boy of about six or seven—breaks away from the group and runs over to her. Folding one arm across his body and raising the other with palm toward Ruth, the child says loudly: "UGH! HOW! OOGEMAGOOGEMA! DO YOU SPEAKUM REAL INJUN?"

Ruth's eyebrows vanish into her headscarf, and she says with some force, "Well, my people say 'Ahneen' to say hello, and you are being rude!" The boy, looking quelled, goes back to his group. Ruth stares after him for a moment, and then moves on toward the encampment to light the campfire and furnish the area with Native artifacts for the day's work.

Introduction

The encounter between elder Ruth Christie and a Manitoba schoolboy that you have just read was the starting point for the present volume. I was at Lower Fort Garry National Historic Site that day because after doing extensive archival research on Cree and Ojibwa peoples in the nineteenth-century community of which the fort had been part, I disagreed with details of the site's depiction of them. After complaining to site managers about the machine-sewn canvas tipis and dubious claims to be "fishing for the tribe" made by interpreters, I had been invited to discuss what was needed for a more accurate representation of Aboriginal lives in the 1850s. If I came on site as an ethnohistorian, though, I left it as an anthropologist. The child's disrespectful behavior went far beyond the usual playfulness that visitors enjoy when visiting such places, and seemed to be provoked by Ruth's historical appearance. It was as if he were programmed to respond automatically to the sight of "an Indian." The encounter made me wonder whether the machine-sewn canvas tipis that initially triggered my ire were a problem not just because they differed from the bark-covered lodges that Ojibwa people used historically, but because they served as powerful symbols against which the sight of "an Indian" would provoke a stereotyped response from many visitors. And then I wondered about the motivations and efficacy of people like Ruth Christie, who is a generous teacher, knowledgeable about her own history and culture, who wants to intervene in the misinformation that many visitors bring with them to these places.

One of the most important—and difficult—recent developments in the field of public history in North America has been the addition of First Nations and Native American people and their histories to existing historic sites. This has been a widespread development, and has occurred in a professional and

political context in which it has become important to make our representations of the past more inclusive. This set of changes has been driven both
from the top down (by heritage agencies, tribal groups, and site managers)
and from the bottom up (by front-line interpreters and visitors). There has
been a great deal of good will for these revisions, and a sense of necessity in
making them. Actually making these changes, however, has been a near-
impossible task: the addition of major themes at a time of falling budgets and
visitor numbers; the dilemmas raised when the addition of tribal histories and
perspectives challenge established understandings of the past; and the essential challenge of confronting visitor misinformation about Native peoples and
Native-White relations. While some public history professionals may rue the
day they opened this Pandora's box, others are powerfully motivated to discuss Native histories in Native voices, and to address the legacies of the past:
"If we can just reach one person, teach one person that we are real human beings, then it's all worth it" (Marie Brunelle, retired Native interpreter at Sainte
Marie among the Hurons, interview July 28, 1995). For Native peoples, implementing changes at historic sites is linked to self-determination, cultural
survival, and sovereignty: teaching about the past in order to change the present and future.

    This book explores the process and implications of adding Native Ameri-
can and First Nations staff and themes to reconstructed historic sites, which
are also known as "living history" sites. There are thousands of such places
across North America. They attempt to evoke and teach about—to "bring to
life," as their marketing departments say—the past, by using period buildings
and furnishings and by stationing in those buildings knowledgeable staff who
are wearing replica period clothing to "interpret" aspects of life in the past to
visitors in the present.[1] The sites I have worked with all have an explicitly educational mandate and are affiliated with public heritage agencies linked in
various ways with state, provincial, or national government departments of
heritage or tourism. These sites, which are funded partly by government and
partly from commercial revenues, market themselves as educational and
recreational venues for schoolchildren, local families, and tourists. They are
very successful in this, for their multisensory form of communication is compelling in the vividness of the physical details experienced by visitors and reinforced by conversations with interpreters.

    Our understanding of life in the past, of course, has changed over time, as
new research findings emerge and new resonances between current events
and those of the past imbue certain elements of history with more weight.
Living history sites have never been frozen in time; their furnishings, costumes, building details, and messages have changed, too. The social history
movement in academic and public history since the 1960s has brought a huge

shift in emphasis from the lives and material details of upper-class people to those of working-class and ethnic backgrounds, as well as a new focus on women, and a corresponding shift from political history to the everyday lives of people engaged in it. Across the same period, popular and scholarly understandings of the dynamics of power within society also affected our understanding of history. Living history sites have changed to reflect this more politicized, socially nuanced view of the past and to show how power and politics affected the lives of all people in society.

The most challenging alterations to living history sites have involved issues of race and culture. Portraying the lives of African Americans, Native Americans, First Nations, and Métis peoples has demanded not only new staff, new costumes, and new props and buildings, but real challenges to the stories that living history sites tell about the past. They also involve acknowledging the damaging legacies of the past that still affect minority peoples.

Such revisionist portrayals challenge underlying beliefs about the past that function to legitimate relations between majority society and minority groups within Canada and the United States today. In particular, the stories told about the colonial past—about the nature of the fur trade and early exploration, about the struggle for and conquest of the frontier—function in North America as origin myths that continue to underpin majority society. Myths are moral narratives that make sense of the world, a framework within which all actions are understandable. Myths can be the most deeply true stories we know, and we cling to them to uphold our identity and to justify our actions. The common assumption by settlers during the colonial era (and by the majority of the middle class since) was that their society was superior to tribal ones; that the dynamics of the frontier had an inevitable plot; that tribal peoples should conform to a certain image of the Noble and Authentic Savage, untainted by adaptation to historical reality, if they wished to maintain a (marginalized) place within North American society—these myths are still woven into our society today.[2] They are most often articulated as stereotypes, as racism, or as a dismissal of the legitimacy of contemporary Native cultures. They have also been articulated in narratives told by historians about the past, stories that, as Laurel Thatcher Ulrich has noted (2001:250), "transformed the violence of colonial conquest into a frontier pastoral." Native peoples are shown only in certain roles within these stories: as savages resisting that frontier pastoral and the "inevitable" march of settler society, or as marginalized, leprechaun- or childlike figures who existed within it. Such roles, and stories, were shown as truths at public history sites (as well as in academic texts) until very recently. Many members of the public continue to believe in these myths and these versions of history. Challenging them directly by giving revisionist interpretations of the past and of Native cultures and histories is crucial. It is also contested, and fraught for those who do this work.

This study is, then, an ethnography of the way that representations of Native cultures and certain kinds of historic Native-White relations have changed at public history sites, and the implications of these changes for the present. I focus on the enactment at reconstructed historic sites of early situations of sustained contact between Native and non-Native peoples. For consistency, I have narrowed my research sites to those depicting fur trade and mission settings of the seventeenth through nineteenth centuries around the Great Lakes: Lower Fort Garry (LFG), a mid-nineteenth century Hudson's Bay Company shipping depot near present-day Winnipeg; Fort William Historical Park (FWHP), a major North West Company post and shipping depot at present-day Thunder Bay, which portrays life around 1815; the North West Company Fur Post (NWCFP), an 1804–1805 wintering post at Pine City, Minnesota, where furs and "country goods" were traded from local Ojibwa people; Colonial Michilimackinac (CM), an eighteenth-century logistical and military nexus for the Great Lakes fur trade, at the Straits of Mackinac; and Sainte-Marie among the Hurons (SMAH), a Jesuit mission dating to the 1640s, near present-day Midland, Ontario. These sites were chosen to reflect a range of historic contact situations, and an equal range of site sizes, visitor numbers, budgets, and institutional affiliations in the present. I desired this range to allow me to see patterns in the representation of Native histories: commonalities in budget and staff allocations in various parts of the reconstructions, visitor responses to Native interpreters, the special approach of Native interpreters to their work, and the problems sites have faced in incorporating Native staff and perspectives.

In analyzing these reconstructions, I ask a series of core questions: How have the Native areas and elements of the sites developed, and what messages are they intended to convey? What do these presentations of Native cultures and histories mean to visitors? How do the additions of Native staff and perspectives merge or clash with the historical narratives these places have traditionally told? To what extent do these places present Native perspectives on the past that may be oppositional to traditional history, and how do visitors receive such challenges? And what does the telling of their histories in these settings mean to the Native people who do this work? These places may depict the past, but as I will argue, they can also be seen as a social phenomenon, with their shifting performances of the past reflecting political and social concerns in the present.

Representing racial and cross-cultural issues in the past at living history sites in the present also presents the formidable challenge of how to show Native peoples and cultures to largely White audiences without falling into earlier, racist patterns of such displays at World's Fairs, zoos, and shows such as Buffalo Bill's. Simply adding Native staff to reconstructions also risks repeating dominant-society narratives about the past by reinforcing them with the presence of Native people and structures at educational, government-affiliated historic sites. Indeed, some authors (e.g., Rossel 1988; MacCannell 1984) would suggest that all ethnic or cultural tourism—firsthand witnessing of lifeways, artifacts, dance or theatrical performances, and other encounters with culture, usually indigenous culture—simply reinforces existing stereotypes and relations of power which surround minority groups.[3]

Such dangers are emphasized by the fact that many visitors bring with them very stereotyped and racist views of Native peoples and their histories. These preconceptions are brought to the fore by the physical appearance of historic reconstructions, with their palisades and spatially separated Native and non-Native areas, which evoke myths associated with the Hollywood version of frontier history: some visitors catch their first glimpse of the encampment area and cry, "Look! Real Indians!" and then sometimes break into war whoops of the kind heard in Western movies. Native staff spend much of their time and energy counteracting such stereotypes. Nevertheless, they are there precisely because they see these encounters as opportunities to correct misunderstanding and address racism. Many encounters between Native interpreters and non-Native visitors involve serious work on both sides, and show that visitors often want to get past the stereotypes and learn.

My approach to the representation of Native peoples at historic sites draws on two different scholarly literatures: that of cultural and heritage tourism, and that of museum anthropology. On the one hand, living history sites are forms of cultural representation linked to museums, whose detailed dioramas, educational purpose, emphasis on material culture, and curator-led messages parallel the fascinatingly material, education-oriented, historian-controlled spaces of historic reconstructions. While museum displays of non-Western peoples have been equally as problematic as those at World's Fairs in some ways, the sea changes that have taken place in the North American museum profession since the mid-1980s in regards to the involvement of tribal members in museum representation have made museums a key arena for debates over authority and power. Since the passage of the Native American Graves Protection and Repatriation Act (1990) and the Canadian Museums Association Task Force on Museums and First Peoples (1992), Native peoples have been acknowledged as having moral and legal rights in the stewardship of their material heritage and in the representation of their cultures and histories. Living history sites have experienced similar pressures and are seen in similar ways to museums by Native peoples.

Museum anthropology, along with anthropology and history more broadly, has also explored the culturally-constructed nature of historical and cultural representations, which are found in ethnographic and historical texts as much as museum displays and historic sites. The five sites I examine in this book are cultural representations, both of the past and in the present, reflecting not only what we think we know about the past but what we value in it, and thus reflecting society today. That they are government-sponsored institutions visited largely by members of the dominant society, and have added representations of tribal cultures and histories to their portrayal of the past, further complicates the politics of representation at these places. Historic sites share these politics with museums that represent non-Western peoples. Within museums, the display of "ethnographic" collections has in recent decades been a focus for intense debate and contestation, largely over issues of authority and voice, with non-Western peoples challenging the former right of curators and museum institutions to speak for them and to exclude them from the decision-making within processes of display. The role of power structures or authority in legitimating certain versions of the past and denying others, noted by Bruner for a "pioneer" site (2005:12), is especially sensitive in this cross-cultural version of the heritage arena.

This focus on power and authority within museums, and between museums and source communities, is part of broader challenges to other forms of cultural representation and their links to colonialism. Scholarly writing about Native peoples became a special focus of postcolonial analysis across the 1980s and 1990s, as the links between colonial relations of power and the production of knowledge about non-Western peoples were increasingly problematized (Clifford 1986, 1988; Said 1978; Trigger 1985). This was precisely the period during which historic sites were adding Native American and First Nations elements to their representations of the past. These historic sites also portray the colonial process itself, in various manifestations, which makes it doubly important that they address the legacies of colonialism within the processes of representation. Adding Native staff, buildings, props, and messages to these places is just the first step of this process.

If issues of power and authority have dominated the literature on cultural representation, the cultural tourism literature has emphasized parallel issues of authenticity and commodification. I say that these are parallel issues in that they all clearly deal with issues of power (in, for instance, who has the authority to declare a representation inauthentic, or a performed culture authentic), although they are seldom articulated in this way. As I discuss further in the chapter on Native staff, *Anishinaabeg*, I find much of the literature on these issues problematic in that it seems to assume the existence of a primeval Noble Savage who somehow becomes inauthentic and "loses" a "traditional culture" because of having the business sense to create a performance to sell to tourists. Some scholars working in the field of the anthropology of tourism have claimed that cultural tourism is a form of oppression in that it relies on the public performance of stereotyped and shallow elements of culture, and that such performances limit the nature of interaction and understanding between Native peoples and audiences: repeating, in essence, the controlling dynamics of colonialism. Most distressingly, despite the emphasis within anthropological debates on issues of voice and representation, I find very few direct quotes in the literature on cultural tourism by indigenous performers, either on what they do and why, or on their own perspectives on these debates.[4]

In contrast, I would argue that the work of Native interpreters at living history sites amounts to cultural performance in a different sense: ethno-protest, a critique of established relationships and received knowledge held by visitors, and a way of resisting authority and the status quo (and see Kapchan 1995:482). More than any other changes to these sites, the presence and work of Native interpreters means that these places are telling different stories about the past than they used to.

Despite my reservations about the literature on cultural tourism, I have worked with several core ideas arising from it. I seek to understand the perspectives of tourists as well as those of Native peoples, and to analyze the encounters between them. I explore whether heritage and cultural tourism does in fact reinforce existing social structure and relations of power between peoples of different social classes and races. I also wrestle with the concept of the "tourist gaze," articulated especially by John Urry (1990), which is useful for its explication of the ways that tourists read (their own) cultural meanings into the places they go to see, but limits our understanding of what else happens at historic sites. The tourists I interviewed certainly tended to read palisades and Native camps in ways that were "socially organised and systematised," as Urry suggests the "tourist gaze" is, and which echoed the relationships they assumed existed between settlers and Native peoples, past and present. What Urry, and the many others who use this idea of "gazing" seem not to see is the return gaze, and the attempts of Native peoples to disrupt tourists' preconceptions. Nor does this literature examine the motivations of Native people who work in the heritage sector, or the broader social benefits that can be gained from encounters such as are examined here. Whether one believes in, or doubts, the hegemonic quality of "the tourist gaze" has much to do with one's beliefs about the efficacy of these encounters, and having seen many such encounters between tourists and Native interpreters, I am a firm believer that these are terribly important moments which can, potentially, lead to change.

There is another set of perspectives that needs to be taken into account when discussing historic reconstructions, and that is the pragmatic realities of public history: funding, budgets, visitor numbers, health and safety issues, and the legalities of hiring only Native people for certain jobs at historic sites.

Indeed, one historic site manager, participating in a discussion on the nuances and theory of issues of cultural representation, once remarked to me, "this is all right for you academics, but I have a program to run on Monday." The logistics of unlocking a site, filling in time sheets, training staff, sourcing and ordering replacement props, dealing with rotting palisades, and implementing directives from higher up in the heritage agency (not to mention budget cuts from state and provincial budgets) means that site managers often feel that analyses such as are the focus of this book are not, frankly, terribly important. I hope in the coming chapters to explore ways in which they are. I don't think that academic and managerial perspectives on historic reconstructions can always be reconciled, but I do believe one should be aware of the ways in which they are entangled.

One way in which all of these perspectives are entangled is that historic reconstructions function as forums for cross-cultural relations, on staff and between staff and visitors. The concept of the "contact zone" is now a core analytical structure within anthropological and historical scholarship, and has been used to understand touristic encounters, especially involving indigenous peoples (Harrison 2003, Bruner 2005:17). As originally defined by Mary Louise Pratt (1992:4), contact zones are "social spaces where disparate cultures meet, clash, and grapple with each other." This "contact perspective" sees "the relations among colonizers and colonized . . . in terms of copresence, interaction, interlocking understandings and practices, often within radically asymmetrical relations of power." James Clifford, extending Pratt's idea to analyze a cross-cultural encounter within the Portland Art Museum, shows how museums and other spaces of cultural representation can become such spaces (1997).

I would add to Pratt's and Clifford's use of this concept that contact zones can also be places of stimulation, where peoples of different cultural backgrounds learn from one another and try to understand each other, however imperfectly. Such spaces are uncertain, and constrained by overarching relations of power, but allowing within interactions the contestation of hegemony, Native agency, and settler dependence (Pratt 1992:4; Harrison 2003:38). I argue that as soon as one adds Native staff to a living history site—especially to a site emphasizing the culture of European settlers—a contact zone is created in which visitors and interpreters interact. Quite often, visitors are meeting Native people for the first time in these spaces: these are, in their own way, first encounters. For Native interpreters, the arena created by these sites offers a space within which to articulate identity and cultural difference: to assert, in the face of centuries of scholarly and popular historical narratives, their ancestors' worth and dignity; to contest stereotypes and misinformation; and to insist on the right to tell their own stories, in their own voices.

More broadly, these historic sites are arenas in which Native peoples challenge majority society in North America: challenge their stories and myths, challenge their histories, challenge structures of power. It was no accident that museums, as institutions symbolic of the controlling authority of the nation-state, became important sites of contestation' for Native peoples in North America. Changing relations of power within museums has been a key part of the process of changing relations of power between Native peoples and the dominant society more broadly across the continent. This process is still very much ongoing, and historic reconstructions that have added Native representations are part of it. Examining how change has proceeded at historic sites functions as a lens through which to see the wider social and political dynamics involving Native peoples in North American society: are they excluded or included? Granted how much power? Do they exercise self-determination? How do they pursue their goals? Where is their agency stymied? What is the nature of the relationship between Native communities and the historic site, and why?

The addition of Native American, First Nations, and Métis people and histories and cultures to living history sites has therefore posed fundamental challenges to the central messages that these places communicate about the past, to assumptions about the intended audiences and functions of these places, and to the expectations visitors have about the past—as well as about Native people in the present. This is also why the public history profession needs to continue this work, and why we need to try to understand what happens when staff, visitors, and the physical elements of historic reconstructions interact.

THE PATH I CAME IN ON

This project arose from my previous research on the cultural histories of Ojibwa and northern Cree peoples (Peers 1994; Peers and Brown 1988). During this time, I became intrigued at the often shallow ways these people have been represented in museums and scholarly texts. My interest in public history stemmed from a desire to communicate new findings about Native histories to a broad audience, and from a dissatisfied response to a specific reconstruction that portrayed a period with which I was familiar from archival research. As I began working with historic sites, I began to understand how complex these places are as forms of communication, and how many agendas are behind what the public sees as "authentic history."

I also began to appreciate the enormity of the revisions that these sites were trying to make. As with their textual parents, historic sites have traditionally emphasized the roles of Europeans in establishing colonial culture in the wilderness, and have minimized the roles of Native participants. When first reconstructed (which for the sites I have focused on, was between 1960 and the mid-1970s), fur trade and mission sites typically had staff representing (and celebrating) historic European traders, priests, and other characters, but tended not to portray the Native sides of these encounters. Since the 1970s, however, in response to academic and political critiques, these sites have added Native encampments, artifacts, and staff. Some are attempting to communicate the European dependence upon and interrelationships with Native people which typified much of the early contact period, a real turnaround in core messages.

Such changes are important for contemporary Native people, for knowledge of traditional life and beliefs informs their identities today, and strengthens their determination to go forward into the future as distinct peoples. The inclusion of their histories at public sites is affirming for these communities. It also has the potential to erode prejudice in the wider society, for by demonstrating that Native peoples coped in the past, one suggests that they can in the present, and by examining cross-cultural relationships in the past, it suggests that these are possible in the present as well.

Historic reconstructions still have far to go before they accurately depict most situations of contact between Native peoples and newcomers in North America. Despite all the research that goes into them, sites depict Native people in limited roles, often less important ones than they actually played: they may only be shown trading furs, for instance, instead of also supplying food or engaging in serious political negotiations. Perhaps most seriously, Native-White relations are still seldom portrayed: relations between Native women and their non-Native husbands, or Native men and their non-Native sons-in-law, or Native people and traders, for instance, are very seldom depicted, especially with any hints at the practical and political implications of such relationships.

It is critical to understand the difference between the messages that are actually communicated by a site to visitors, and those that are supposed to be communicated, and to work to resolve discrepancies. If we do not, then Native areas and staff will simply suggest that Native people played supporting roles in North American history; that interaction between Natives and Whites was limited and unusual; that Native material cultures were technologically inferior to European ones; that pristine Native cultures were shattered by contact with Europeans; and that peoples of European descent "naturally" dominate Native peoples. If I am sometimes critical or impatient in my analysis of the development of Native interpretive programs, then, it is because I think that these programs matter, and that they can potentially challenge such disempowering assumptions.

In order to understand what these sites are trying to do, one needs to understand the different motives of the staff who have brought such programs into being. While many non-Native site administrators and interpreters have participated in change, and see themselves as contributing a revisionist view of the past which includes Native peoples, Native staff themselves have a distinct set of perspectives on their work. Quite often, Native interpreters stated to me that they felt they were "playing themselves." "We are playing ourselves," Cecilia Littlewolf-Walker said at Fort William: "the real First Nations people." Other Native interpreters used similar phrases. Despite their use of the word "playing," their sense was that they were not exactly acting—and certainly were not "playacting"—when they donned historic clothing, but that they were representing themselves in the present as well as their ancestors in the past. The phrase also suggests their intimate connections to the history they depict and the importance they place on being themselves in the face of the stereotypes through which many visitors see them. These qualities of interpretation are generally not true for non-Native interpreters. The implications of the notion of "playing ourselves" suggest that the addition of Native people and perspectives to historic sites also involves the addition of some very serious work that goes on in these otherwise somewhat ludic, fantastic, entertaining places.

The Native interpreters' statement that they are "playing themselves" is an indication that these sites are points of intersection for multiple and complex agendas and histories. The processes by which these complex representations of the past come to exist, to change, and to be communicated to the public, and the different ways in which Native and non-Native staff and visitors derive meaning from the site, are central to my analysis. I have also tried to answer the questions of Bruner and Kirshenblatt-Gimblett (1994:436):

> What is being produced here and how? How did the site arise historically? How is it staged, who has artistic control, and how does the performance develop in space and time? How is the production organized in social and economic terms, and who gets what from the event? As the [performers], . . . the tourists, and the [administrators] do not experience the site in the same way, we ask, what does the event say and what does it mean to its varied producers and audiences?

At these places, representations always have multiple interpretations; nor are they ever finalized, either in their creation or in their reception. These sites are always works in progress, continually revised through contestation, negotiation, and compromise. This struggle takes place between Native and non-Native staff, interpretive and administrative staff, administrators and government agencies, and visitors and the site in all its human and material manifestations. The expectations and meanings of historic sites may originate from each of these groups, but are revised in the communicative process that takes place between all of them.

Such complexity makes historic reconstructions an unwieldy medium in which to communicate, but their basic nature makes them a very compelling one. With their large visitorships (combined, the five sites I worked at have an annual gate of approximately 350,000), historic sites offer the potential to communicate important information about the past to large audiences. They have the potential to communicate something of the fascinating conjuncture of cultures involved in North American history, and the adaptations that the peoples who met on this continent have made to each other. They can also teach visitors about Native cultures, and about the crucial roles that Native peoples have played in the history of this continent.

METHODS

The present work has evolved over a decade that began in 1994 with an intense period of fieldwork at five sites. Since then, I have revisited sites, testing findings, training staff (several sites asked me to design or participate in training for interpreters), and doing further interviews. Crucially, this research project happened after I had established myself as an ethnohistorian with a focus on cultural continuity and change in tribal societies of the late eighteenth and early nineteenth centuries. I had written a tribal history before beginning this project (Peers 1994), and was hired by one of the sites (LFG) for the present project, to research and write a report on the nature of the Aboriginal presence on the site to underpin historic interpretation there (Peers 1995). This background proved to be most useful during the anthropological research.

During the initial period of research in 1994, and in revisits since then, I have worked with a broad spectrum of people at each site: senior administrators, staff supervisors, curators, interpreters, and visitors. Using a standard set of questions, I did informal interviews with administrators about the history and development of the Native interpretation program at each site. I did similar interviews with the senior interpreter in the Native area of the site and recorded many partial conversations (almost always interrupted by interactions with visitors) with as many interpreters as possible, Native and non-Native (and some retired interpreters), in all areas of the site. I asked about such things as their goals for the site's future; about what the historic themes for the site were, and who had decided them; about the dynamics between Native and non-Native staff; about visitor responses to various aspects of the site; and about the joys and frustrations of public history. I was made privy to a surprising amount of the politicking and gossip involved in the evolution and administration of bureaucratic institutions.

Staff were without exception enthusiastic and helpful, but the interpreters were extraordinary co-researchers. They suggested questions to ask visitors, asked questions of their own, saved up stories about incidents with visitors, and contributed crucial information and perspectives. They also made me their personal historian, and gave me questions to find answers to in the archives, which I did my best to do. This in itself helped me to understand the role these sites can play in mediating past and present: elder Ruth Christie, who portrays her own great-grandmother at Lower Fort Garry, asked me to go to the Manitoba archives and find this woman's name, which had been lost across family history; several experienced interpreters who were trying to revive traditional skills asked detailed questions about material culture which I had not considered in my earlier career as an historian of Ojibwa culture. Questions such as "as a Native interpreter working at a site portraying the 1850s, is it historically accurate for me to knit?" also turned out to be tied to broad narratives and assumptions about the past, and about Native peoples, as much as they were questions of fact, and debates about such questions have been extremely revealing.

I also worked extensively with visitors, whom I interviewed after (and sometimes during) their time in the Native area of each site, after their conversations with Native interpreters, and in the exit area of the site. For these conversations, I also used a core set of questions, which I flexed to work into the conversations. I also observed interactions between interpreters and visitors in the Native encampments, taking notes and pictures and sometimes recording. At each site, on each research visit, I accompanied daily tours and taped the interpreters' remarks and visitors' questions. These activities were crucial to understanding what goes on at the heart of these places, how information and narratives are communicated, what visitors bring with them, and how interpreters communicate their own perspectives and knowledge.

I also took a turn at being an interpreter myself. During my first stint at LFG, staff decided that my presence would be less obtrusive if I donned period clothing, so for a week I portrayed a Red River settler's mixed-blood wife bartering for moccasins with the Native women in the encampment. I was allowed to assist with interpreting, an experience which opened my eyes to the difficulties of such work and the communications skills of those who do it regularly. At other sites, when I was observing but not in period clothing, interpreters often brought me into conversations with visitors, introducing me as an historian with considerable experience in archival research on the fur trade who might have an answer to a particular question. Again, it was educational to hear the range of questions visitors ask, and to discuss with them why they were interested in such things, even if I did not have all the answers.

Speaking with visitors has proven, for me, to be the most challenging element of the methodology for this project. I have conducted hundreds of interviews with visitors at historic sites across the past decade, and found every one of them difficult. With very few exceptions, visitors to historic sites do not make site visits the sole activity of a day. They are en route to somewhere else, need to pick up a child from a play date or get to the grocery store, and are often reluctant to add more than a few minutes to their visit for a chat with an anthropologist. Indeed, site managers sometimes asked that I limit the duration of my interviews with visitors to avoid "hassling" them or leaving them with negative impressions about the site (see Harrison 2003:5). On the whole, walking up to a family group at a historic site and asking about their knowledge of Native peoples and Native-White relations, and how this had been challenged by their visit, did not produce terribly useful results. Some discussions, however, went as long as twenty minutes, and in several cases I was invited by visitors to accompany them around the site, or taken by them back to particular points on the site. I shifted the nature and wording of my core questions several times across the entire research period to improve matters, but never encountered the magic situation encountered by Julia Harrison, who—after experiences very much like mine, at tourist sites in Hawaii—found that when interviewing tourists at their homes, after their travels, her interviewees essentially wouldn't stop talking (2003: 41). In the summer of 2005 I attempted to get interviewees at historic sites to give me their contact details so I could try Harrison's technique, but found that visitors were uniformly reluctant to commit themselves to such engagement.

Photographs proved crucial to record and analyze the physical elements of these places and aspects of visitor behavior. My husband, Drew Davey, who is a professional photographer, undertook the majority of this documentation, taking hundreds of images of buildings, props, and people at each site. Drew also did large-format portraits of interpreters in historic clothing, working with them to produce collaborative portraits, a process which enhanced my understanding of the motivations and self-investment of interpreters in their work.

At each site, I have analyzed the physical layout and representations shown to compare them with known historical realities and to understand the decision-making process which resulted in what visitors actually see today. As part of this work, my archival research for Lower Fort Garry National Historic Site, to use archival materials to reconstruct the specific social, economic, and material nature of the Native presence at the fort in the mid-nineteenth century (Peers 1995), proved invaluable in understanding how historic and reconstructed versions of places differ. With this information in mind, I brought to each site the same techniques of visual analysis used by museum anthropologists to understand how the techniques of display create and confound meaning. I inventoried buildings and their contents, noted the physical positioning of elements of the site in relation to others, looked at what was actually visible to visitors rather than intended by managers, and worked with visitors to understand how the intended messages of buildings and furnishings can often be interpreted quite differently.[5] Documents that I obtained at each site about the history of the reconstruction, the development of the Native interpretation program, and plans for the future also proved helpful.

I have continued to correspond with site staff and administrators, and returned to several sites to present research findings to site staff and to do further fieldwork. On several occasions I have returned to these sites at the start of a season to assist in training staff, especially in techniques to deal with racist comments from visitors. In the summer of 2005, I did further fieldwork at Lower Fort Garry and the Northwest Company Fur Post to see what had changed over time, to test my findings, and to refresh my perspectives. E-mail and telephone communication across 2005–2006 with staff at Fort William Historical Park, Colonial Michilimackinac, and Sainte Marie among the Hurons helped me to update my understanding of those sites. All of these revisits were important opportunities to test my research findings and to keep me in touch with the sites as they have developed since the mid-1990s. I have also benefited from opportunities to present my work to public history professionals, including presentations to the members of the Ontario Museums Association at their annual meeting in 1999; at a workshop on interpreting fur trade history sponsored by major U.S. and Canadian public heritage agencies (Peers 2000); to a workshop sponsored by the National Parks Service in West Virginia in 2001; and to staff at Colonial Williamsburg when they launched a new American Indian Initiative in 2004. Feedback after these presentations has been terribly helpful. Anonymous reviewers and remarks by colleagues on articles published in *The Public Historian* (Peers 1999a), the proceedings of the Seventh North American Fur Trade Conference (Peers 1998), and the 2000 Association of Social Anthropologists conference in England (Peers 2002), have further developed my thoughts.

ON THE POLITICS OF RESEARCH

Given the challenging nature of the shifts in public history surrounding the addition of Native staff and narratives, it was perhaps inevitable that my research at these five sites tended to become part of the ongoing struggles for power and control that these revisions had sparked. Gable and Handler's statement (1993:30) that "we learned that it was not possible for us to comment, as neutral observers, on Colonial Williamsburg's history—that our interpretations would have political consequences . . . within the very 'field' to which they referred" was also true in my case—perhaps doubly so, because I was also an historian whose work was closely related to the site or was seen as a kind of historical research resource by interpreters. That I was trying to understand both the interpreters' and the administrators' perspectives, and that I would be publishing my findings, made me potentially useful to both groups, between whom I often found myself mediating. Interpreters frustrated by the lack of budgetary support for continued development of an encampment hoped I would criticize the site and its administration; administrators sometimes asked for my advice in "dealing with" Native interpreters about various issues. Public history sites involve a great deal of politics, and the "authentic reconstructions" into which visitors step are formed by "the politics of administrative culture" (Gable and Handler 1993:26) as much as by historical research, budgets, or popular assumptions about the past.

Site administrators were by and large excited about my work, and hopeful that it might enable them to improve programs. Some held a "debriefing session" with me before I left to discuss my initial findings; others made it clear that they did not wish to be given—in the words of one administrator—a "report card" when I left, and that they were already the target of enough lobby groups riding hobby horses. After realizing that some staff were convinced that they were somehow causing negative comments from visitors, that site managers were unaware of the racist comments faced by Native staff on a daily basis, and also that Native interpreters were not being trained to deal with such comments, I went back to several sites and gave training workshops and developed staff training materials.

Even choosing the words in writing this volume has underlined how political and engaged this work has been. Since the historic sites considered here exist on both sides of the international border, they represent peoples who in Canada are usually termed First Nations or Aboriginal, and in the United States are termed American Indian or Native American. There is no single term used across North America to designate all of the indigenous peoples across the continent, and rather than using all of these terms every time I refer to the tribal peoples represented at historic sites, I have chosen to use the term "Native peoples" or "Native," as in "Native interpreters"—unsatisfactory in some respects, but necessary. I have occasionally used the term "Indian" to signify the stereotyped, inaccurate, racist image of Native peoples created by outsiders, and when discussing Canadian sites sometimes find "Aboriginal" and "First Nations" more appropriate. Words matter, and being able to choose or reject terminology signifies power. I hope that the tribal peoples whose work I discuss here will understand why I have chosen this shorthand term. The term "Métis," used throughout this work to designate a range of peoples of mixed European and Native descent who historically used an equal range of terms to signify themselves, is also a choice made from several possibilities, but reflects increasingly widespread usage of this term today.

Finally, I have also chosen the term "interpreter" to describe those who work at historic sites, wear period clothing, and interact with visitors on site; they are trained and paid by the site. Some sites use other terms such as "animator" to describe such staff members; I subsume those terms into "interpreter," since what these people are doing is not actually "bringing the past to life" (as historic sites would like visitors to believe), but rather translating from past to present and back again: interpreting. I distinguish, as well, staff members who are interpreters from hobbyists and volunteers who are reenactors, who dress up at weekends in period clothing largely for their own purposes of entertainment, and do not deal here with reenactors (on which see Deloria 1998).

SITE MAP

Visitors to historic reconstructions are issued with a map of the site that tells them something of the layout and history of the site. I hope to provide similar information for the reader, explaining the nature of this work and how it is structured.

I have chosen to preface some chapters with a vignette—a transcription/description of an actual moment (or a composite of several moments) that I experienced on site during my fieldwork—to provide context for the reader, giving a slice of typical interaction at these places and so assisting the reader to follow me in the course of analysis. The encounter between Ruth Christie and a child at Lower Fort Garry that preceded this chapter worked in this way.

The first chapter, "Landscapes," describes each of the five historic sites at which I have worked, placing them each in their individual historical and institutional trajectories. While laying out their individual histories, I also look at these sites as a coherent group representing contact situations. This chapter introduces the idea that historic reconstructions, like landscapes, are culturally shaped and understood, and that they are cultural representations laden with meaning in each of the moments of their histories. It also introduces the idea of landscape as performance space or arena, a site of articulation of cultural myths, a site of cross-cultural encounter, a "contact zone" between peoples of different backgrounds and between past and present.

In the next chapter, "Cosmologies," I examine the way in which North American historic reconstructions have tended to articulate dominant-society myths in the form of historical narratives. These myths justify certain treatments of Native peoples, both in the past and in the present. Through historical commemoration, these myths were deployed to enshrine dominant-society experiences in the past that were seen to have contributed to nation-building. The first part of this chapter sets out the ways in which the fur trade and mission sites I worked at have tended to be developed within this intellectual and mythical framework, and explores how the representations of Native people at these sites has supported these myths. These representations have of course been substantially revised at the sites I examine. The second part of this chapter therefore discusses the theoretical processes of such change, and the implications of the addition of Native elements—and perspectives—to the stories these places tell.

We then turn to the visitors at these sites: who are they, what do they already know, what do they want from these places, what do they learn and how? The chapter on "Visitors" discusses the visitor profile for these sites and examines how visitors experience these places and how the knowledge and perspectives they bring with them intersect with information communicated by the site and its staff. I explore the typical visitor responses of nostalgia and the use of the "tourist gaze" to deploy historical and moral myths about Native peoples and Europeans. Typical assumptions about Native peoples (that they existed only in the precontact past, that their cultures were less "advanced" than European civilization) are also discussed. Finally, I note the development of more diverse audiences and modes of delivery by some of these sites, especially Fort William, and how the living history program has in some cases been repackaged for very different kinds of visitors. These new packages offer revisionist messages, but as with the traditional forms of historic interpretation, their messages are mediated by the form of delivery and by audience preconceptions.

Visitors respond strongly to the physicality of historic reconstructions: their buildings, props, costumes, trade goods, and food. The next chapter, "Authenticities and Materialities," examines the physical elements of these sites, how they arise and are modified, how they are legitimated or disauthenticated, and how and what they communicate. The issue of authority as the most important meaning of authenticity, raised by Bruner (2005:12), becomes very important in understanding the meanings of these physical elements of historic reconstructions in this cross-cultural setting.

I use techniques derived from visual and museum anthropology to analyze the conflicting and problematic messages communicated by the physical aspects of the reconstructions, such as the palisades and the spatial separation of the Native areas. I join this visual analysis with historical research to discuss the patterned minimization of the numbers and roles of Native peoples depicted at these sites, and how these patterns are communicated through props, buildings, and spatial relationships. If this chapter suggests that historic reconstructions are compromised by their physical nature, however, it also suggests the ways in which the buildings, furnishings, and costumes at these places act as crucial nodes for communication between people: the objects themselves become the focal points for multiple sets of meanings and competing agendas. I look at the ways in which these material elements are invested with important meanings by Native and non-Native staff and visitors. The material culture at historic reconstructions is instrumental to the construction of identity for staff and visitors, to the reclamation of traditional knowledge for Native interpreters, and to challenging visitors' stereotypes as much as it works to evoke these.

Of all the staff working in these complex spaces, Native interpreters have, I think, the toughest time. They have the most invested in their work, and are more often the focus for debates over authenticity (and issues of authority) than most non-Native staff. In *"Anishinaabeg,"* I set out the essence of what Native interpreters at all sites told me about their motivations, the peculiarly conflated nature of their work, and some of the typical dynamics of their encounters with visitors. I explore, as well, their personal investment in historical education, and set their work within the alternative tradition of cultural performance in which—in contrast to the disempowering colonial tradition discussed in "Cosmologies"—Native interpreters think of themselves as working.

The most powerful moments that happen at these places occur when non-Native visitors encounter Native interpreters, when the face-to-face nature of this encounter brings conflicting myths and histories into direct proximity. In "Encounters," I analyze these often fraught interactions. I use the concepts of "borderlands" and "contact zones" to understand the complexity of these confrontations which occur among historical eras, cultures, and individuals, and also to understand how historic reconstructions can serve as arenas for articulating not only dominant-society myths and expectations, but Native perspectives as well, and for challenging broader social dynamics in every face-to-face conversation. It is in these encounters, most of all, that the potential of Native interpreters to challenge the preconceptions of mainstream visitors emerges most strongly. In these events, the dynamics of the "tourist gaze," the tourism literature's obsession with authenticity, and of assumptions about Native participants in cultural tourism as passively controlled by external forces and preconceptions, are matched by the vigor and force of Native interpreters who insist on the right to speak in their own voices, to tell their own version of history, to gaze back.

Finally, in the concluding chapter, "The Living and the Dead," I evaluate the work these places do in terms of Native and non-Native agendas; the uses of the past; the needs and expectations of various audiences; their potential as foci of communication and agents of social change; and the realities facing them in terms of budget cuts and declining visitor figures. When we revise the past, what are we saying about the present? It asks, finally, what the present-day implications of these revisions of the past are, and to what extent sites are successful in communicating these messages.

LOOKING THROUGH THE GATE

As someone who works in the space between anthropology and history, I have been inspired by Jonathan Hill's 1992 call for a rethinking of anthropology as the "historically situated process of listening to, contextualizing, and interpreting the historical discourses of contemporary peoples" (Hill 1992:815). I hope that this is such a work.

I hope, too, that interpreters and administrators will use this study to think about the messages they communicate about Native people and Native-White relations in the past, and to find ways of creating increased understanding, respect, and dialogue between Native and non-Native staff and between staff and visitors at these sites. I hope that it will lead to the proposal of ways to communicate a broader, more realistic range of relations between Native and non-Native peoples at these sites, and to further questioning by scholars, staff, and visitors about the precise nature of these historic relations. Living history sites have the capacity to inspire wonder in their visitors, and to challenge received and racist ideas about the past as well as to delight with their textures and smells and characters. They can serve both the Native and the non-Native communities in different ways, can encourage cultural preservation as well as cross-cultural understanding. These are opportunities available to few of us, and in analyzing how Native interpretation programs have developed and how they function, I encourage site staff at all levels to make the most of them.

Since beginning this research, I have encountered three works that have helped me to keep going with it for over a decade. One is Rosenzweig and Thelen's study of the uses of the past in popular society, in which they note that a very large segment of American society feels the need "for history that actively assists them in making connections between the past and the present," a history that "can be used to answer pressing current-day questions about relationships, identity, immortality and agency" (1998:178). It also noted the emphatic rejection by many Americans of simplistically patriotic historical narratives, the desire for narratives which explain the complexity of lives lived, and because of this, the turning away from academically based history to historically based hobbies such as genealogy (179). This should bode well for historic sites that are trying to make their portrayal of the past more inclusive; it certainly underscores the importance of the work that Native interpreters can do.

I link their conclusions to work by Ruth Abram and Martha Norkunas, who both write about different aspects of the moral, social, and political elements of social history representations. Abram came to the Tenement Museum in New York having worked on equality issues, and asking how society can cope with the cultural and racial differences of its members; she also asked how society could stop using such differences against its members (Abram 2005:20).

She has begun to answer these questions through the explicitly educational work of the Tenement Museum, making it a vehicle to eradicate prejudice, and went on to instigate the founding of the International Coalition of Historic Site Museums of Conscience. Each of these sites asks "compelling questions" intended to provoke thought and dialogue about the legacy of the past in the present: what forms of slavery exist today? could the Holocaust happen again? what would a society of equality be like? (Abram 2005:40). I would argue that Native histories, told at contact sites such as those I have worked with, have similar potential for affecting our society in the present and future, and potential, as well, for healing Native communities so long denied the ability to tell their own stories (see Sandell 2002:4).

Martha Norkunas, writing about the work of retrieving the effaced histories of minority communities, asks what happens when the historical community doesn't try to do this, when reconstructions and museums simply communicate older, hegemonic narratives: "But what happens when you don't resist? . . . You allow others to control the present through their interpretations of the past" (2004:115). However fraught this work of adding Native histories to these representations may be, then, we need to try: "If we can just reach one person, teach one person that we are real human beings, then it's all worth it" (Marie Brunelle, retired Native interpreter at SMAH, interview July 28, 1995).

NOTES

1. Interpretation is broadly defined as "any communication process designed to reveal meanings and relationships of our cultural and natural heritage to the public through first-hand involvement with an object, artifact, landscape, or site" (Association of Canadian Interpreters, cited in FWHP Interpretive Manual n.d.:1; cf. Tilden 1977 [1957]:8). Interpretation at historic sites generally involves staff in replica historic clothing representing a typical person from the past who engages in period activities and in conversations with visitors, answering questions and imparting information. See also Goodacre and Baldwin 2002 for an excellent overview of historic interpretation.

2. Cf. Robert Hewison 1989 cited in Goodacre and Baldwin 2002:173.

3. On the definition of ethnic or cultural tourism, see MacCannell 1984:344; Moscardo and Pearce 1999:417; Smith 1977; van den Berghe 1994; Boniface and Fowler 1993; Stanley 1998.

4. This point is also made by Burns (2004:14), in a recent review of the literature on anthropology and tourism: "voices from the host perspective, particularly indigenous hosts, remain in the minority. . . ."

5. On visual analysis, I have relied on Banks 2001; Pink 2001; Mirzoeff 2002; Morgan 2005:2–6, 27–35.

Chapter One

Landscapes

> Relics of what happened in the past are cultural artifacts of the moments
> that produce them, but they also become cultural artifacts of all the mo-
> ments that give them permanence. . . . They gain meaning out of every so-
> cial moment they survive. (Dening 1996:43)

In an evocative article, Margaret Rodman (1992) discussed the idea of landscape as something experienced in different ways by different members of societies. "A single physical landscape," Rodman wrote, "can be multilocal in
the sense that it shapes and expresses polysemic meanings of place for different users" (1992:647). She noted that if one discussed landscape with different members of a village in Vanuatu, her research site, one would get completely different ideas: a child might map all the forbidden coconut trees he
had raided, places he played; an old woman might remember birthing sites
and gardens she had created. Rodman made the crucial point that landscapes
are, as she phrased it, "multilocal," that they exist differently in the minds of
different people. In settler situations such as North America, Europeans who
had no idea of the meanings and uses of landscape to tribal peoples made their
own associations and reshaped landscape according to their own cultural conventions.

Landscapes are not only shaped by cultural knowledge, but are places to
articulate and perform cultural beliefs; they are performance spaces where
core beliefs underpinning society are enacted. Because these beliefs and behaviors are held unevenly and are contested within and across cultures, landscapes can also be places where multiple cultural performances occur simultaneously.

Reconstructed historic sites are landscapes in themselves. They are places
that have been excavated, researched, reconstructed, furnished, peopled,

"brought to life": thought about, fought over, and physically constructed. In their historic incarnations and in their contemporary reconstructions, they articulate cultural beliefs: how much personal space should a voyageur have? Or a priest? How are social hierarchies reflected in furnishings? They are performance spaces, theatres, where culture is enacted, in much the same way that Elizabethan theatres encoded belief systems in their painted Heavens and English culture in their performances. At historic reconstructions, the culture enacted—what is "brought to life"—is not just that of the past but of the present: what we reconstruct, how we revise these places, is an enactment of culture in the present.

Historic reconstructions also bring together past and present; locals and tourists; scholars and the public; managers and interpreters; and, at the sites I am examining, Native and non-Native peoples. Just as the landscape of Vanuatu may be seen differently by different community members, so too are these sites understood differently by each of these groups. (And, of course, none of these groups is monolithic in its ways of perceiving things; there are multiplicities of perspectives here.) Each of these groups wants certain things of the site, ranging from the need to increase visitor numbers, to the need to show an inclusive history, experience nostalgia, or speak in one's own voice about tribal history.

As places where all these perspectives and needs come together, as arenas for simultaneous interacting cultural performances, historic sites are extremely complex spaces. Across this volume I will develop the idea that such spaces are "contact zones" or "borderzones," where peoples from very different backgrounds, with different agendas and perspectives, come together and engage (Bruner 2005:17; Pratt 1992). I raise the idea here to emphasize the complexity integral to these places, to be borne in mind as I describe their physical entities and their histories. These places are incredibly mediated: what we experience at them is the product of many intentions and needs, and it all changes over time.

If what we show, what we reconstruct, how we revise these places, is an enactment of culture in the present, then what is actually shown and what is not shown? How does the reconstructed reality relate to the historical realities?

The fur trade and mission sites analyzed here reflect both site-specific historical research and broad historical themes that have shifted drastically within scholarship on Native-White relations over the past several decades. Both the exchange of European goods for furs and the attempts by Christian missionaries to harvest souls began in a sustained way in the early seventeenth century in the northeast, and involved long-term, often daily and intimate relations between tribal peoples and Europeans. Intermarriage between fur traders and Native women was common, and many fur traders and missionaries spent much of their adult lives living within Native communities.[1] While the fur trade and missions were part of the overall processes of colonization, then, they also had dynamics quite distinct from later processes of settlement. Our views on these dynamics have changed over time. Where early studies of the fur trade (Innis 1999 [1930]), Hickerson 1988) concluded that Native peoples became dependent on Europeans and the goods they supplied, recent work has emphasized that the trade was just one component of Native life, and that the adoption of European goods did not destroy core elements of Native cultures. Similarly, studies of missionization have explored the ways in which Christianity did not necessarily displace older belief systems (Peterson and Peers 1993; Long 1987; Grant 1984). All recent scholarship on Native societies in encounters with Europeans has emphasized the ways in which Native peoples pursued their own goals. Rather than seeing the European presence as an inevitable, hegemonic steamroller, these studies (e.g., Peers 1994; McConnell 1992; Merritt 2003; White 1991) have explored Native agency and the nuanced details of shifting relationships between Native peoples and Europeans.

I explore in the chapter on "Authenticities and Materialities" some of the problems of representation involved in implementing such scholarly paradigm shifts. First, though, I wish to examine each of these sites in detail, placing them in the contexts of their particular histories, their contemporary situation within funding agencies, and the relationships between their representations of the past and "the politics of administrative culture" (Gable and Handler 1993:26). I have also tried to answer Bruner and Kirshenblatt-Gimblett's questions (1994:436): "What is being produced here and how? How did the site arise historically? How is it staged, who has artistic control, and how does the performance develop in space and time? How is the production organized in social and economic terms, and who gets what from the event?"

The five historic reconstructions on which this study is based are scattered around the Great Lakes, on both sides of the international boundary. They are of different sizes, with different visitor numbers, and portray a range of eighteenth- and nineteenth-century contact situations. I want to introduce them separately here, to give a sense of their distinct shapes, histories, and messages, before considering in the chapters ahead the many similarities of what goes on at these places.

LOWER FORT GARRY

Lower Fort Garry (LFG) was built in the 1830s on a high bank of the Red River between the present-day city of Winnipeg and Lake Winnipeg. It is now

near the present town of Selkirk. The fort was built with a high stone wall
with corner bastions and a central, gracious house in a vernacular Georgian
style which was intended as a residence for George Simpson, Governor of the
Hudson's Bay Company, and for senior company staff. Simpson used it only
briefly, although it continued to house senior officers and clerks. The fort
served as a crucial trans-shipment point for the company's western fur trade,
and as a shop for the population at the north end of Red River settlement. After 1850, a large farm, brewery, and other facilities were begun there to supply the company's needs, providing labor opportunities for local people
(Coutts 1993:5–7). In 1871, the first western treaty with Canada's Native people was negotiated and signed at the fort with bands of Ojibwa and Cree.

Activity at the fort decreased across the late nineteenth century, and LFG
officially closed as a Hudson's Bay Company post in 1911. The Manitoba
Motor Country Club used the buildings as its headquarters until 1963; the
buildings were also used at various times as a penitentiary and an insane asy-
lum. In 1929, the federal Historic Sites and Monuments Board erected a
plaque at the fort commemorating it as an historic site—but for its role in the
treaty-making process rather than in the fur trade. The text of the plaque read,
in part, that the treaty "ended the restlessness of the Natives and left the way
clear for peaceful settlement." As Robert Coutts has written, early ideas about

**Figure 1.1.   Warehouse and laborers, Lower Fort Garry National Historic Park. Image
courtesy Parks Canada/A. Cornellier.**

heritage and reasons for commemorating sites "were inextricably linked to the perceived 'triumph' of Anglo-British culture and institutions in Canada." This plaque emphasized such beliefs, and "made clear that the settlement and 'civilization' of the 19th century Canadian West were the dominant commemorative themes at LFG" (Coutts 1993:1–2).

As tourism expanded after World War II, there were increasing calls for LFG to be purchased by the federal government and turned into a heritage site. This happened in 1951, and the site has been administered by the heritage department of the federal government ever since, as a National Historic Site. In 1963, an extensive restoration program was begun and "over the next two decades the rest of the extant buildings at the fort were restored to their 19th century appearance" (Coutts 1993:3). The interpretation program also grew, and in the 1970s became "a full scale animation program which saw costumed seasonal interpreters role-playing a variety of historical personalities who lived and worked at the fort in the 1850s and 1860s" (Coutts 1993:3).

In keeping with the early commemorative theme of the triumph of British civilization over the wilderness, the expansion of the interpretive program turned LFG into a sort of pioneer village with fur trade associations. In Barbara Johnstone's planning document of 1962, Native subjects for interpretation ("Cree and Ojibway neighbours") came last on the list, after "Garden Parties" and "Crafts Associated with the Fort" (blacksmith shop, brewery, saw mill, grist mill) (HBCA E.97/53). Native people were discussed only as a minor point within the discourse about the establishment of British society in Red River. During the 1970s, interpretation focused on senior fur trade officers at the fort, and their wives. Since the 1980s, the animation program has emphasized class and race relations in Red River, and interpreters have portrayed male and female mixed-blood and European laborers, employees and settlers; the temporal framework for interpretation has also focused mostly on the 1850s.

The modern visitor center, with an orientation display, visitor facilities, conference space, and café and shop, was opened in 1980. (The orientation display appeared to be closed during the time of my visit in 2005, and visitors simply took the site leaflet and proceeded outside.) The site consists of a fairly large acreage (much of it with archaeological resources which are not interpreted), the stone walls which enclose a range of period buildings, and outside the walls two cottages and the Native encampment. The animation program has continued, underpinned by a range of historical research on life at the Fort and in Red River more generally, which incorporates revisionist perspectives from Canadian fur trade scholarship about the roles of Métis and Aboriginal people in the trade, and the multicultural nature of the settlement.[2]

About 1990, managers of the interpretive program (one of whom was of local Métis ancestry) decided to add a Native component to their program,
which would focus on local Ojibwa and Cree[3] cultures, and the interactions
between these people and Lower Fort Garry. Without budget for research,
costumes, and furnishings, these two staff members managed to hire several
interpreters (initially, about half of them Aboriginal) to staff the encampment,
and purchased or borrowed from around the site several canvas tipis, buffalo
hides, furs, beading equipment, kitchen gear, and other furnishings. The plan
was to get the encampment up and running, and gauge public response to it.
If this was favorable, then Parks Canada would hopefully fund specific research on the Native presence at the fort and the interpretive presentation and
furnishings could be refined. This has in fact been the manner in which the
encampment has progressed, although change is occurring in a more complex
way than anticipated. When the encampment was first created, several scholars both within and outside Parks Canada, including myself, voiced disap-
proval at the inaccurate canvas tipis, the interpreters' dubious claim that Native people brought fish in large quantities to sell at the fort "for the tribe,"
and other unresearched aspects of the interpretation. Unusually, photographs
exist of Native people and dwellings in Red River in 1858, along with detailed archival references to Native life there. While appreciative of the staff's
initiative in getting the encampment together, I was disappointed that Parks
Canada had not invested more research time or funds on the area. Ultimately,
I was hired by Lower Fort Garry in 1994 to research the material, social, and
economic nature of the presence of Native people around the fort in the mid-
nineteenth century, and delivered a report (Peers 1995) that now serves as the
basis for interpretation at the encampment, a copy of which is given to every
interpreter working in the encampment area. The canvas tipis have remained,
as it is unfeasible to pay for construction of bark-covered structures. However, the site has made progress toward providing more accurate information
and props for interpreters, and toward integrating the presence of the Native
interpreters into the rest of the site as a whole. On very rainy days, for instance, some of the Native staff work in the farm cottages on site as "day laborers," and all interpreters from the encampment spend part of their work
week inside the walls of the fort portraying other characters: mixed-blood laborers, clerks, or wives of senior traders. As of the summer of 2005, one canvas tipi stood, partially furnished, with a work/cooking/activities area around
a campfire nearby.

   Interpreters sit on low folding camp chairs that are covered by trade blankets, and engage in beadwork and other crafts. A *tikinagan* (baby carrier), a
wooden trunk with cooking and domestic items, and some obviously Aboriginal objects—a quilled knife sheath, a deerbone cup-and-pin game—are laid

Figure 1.2.   Tipi, interpreters, visitors. Image courtesy Parks Canada/V. Lockett.

out for visitors to see and touch, and interpreters explain these items. The tipi is furnished inside with a dew cloth and pallets covered in buffalo robes and blankets, with furs and objects hung from the tipi poles. Interpreters greet visitors in the cooking area outside, and then after an initial discussion explain the contents of the trunk, and then invite the visitors to come into the tipi with them, giving an explanation of how to move in the culturally-appropriate direction (clockwise, turning left as one enters the tipi), and who in the family would have slept where in the tipi.[4] By 2005, Ruth Christie, the Cree elder who worked with this camp for a decade, had retired and all the interpreters were young adults. Most were women from the Winnipeg area, with one man from Saskatchewan; one of the female interpreters was Filipino.

The presence of a Filipino "Native" interpreter raises the problematic issue of employment legislation, within which it may be illegal to appoint only staff of Native descent to work in the encampment, and within which it may also be illegal to restrict staff of Native descent to working solely in the Native area of the site. All historic sites wrestle with this dilemma, but as a federally designated site within a national heritage agency, dealing with the incredible amount of bureaucracy that a major heritage agency creates, LFG exemplifies the problem especially well. Indeed, so cumbersome is the administrative burden at this site that interpretive staff are given no training in either the history of the site or in interpretive techniques. Their single week of preseason training includes information on fire drills and pensions, and in 2005 included a session from the federal department of Indian and Northern Affairs on the nuances of ethnic terminology, but they are expected to teach themselves the basics of their jobs by reading site manuals and through mentoring between experienced and new interpreters. Despite this, staff across the site in both 1994 and 2005 were impressively knowledgeable about period material culture and intergroup relations at the fort in the mid-nineteenth century, and pursued a program of research and presentations to each other and the public.

By the time I arrived in late July 2005, one of the Native staff had already resigned, having decided that historic interpretation was not for her. This, too, is a common pattern at living history sites with seasonal employees. The site has informal relations with the Peguis First Nation, whose ancestors lived near LFG. Peguis band council will normally pay a student from the band to work at the fort during the summer season, an arrangement that resulted from a personal friendship between an LFG site manager and a member of the band council. It has, however, proven difficult to fill this position. As I will explore in a later chapter, this is typical of relations between heritage agencies and Native communities: these relationships have not developed strongly across the past decade, largely due to the different agendas of the different parties.

LFG can be an awkward site to interpret. It is associated with the fur trade, yet was not a stereotypical fur trade post; it is the closest thing to a pioneer village that Winnipeg has, yet it was tied more to the fur trade than to agriculture. More importantly, the interpretation of the Native presence on site does not always mesh with the site's reasons for being designated as a national historic site. In 1950, when this occurred, the reasons given were:

- it was the place where Treaty One was made
- it is one of the finest collections of early stone buildings in Western Canada
- as a HBC post, it was a focus for industry and transport, as well as a supply and distribution center for the fur trade
- it was used by the federal government for public purposes in the 1870s, notably as the first training base for the North West Mounted Police (LFG Commemorative Integrity Statement 2004:4)

In the 1990s, Parks Canada introduced a policy of Commemorative Integrity, intended to ensure that historic sites are managed to protect and communicate the reasons and cultural resources for which they were originally designated. Each of the thousands of sites in the federal system has had to produce a "Commemorative Integrity Statement" outlining the original reasons for commemoration, the resources designated, and how each resource (building, landscape) is managed to protect it and to communicate its important heritage features.

LFG's Commemorative Integrity statement is an intriguing study of how the original reasons for designation as a heritage resource may be very different from the importance of the resource as seen today. The statement begins by reiterating the reasons for the 1950 designation of the fort as a National Historic Site. All buildings within the walls and the walls/bastions themselves are described in the statement as being related to the reasons for designation; only one building outside the walls, the Ross Cottage, is described as such and it is noted as not being rated as a heritage building under the Federal Historic Buildings policy. Today, Ross Cottage plays an important role in communicating to visitors the idea that many settlers and laborers were Métis, who had kin in Aboriginal groups such as those represented in the nearby encampment, but this is not reflected in the statement.

None of the buildings or archaeological resources listed in the statement are Aboriginal; they all pertain to European and Métis activity on site. Despite the archival documentation of the presence of Aboriginal people at LFG and in the surrounding area as part of the local community, there are no original material resources pertaining to their activities extant at LFG. Aboriginal people are explicitly noted in the statement only as signators to Treaty One. The parish of St. Peter's is mentioned (LFG Commemorative Integrity Statement 2004:19) as having supplied tripmen for fur trade transport, but the fact that the majority of residents of St. Peter's were Ojibwa and Cree is not mentioned. The emphases of revisionist social history scholarship since the 1950s—on Red River as a multicultural and multiracial community, and on the fur trade as a broader cross-cultural phenomenon—are excluded from the statement. Parks Canada would be entirely within its rights to remove the Aboriginal encampment and staff, unless these interpreted the signing of Treaty One. The celebratory emphasis on LFG as the site for this treaty signing that became part of its reasons for commemoration, however, is not shared by Aboriginal people in Manitoba or Canada, who tend to see this first treaty as the first moment in western Canada when Aboriginal sovereignty was threatened and external control began to be imposed over them.

Despite these difficulties, the encampment and its messages have proven very popular with visitors. LFG is one of the most important reconstructions in Parks Canada's roster: it received huge amounts of funding for reconstruction, and still has a large visitorship—although due to reduced American visitation after 9/11 and shrinking school trip budgets, visitor numbers have fallen from seventy thousand in the early 1990s to about thirty-one thousand in 2004–2005 (interviews with Ken Green and Giselle Gauthier, LFG 2005). LFG is a complex site that has already redefined itself several times to reflect shifting academic historiography. It is now pursuing local audiences to raise visitor numbers, and is developing educational programs to meet school curriculum and field trip needs as well as focused tours for local seniors and other groups. The annual payment of treaty monies to descendants of signators to Treaty One was made at the fort one year, and it has hosted an Aboriginal art show. As a site designated in 1950, reconstructed with its animation program launched in the 1970s, revised ever since, and now coping with declining visitor numbers, it will be interesting to see how the site develops in the future.

FORT WILLIAM

With forty-two buildings, "2780 feet of 10 foot high wooden palisade" (Visitor's Map 1994), dozens of summer interpretive staff, and visitor numbers of about ninety thousand annually, Fort William Historical Park (FWHP) is an ambitious reconstruction. It is a daunting site even for the casual visitor: a walk through the forest or short bus ride brings one to the Native encampment; another stroll brings one inside the gates; there are many buildings inside, and a farm, with livestock and gardens. The buildings include everything from the Great Hall and fur store to the Indian trading shop and a hospital. Funded by the Ontario Provincial Government through the Ministry of Tourism, FWHP was reconstructed in the early 1970s about nine miles from its original site on Lake Superior. The original site, first Fort Kaministiqua (by 1803) and later Fort William (1807), was the North West Company's main shipment point for furs coming from the west and trade goods coming from Montreal. The fort was seized by Lord Selkirk after the Red River troubles of 1816, and transferred to the HBC when the two companies merged in 1821. It closed in 1883.

Fort William was a tourist site as early as the 1830s. As Patricia Jasen has noted, its position at the Lakehead (the gateway to the west and a transportation terminus for the Great Lakes), its romantically decaying buildings, and its association with the declining western fur trade made it a "must" for early tourists (Jasen 1990). The fort was also on the main water route (and, later, the main rail route) from east to west. As early as 1876, years before the fort closed as an operating fur trade post, the *Thunder Bay Sentinel* stated that "Fort William's early days would be sure to capture the imagination of the public if, through the artifacts that survived at the old fort, its history was properly placed before them" (Jasen 1990:8).

In 1902, the last of Fort William's original buildings was demolished. The Thunder Bay Historical Society commemorated the site with a plaque: like many such societies, they desired to record their area's contribution to the making of Canada, to reinforce civic (i.e., British-Canadian) virtues, and to encourage tourism and economic development (Jasen 1990:12). In the 1930s, there were plans to build a replica of the fort, but disagreement over the location, and the interruption of the war, prevented progress.

Increasing interest in tourism as a form of revenue for the Thunder Bay area led to a commitment to the reconstruction by the Ontario government in the 1960s. By the end of the 1960s, archaeological excavations of the original fort had been completed and a site was chosen for the reconstruction (Jasen 1990:17–18). The 1971 feasibility study was entitled "Hinge of a Nation," another reference to the view of the fur trade as an episode in national history. Academic and public history consultants hired in the early 1970s researched the social history, material culture, and appearance of the fort, and a decision was made to portray the fort as it would have looked in 1815. Construction commenced in 1971, and the site opened in 1973; the reconstruction was finished in 1975 (OFW Management Plan). The site is now known as Fort William Historical Park (FWHP).

Like LFG, Fort William emphasizes class and cross-cultural relations in the fur trade, with staff portraying top-hatted gentlemen in frock coats, voyageurs, farm hands, and the Métis and Native women who were the workforce within the walls.[5]

The daily dramas enacted by staff, and standard lines given to visitors by staff, are about relationships and differences between these groups: a Métis woman working in the surgery, for instance, tells visitors that the European

Figure 1.3.   Stairs, Great Hall, Fort William Historical Park. Photograph by Drew Davey.

doctor despises the herbal medicines she learned from her Native mother, and that all she is allowed to do is clean. Another drama involves staff who pick up furs at the Native encampment and take them along with visitors to the trading shop where visitors are coached to trade for necessary goods. A new drama introduced in the past few years allows Native women interpreters to reflect in the presence of visitors about the implications of White wives of senior fur traders arriving at the Red River Settlement. The dramas underscore the site's designated interpretive themes and help to unify the disparate elements of a large site. The site also has a sophisticated manual to train staff in techniques of interpretation, and annual training weeks include sessions on the history and cultures depicted.

The Native encampment was begun about five years after the reconstruction of the main fort, and is intended to interpret the way of life of the Ojibwa people who historically traded, visited kin, and labored at the fort.

When Freda McDonald (an Ojibwa elder originally from Fort Alexander, upriver from Thunder Bay) began work there in 1977, the site had a single lodge. In 1994, there were three *wigwassikamikag* (conical structures covered with birch bark); in 2005, the area held three such structures, the Learning Wigwam, and three bark-covered work shelters. Eight to ten Ojibwa men and women from all over northern Ontario and beyond work there, engaging in crafts, sewing, carving, and cooking as they talk to visitors. Since 2002, the

Figure 1.4.   Native encampment, Fort William Historical Park. Photograph by Drew Davey.

site has also had a Learning Wigwam for the increasing numbers of visitors on booked educational programs.

This has always been a very political site, where different groups have argued strongly for their own versions of the past. This began with the notion of the "romantic fur trade" (Jasen 1990:2–9) in the nineteenth century, and shifted, at least in local, popular representations, to a vision of the site as a Wild West frontier outpost (with a Mountie and the Union Jack thrown in to uphold British law and order) by the 1950s (see figure 2.1, in chapter 2). Academic consultants in the early 1970s suggested quite a different view of Fort William in their research reports. While drawing on popular stereotypes (the French-Canadian voyageur as strong, courageous, and skilled, the dandified Scottish officer, and the fur-trapping Ojibwa), their reports were well-documented profiles of the range of peoples and their interactions.

This material has been augmented as fur trade historians have done further research (e.g., Van Kirk 1980, Brown 1980). Research material has developed into a series of detailed interpretive themes or messages for every single building on site that encompass the sweep of fur trade history. Some of these, taken from the "Thematic Guide to Old Fort William Structures and Areas" training manual in 1994, are listed below:

Theme: Operations and Management
Location: Counting House
Interpretive Messages:
Major:

1. North West Company profits
2. Role of clerk in North West Company
3. Types of records kept at Counting House
4. Quill pen making

Minor:

1. How profits affected by logistics of fur trade, War of 1812, competition with Hudson's Bay Company, Lord Selkirk, extravagance, etc.
2. Terms of employment of engagés through discussion of contracts, men's accounts, etc.
3. Trade routes

Theme: Commerce and Warehousing
Location: Indian Shop
Interpretive Messages:
Major:

1. North West Company trading methods—Indian debts; Indian presents; the *plus* and the barter system in general

2. Impact of European manufactured goods on Indian culture in general
3. Contribution of Indian culture and Indian labor to the fur trade

Theme: Native Life
Location: Indian Camp
Interpretive Messages:
Major:

1. Culture, customs, skills, beliefs of the Ojibwa
2. Influence of fur trade on native culture as reflected in clothing, axes, kettles, guns, and so on
3. Role of the native in the fur trade

Other research to support the Native encampment area provides a detailed, archivally based picture of the local Ojibwa community in the early nineteenth century; a background summary on Ojibwa culture and history; information about appropriate crafts; and information on the roles and presence at the Fort of Ojibwa men, women, and children (FWHP Indian Encampment Manual, 1986). Within the research reports for the site, and as communicated by day-to-day interpretation, Ojibwa people at FWHP appear mostly as part of a European-oriented fur trade: they contribute to it in the form of furs, country provisions, and wives. Another interpretation support guide, "Daughters of the Country: a guide for female interpreters" (site document for internal use, 1992), skillfully digests and re-presents fur trade scholarship on the important roles of Aboriginal and mixed-blood women in the fur trade, giving a lively combination of text and extracts from archival documents. The limitation of such manuals—common to most sites interpreting fur trade and Aboriginal history—is that virtually all such scholarship has been written from non-Aboriginal perspectives and often within non-Aboriginal categories such as the fur trade, which was only a part of Aboriginal history. As with other sites, FWHP makes clear that the contributions of Aboriginal people were crucial, but struggles to interpret the fur trade and Aboriginal history from Aboriginal perspectives. It does so very well in the Native camp, where interpretation focuses on Ojibwa culture, and where the interpreters convey a strong sense of Ojibwa perspectives on the fur trade and its impact on their lives and history.

Aboriginal people comprise very few of the regular visitors to the main site, which is typical of the visitor profile for historic reconstructions generally. They do, however, visit in large numbers during the annual "Ojibway Keeshigan" festival, which brings in tradition-bearers from local bands for powwow and other activities. Native staff told me about this event with great enthusiasm, saying that they feel that this event brings their history to life, showing the links between past and present. This long-established event has been joined by other special events that reflect the site's commitment to increasing its involvement with the local Aboriginal population. FWHP has partnered with several Aboriginal organizations for developing and advertising events, and has hosted an Aboriginal youth conference. The site's classes in moccasin- and mitten-making, quillwork, and other traditional skills have been offered for two decades now, and continue to be popular.

As an early Management Plan (ca. 1976: section 2.44) states, the Native encampment at the fort was designed "to meet the demands of certain groups of people in the community . . . provides a unique opportunity for the local native community to establish its own interpretive unit at the Fort." Another early planning document suggested that an "Institute of Native Canada" be built on the grounds to train Native staff for the site. That plan was revived in the early 1990s by Native advisors, who wished to create a healing and cultural center. Given the site's reduced provincial funding since then, this plan has not come to fruition,[6] but a "Learning Wigwam," a teaching space for Native classes, has been constructed to broaden the site's historical program and involve more Aboriginal audiences. This has not resolved the question of "whose history" this site portrays, or reconciled the differences between Native and non-Native, scholarly and popular, understandings of fur trade and Native histories, which all these sites wrestle with. The site has, however, been willing to wrestle with such questions and to consider the needs of the local Native community, which makes it stand out in the field of public history.

Like other historic reconstructions, Fort William's budget, visitor numbers, and staff complement have changed significantly since 1994. The site was severely flooded in 2003, and implemented a CDN$7 million recovery program since; flooding in spring 2006 was at least as serious. In addition to these events, general visitors to the living history part of the site during the main season have dropped significantly. Peter Boyle, Historical Operations Manager, notes that "the majority of visitors to our living history program come from the USA," and that the combination of 9/11, SARS, and the increasing value of the Canadian dollar has affected tourism in Canada very badly across the past decade (e-mail, Boyle to Peers, October 27, 2005). The site has compensated by pursuing local secondary, post-secondary, and adult education markets, developing a host of new programs for them as well as for Scouts, Guides, Brownies, and young children. School programs range from "Fur Trade Natural History," "Life in a Wigwam," and "Women in the Industrial Revolution," to "Aboriginal Cultural Expedition" and "Snowshoeing." Many of these are geared to specific parts of the provincial curriculum, and many focus on Aboriginal themes. Guiding and Scouting programs are also keyed to stages in those groups, and include natural history, Aboriginal culture, fur trade history, and crafts. There are also a host of "artisan" programs operating as a sort of community outreach or further education college, and these include bread baking, patchwork, bannock-making, working with draft horses, moccasin-making, and porcupine quillwork (FWHP booked program guide, 2005).

Fort William's representation of Aboriginal heritage is quite strong. The site communicate core messages about the roles of Aboriginal people in the fur trade, the impact of the fur trade, and relationships between peoples in the trade, as well as fur trade material culture, much of which is Aboriginal. Where in 1994 some of the Native interpreters commented that they felt the site does not offer a sufficiently critical perspective on Ojibwa history, that it glossed over the damage done to Ojibwa culture and people during the fur trade era, by 2005 managers Boyle and Magiskan both reported a sense of deepening in what was communicated about fur trade history and its legacies for Ojibwa peoples, and felt strongly that staff "have invested a good deal of time and energy attempting to address the dark issues [of history] and have done much to educate the general public in an effective way" (Boyle to Peers, comments on draft text, November 17, 2005). There is a full-time, year-round position of Native Heritage Coordinator; a seasonal (ten-month) senior artisan; a seasonal (ten-month) education specialist; six to eight summer students, as well as some four to six additional Métis and Native staff working elsewhere throughout the site in various capacities, including support staff. The site has seen a significant increase in Aboriginal participation in booked programs and special events. Non-Native visitors to the site continue to express interest in Native cultures as one of the primary interests at the site. Still, there are frustrations on staff, with the difficulty of maintaining core traditional skills such as Native woodcraft, coopering, and tinsmithing on staff surfacing as a key issue related to budget and staff cuts (Peter Boyle, Manager, Historical Operations, Fort William Historical Park, e-mail to Peers October 27, 2005). Despite significant difficulties across the past decade, FWHP has developed very strongly indeed.

THE NORTH WEST COMPANY FUR POST

This reconstructed wintering post, located in Pine City north of Minneapolis, is the smallest of the sites examined here. It was used by Northwest Company trader John Sayer, his Ojibwe[7] wife Obemau-Onoqua, and his staff during the winter of 1804–1805. A log rowhouse of five rooms, with a small palisaded area around it, it is a far cry from the size of FWHP.

The NWC post is one of twenty-five Minnesota Historical Society (MHS) sites. It was reconstructed in the 1970s and, because of its small size and vis-

Figure 1.5.   Wintering house view from bastions, Northwest Company Fur Post. Photograph by Drew Davey.

itor numbers (about 20,000 annually), it is threatened with closure every time the state legislature cuts the MHS appropriation. Elements of the site have changed dramatically across the past decade. In 1994, the site had no visitor center, no running water, and the interpreters also did maintenance (doing the lunch dishes, cleaning the outhouse) in addition to their duties with the public. At that point, there was one manager and about six seasonal staff. A new visitor center was opened in 2003, along with a large exhibition on the fur trade and on relationships with Native peoples. There is now a gift shop and meeting and staff facilities in the center, and the senior manager, Patrick Schifferdecker, now works with a staff of fifteen including several maintenance people. This has had knock-on effects, one of which is that Schifferdecker—an extremely knowledgeable historian—has less time to research and to link research to staff training. The site is still under threat in the long-term because of its visitor numbers, and the manager's goal is to work to increase the range of audiences as well as visitor numbers.

This site does more with fewer staff members and resources than many larger reconstructions. As well as knowledgeable historians and artisans on staff and within MHS, the site has drawn on cutting-edge scholars in the field of fur trade and Ojibwe history, including Douglas Birk, Carolyn Gilman, and Bruce White. The site has the advantage of a daily journal kept at the post during the year it depicts. In 2005, staff began each day by reading the historic journal entry, planning particular activities to relate to the events of that day in 1804–1805, and ended the day by writing their own version of the entry to reflect the day's actual events. The new exhibition and interpreters' discussion incorporate detailed research, emphasizing Ojibwe perspectives on the trade and the lives of laborers as well as the workings of a wintering post. Staff use first-person interpretation (acting the role of a typical historical character, which every staff member creates after research), but also switch into third-person (informal discussion) as needed. Every visitor is escorted through the site by a single interpreter-guide and given a customized tour. There are opportunities for visitors to participate in historic activities, such as scraping hides, knotting fishnets, or playing games.

In the early 1990s one of the staff members very carefully "dressed" each of the rooms, so that they really do look as if their occupants have just stepped out: something that other sites try to do but seldom achieve.

There is a denseness of furnishing and decoration here that seems very believable, unlike the nearly empty rooms at many other reconstructions. Beds are not always made; clothes are hung on pegs; rough shelves crammed with food and sewing items, candles, and personal objects contribute to the sense of life in a hastily-built, cramped post intended to be used for just one season. Rooms belonging to fur trade employees of different rank reflect these differences in their furnishings, and the trading room overflows with furs and goods.

Staff at the NWCFP includes a core of highly talented interpreters. Audrey Wyman, who played "Nokie," an Ojibwe grandmother, worked for years at

Figure 1.6.   Trading shop, Northwest Company Fur Post. Photograph by Drew Davey.

the site, retiring in 1997; she and her adult daughter Mary Vanderpoel (initially a long-term interpreter, now Historic Site Technician) who depicts a Métis/Ojibwe woman, "Binekwe," at the site, are both of Ojibwe descent, and knowledgeable about regional history and culture. Staff have begun to establish relations with local bands, and tribal members have sometimes worked as interpreters. The manager also arranged to hire Sandra Goodsky, an Ojibwe woman who had worked at the site as an interpreter, as a research consultant to refine the site's portrayal of Ojibwe themes (Goodsky 1993).

Ojibwe material culture is woven throughout the site, from the hide being scraped in the yard to bark mokuks holding European objects: these things help tell the story of European reliance on Native people in the fur trade, and are actively used by interpreters to link to broad contextual information about relationships and cultures. The site also has a carefully furnished wigwam and items in the trader's room representing his Ojibwe wife. Interpreters learn to make their own moccasins, and there is an extremely high level of knowledge about period-appropriate Ojibwe craft production among the staff.

The combination of historical knowledge and mentoring, with good training in interpretation, and the use of the interpreter-led tour, enables this site to deliver a very high quality experience for visitors, who receive much more contextual information about the things they see than self-guided visitors do

Figure 1.7.   Wigwam interior with women's clothing and accessories, Northwest Company Fur Post. Photograph by Drew Davey.

at larger sites. I consider it a model for others to follow, and hope that staff will be able to increase visitor numbers to ensure its longevity.

COLONIAL MICHILIMACKINAC

Fort St. Phillipe de Michilimackinac was built in 1715 on the south side of the Straits of Mackinac between lakes Huron and Michigan. Its central position in the Great Lakes and at the nexus of canoe routes from Montreal and to the far west made it a major depot for Montreal-based trading companies. Michilimackinac bought large quantities of corn grown in the nearby Odawa (Ottawa) villages to feed voyageurs, further enhancing its importance for the fur trade. Its position also made it a natural meeting place for Native peoples of the Great Lakes. European and Métis traders based at Michilimackinac were thus well positioned between two worlds and maintained kin ties with tribes throughout the region that enabled them to trade. Hundreds of Native people came to the fort each summer from across the Great Lakes to visit kin, trade, and hold political councils to plan trade and warfare strategies. For decades, this community was the heart of the Great Lakes fur trade (Armour and Widder 1978, 1990:31–35; Peterson 1985).

Michilimackinac was surrendered to the British in 1760. The transition was not smooth. The incoming British had few kin ties to Native people, were arrogant in their dealings with chiefs, and insulted them by reducing the gifts traditionally given as diplomatic gestures during trade. In Native thought, ceasing to give these presents expressed distrust and the desire to end an alliance (White 1982, 1987; Armour and Widder 1990:35). When Pontiac's rebellion broke out in the spring of 1763, news of Native attacks on British forts to the south gave the local Ojibwa resolve to act on their grievances. On June 2, 1763, chief Matchekewis and his men captured the fort, killed some British occupants, and took others captive. The French and Métis inhabitants of the fort were not harmed. The fort was run by the remaining French and Métis until it was regarrisoned by the British in the fall of 1764 (Armour and Widder 1990:36).

Michilimackinac proved to be politically important during the American Revolution, for continuous negotiations with the Odawa, Ojibwa, and other tribes were vital to maintain their loyalty to the British throughout the conflict. Large war parties left from the fort throughout the Revolution to fight for Britain (Armour and Widder 1990:40–42). In the late 1770s, the fort was moved to the more defensible site of Mackinac Island, on the north side of the straits.

The site of the old fort was turned over to the state in 1904, and archaeological excavations have proceeded almost continuously since the 1930s. The reconstructed palisades and buildings are located in their original places and rebuilt according to archaeological evidence. The site has an active archival research program, and has published many works on the fort's history and material culture. The current reconstruction was done in the 1960s and 1970s, and interprets the fort as it was in the 1770s (Armour and Widder 1990:42–43). Approximately half the original structures have been reconstructed.

Now managed by Mackinac State Historic Parks, a division of the Michigan state government (in 1994, the site was under the aegis of the Department of Natural Resources; in 2001, it was shifted to the new Department of History, Arts and Libraries), Colonial Michilimackinac (CM) attracts between about one hundred and five thousand and one hundred and twenty thousand visitors a year, a figure which has tended to decline over the past few years (Steve Brisson to Peers, e-mail, October 26, 2005). The site emphasizes the British military presence at the fort, along with elements of the remaining French community in the 1770s (the church is staffed by an interpreter portraying a French-speaking Jesuit, and Métis weddings are reenacted daily) and the lives of Métis and Europeans within the fort.

Figure 1.8. View of main buildings, Colonial Michilimackinac. Photograph by Drew Davey.

There has been a strong emphasis on relationships between different peoples at the fort. The reconstructed buildings include rowhouses, traders' storerooms, officers' quarters, the priest's house, and the church. The site employs about twenty interpreters each summer, who portray soldiers, officers, voyageurs, Métis and European wives, the priest, and traders.

In the late 1980s, site administrators added a Native American encampment to the reconstruction. They had known it was important to include the roles of Native people in their interpretations of Michilimackinac's history, but were nervous that by doing so they would somehow offend local bands. In 1989, Dr. George Cornell, a Native American scholar, was hired as a consultant and reviewed the site. His report recommended that the site emphasize the presence of historic Native Americans and their roles in the trade and in politics. A *waginogan* (a substantial winter dwelling), a summer *nasaogan*, and several work shelters were built in 1991–1992. Phil Porter, then Curator of Interpretation for the site and a professional historian, compiled a training manual for the encampment that brought together information about the Ojibwa and Odawa of the region and their roles at the site.

Because of the small size of the Native American staff, only one lodge was furnished, and this had to be closed periodically (if, for instance, one interpreter is on break and the other must leave the camp to do a walking tour).

Figure 1.9.   Odawa Lodge, 1994, Colonial Michilimackinac. Photograph by Drew Davey.

Native staff worked in 1770s costume that in 1994 included, at the male interpreter's personal decision, shaved head with roach, multiple earrings, and trade silver nose ring. I was especially impressed by the enthusiasm of staff in the 1994 season for researching eighteenth-century tribal life and material culture. Interpretive activities included making hominy corn, bark containers, finger-woven sashes, and plant-fiber cord. Staff introduced trade items into the lodge (a tin lantern, a carrot of tobacco, a musket, blankets) and talked to visitors about the incorporation of European material culture into Native life. Despite their enthusiasm, the Native staff expressed frustration that so few structures had been built when historic summer encampments at the fort were so large, and were concerned in 1994 that the site might not wish to fund continued development of the encampment. Sadly, the size of the Native representation has become much smaller: budget cuts have led to the elimination of the core Native interpreter position from 2006, and there will be no live interpretation of Native peoples for the next few years until the budget situation is resolved. Since the lodge cannot be staffed, it is unlikely to be furnished, and will sit, empty, outside the walls of the fort.

Colonial Michilimackinac received a grant from the National Endowment for the Humanities in 1989 to plan a new exhibition exploring relations among Native Americans, French, and British during the site's history. Native and non-Native consultants emphasized the need to focus on the Native perspective on the site. The initial title for the proposed exhibition, "Enemies to Allies," was rejected by the Native consultants (Andrews 1995: n.p.) and eventually the planning team proposed a more ambitious exhibition that would examine the coming together of cultures as a window on the whole site. This has not yet been implemented but is still part of the site's plan. A major long-term exhibit opened in 1997 at a nearby MISPC site, Fort Mackinac, on Mackinac Island across the straits from CM, which covers the history of the Island with an emphasis on Native and Métis peoples in the area. Another exhibit specifically on Native peoples in the region is planned, pending funding, for the Indian Dormitory building, also on the Island.

The development of the Native encampment has been affected by relationships with local bands. One local band was only recognized (given official status) by the federal government in the early 1990s, and has ambitious plans for economic and cultural development in the region. While the tribal council has stated that researching and presenting their history is an important priority, they were also concerned in 1994 that Native Americans tended to be hired only as summer staff and for little more than minimum wage (Frank Ettawageshik, interview, 1994). This has certainly changed, as one assistant manager and several support staff are now Native, but the Native interpreter position has been cut. However, Steve Brisson, curator for the MISPC, noted that local bands offered formal support for the Indian Dormitory redevelopment grant application to NEH (Brisson to Peers, e-mail, October 27, 2005).

A serious point of contention between the site and local tribes has been that the site hosts an annual reenactment by townspeople in Mackinac City of the 1763 attack on the fort (Andrews 1995: n.p.). In front of large crowds, non-Native people dressed as Ojibwa "warriors" reenact elements of the historical event, including entering the fort and then tomahawking and scalping other actors who are dressed as British soldiers. The reenactment turns an extremely complex historical event into a caricature, including getting the audience to laugh when someone is "scalped" and has his wig pulled off. When the site commissioned a report from a Native American consultant on how to develop working relations with local bands and how the site might approach the representation of Native perspectives on the past, the consultant noted that:

> Some Anishnawbek [literally "Ojibwa," but used in this sense to mean Native people] stated that they will not go to any of the exhibits, facilities or activities of the MISPC [Mackinac Island State Park Commission] because of the negative attitude generated in the past and from the continued policy by MISPC in regard to the exhibits and activities, especially the reenactment of the 1763 capture. . . . The continuation of the reenactment by the non-Anishinawbek community at the fort is an issue that will sustain negative tensions on the MISPC's relationship with most of the conservative element of the Anishinawbek in northern Michigan. . . . Until something is done about this issue, the Anishinawbek believe that the MISPC is not taking their concerns seriously. (Andrews 1995: n.p.)

As of 2005 the event is still held, although it is deemed by Fort staff to be better than it was, and the overt references to "massacre" have been dropped. Steve Brisson, the curator for MISPC, is optimistic about the future of CM and related historic sites within the agency in terms of its representation of Native peoples:

> Many visitors have questions about Native people today. They are often surprised that a vibrant community still exists; that several of my coworkers are tribal members. At break, the conversation among some employees sometimes turns to tribal issues, such as upcoming elections. I would love to share this with our visitors. . . . For several years we have hosted a Native Women's Gathering on Mackinac Island each fall. . . . They begin each year by cleansing the building and lighting the sacred fire. I often think of that sacred fire when pondering these issues.

The future of the Native interpretation program at CM seems very uncertain.

SAINTE-MARIE AMONG THE HURONS

Sainte-Marie was a Jesuit mission within Huron territory on the edge of Georgian Bay (present-day Midland, Ontario), which served as a respite for priests posted to remoter communities and where Huron converts came for further instruction in Christianity. Construction began in 1639. At its height, the palisaded community housed some sixty Europeans (priests, donnés, lay brothers, and engagés); in 1648–1649 about three thousand Huron[8] visited the site. Sainte-Marie was not attached to an existing Huron village and had no permanent Native residents (Tummon and Saddy 1993:5).

Sainte-Marie was a pivotal point in the expansion of French civilization, trade, and religion into the continent's interior. Allied with the French, the Huron found themselves embroiled in warfare with their traditional enemies the Iroquois, who were supported by the English and Dutch, enemies of the French. The Iroquois launched a war of destruction against the Huron in a bid to capture fur-rich territory, and the Huron, decimated by epidemic disease and politically split between Christian and traditional factions, were unable to resist. Across the 1640s, priests were killed as well as Hurons: the remains of Jean de Brébeuf and Gabriel Lalement were buried in the church at Sainte-Marie in the spring of 1649. Shortly afterward, the remaining Jesuits made the painful decision to burn Sainte-Marie to prevent its capture by Iroquois. The Jesuits and some of their converts spent the rest of the year, including a winter of terrible starvation, on a nearby island in Georgian Bay. In the spring of 1650, those left alive returned to Quebec (Trigger 1987 [1976]).

Sainte-Marie is a sad place: the end of Jesuit dreams of conversion, of French dreams of colonial expansion, of the Huron confederacy; a symbol of Native conversion, of intertribal warfare fuelled by imperial rivalry, of epidemic disease, starvation, and dispossession touched off by European contact. It is, for these reasons, also a terribly important place that has the potential more than any other historic site to communicate some of the nuances and consequences of colonial contact, topics that many historic reconstructions shy away from. The site was excavated between 1940–1960, and was reconstructed in the 1960s as a Canadian Centennial project with funding from the Society of Jesus, the University of Western Ontario, and the Ontario government (Hawkes 1974:23). The site itself is on a 100-year lease from the Jesuits, and is run by the Ontario government.

The reconstructed palisade (to which another layer was added for security when the Pope visited in the 1980s) encloses two longhouses, the Jesuits' quarters, two chapels, and work buildings.

Figure 1.10. Empty longhouse interior, Sainte-Marie among the Hurons. Photograph by Drew Davey.

Interpreters portray Jesuits, donnés, traders, and Huron, except that the Huron are represented by Ojibwa, who moved into the area after the Huron left. Budget cuts in the 1990s have reduced interpreter numbers, leading to reductions in building furnishings (which tend to be stolen by visitors when there is inadequate supervision). Remaining interpretive activities include food preparation and cooking, animal care, log squaring, and craft work: the site transforms European colonialism into a French-influenced, very early "pioneer" setting. Its interpreters also attempt the difficult task of communi-

Figure 1.11. Longhouse interior with furnishings, Sainte-Marie among the Hurons. Photograph by Drew Davey.

cating the goals and worldviews of both the Jesuits and the Hurons. The Native interpretation program was begun in 1982 with a grant from the Georgian Bay Tribal Council to hire ten costumed Native staff. Staff funding was later assumed by the site, but this early grant worked well to establish relations between Sainte-Marie and local bands (Lunman 1995:19; Lefaive, Brunelle: personal communication 1994). Levels of Native staff have been maintained recently despite budget cuts: staff have been cut in administrative and other interpretive positions.

The site has faced staffing challenges in addition to the lack of Hurons. There were no European women present at Sainte-Marie in the seventeenth century, and women were initially hired at the reconstruction to work as tour guides wearing "park ranger"-style uniforms. When they demanded to wear costumes, equity laws enforced it, and the site has since put women in men's costumes. Administrators are dreading the day that a woman asks to portray a Jesuit, especially as Sainte-Marie is a Catholic pilgrimage site and has generally good relations with the nearby Martyrs' Shrine. As well, to cope with requests by Native staff that they not be "ghettoized" by being assigned only to the longhouse area, all staff are now rotated through all buildings. Visitors are as likely to find an Ojibwa woman in a European building as a white woman dressed as a donné in the longhouse. My own observation on-site suggests that this strategy leads, unfortunately, to a good deal of confusion among visitors, who ask if the Jesuits "kept women" or why there are no Native people in the longhouse.

Sainte-Marie does tackle some of the difficult aspects of its history in public interpretation. Dramas enacted by interpreters consider the issues around conversion and cultural change, the splits within Huron communities as the result of this, and the relationships between Jesuits and the Huron. Elsewhere, dried corn in large quantities reminds visitors of the dependence of Jesuit people on the Hurons. Given the sparse nature of the props in many parts of the site and the site's struggle to maintain interpreter numbers, however, it is hampered in what it can portray.

Sainte-Marie is concerned about its financial survival and has considered many strategies to counter declining visitation rates. An historical dinner theatre now takes place at the site, and a Friends of Sainte-Marie group has begun fundraising. The site updated its introductory video in 1986 (the original portrayed Iroquois as marauding savages and the Huron as primitive, and resulted in complaints by Native groups to the Human Rights Commission). The Jesuits themselves have received the new video well, but many Catholic visitors seem to be offended by its pro-Native perspective (Lunman 1995:20–22). Given the political furor of the 1990s over European missionization of Native peoples, this site is going to continue to be very difficult to manage; given the continuing budget cuts, it will have to cope very creatively indeed. Given the potential importance of the messages this place can communicate, it stands to make a crucial contribution to public history in Canada, and deserves to succeed. Whether it can communicate some of the difficult messages associated with its particular history in the face of the pressure to increase visitor numbers remains to be seen.

NOTES

1. Major works on Native-White interactions include Axtell 1981, 1985; Grant 1984; R. White 1991; B. White 1982; Van Kirk 1980; Brown 1980.

2. Works such as Van Kirk 1980, Brown 1980, and research by Bob Coutts of Parks Canada have been central to interpretation at LFG.

3. The Cree in Red River were mostly northern Muskegowak peoples from the area between Lake Winnipeg and Hudson's Bay, who had chosen to relocate in the settlement.

4. Historically, there were no tipis on this site. Conical lodges of birchbark over poles (*wigwassikamikag*) or oval bark lodges were recorded in the settlement during the nineteenth century.

5. I am grateful to Peter Boyle, Manager, Historical Operations, and Ann Magiskan, Native Heritage Officer, at Fort William for information provided in October/November 2005 on the direction of Native interpretation at the site, and site operations generally, since 1994.

6. The site hopes, however, to engage in a planning exercise for this venture in partnership with the local Aboriginal community within the next few years.

7. Ojibwe is the commonly used spelling of the tribal name in Minnesota.

8. The Huron people today term themselves Wendat in Canada. I use the historic term to avoid confusion with the name of the site.

Chapter Two

Cosmologies

The "theatricality of history making" involves the notion of viewing in a space so closed around with convention that the audience and actors enter into the conspiracy of their own illusions. (Dening 1993:74)

Beyond these images, whether their users knew it or not, lay a particular ideological agenda—the imagery constituted a kind of language for signifying the meaning and fate of the Native population of North America. (Jasen 1995:17)

Historic sites often advertise with claims of authenticity: "Come and see the past as it really was!" However, reconstructions are in many ways not like the historical communities on which they are based: they are not just reconstructions, but constructions. They show selected aspects of life in the past, and their carefully researched authenticities are shaped by ideologies as much as political and pragmatic considerations. While each site has its own particular history, these places also have much in common about how they have developed and the messages they emphasize. This chapter explores the collective histories and meanings of historic sites and their representations of Native people. I argue that reconstructed historic sites articulate core beliefs about "the frontier" in North American society, and about the relative worth of settlers and Native peoples. These beliefs have legitimated historic processes of colonization; they remain pervasive throughout North American society; and they continue to affect social and political relations in the present. At the same time, these sites have begun to change, and their shifting representations of the past suggest that there is more than one set of beliefs in play at historic sites. One of the main reasons that the revisions of historic sites to include Native peoples has been difficult is that Native perspectives are in complete

31

opposition to the dominant-society ones which have shaped these places, to the extent that they call into question the purposes and audiences for historic commemoration. However contested they may be, though, these revisions have been happening for some time. The relationship between historical representation and social hegemony that I set out in the first part of this chapter is thus questioned in the second part of the chapter. As Bruner reminds us, hegemony is "something strived for rather than finalized or achieved" (Bruner 2005:127); there are "always dissident voices and challenging readings," alternative voices telling other histories (Bruner ibid.). In this chapter I begin to tell a few of these stories; in later chapters I will examine how such broad structures of meaning play out on the ground, in the work of Native interpreters, the experiences of visitors, and the encounters between them.

Since the late 1970s, the nature of public memory and public history representations has shifted along with public debate and academic research in North American society, as these began to emphasize the inclusion of minorities, immigrants, women, and laborers to a far greater degree than had been the case in earlier decades. Combined with the determination of Native peoples to gain greater control over their lives and the representations of their cultures, this shift has led to the revision of historical narratives communicated by public history sites. These changes suited—at some levels—the official policy of multiculturalism in Canada, and the growing emphasis on ethnic identity in the United States. The politics and pragmatics of the implementation of Native interpretation have, however, limited the extent of this important revision at historic sites, and the implications of this shift for North American society more broadly. So has the continuing importance of the mythical cosmology that many historic reconstructions perform in North American society.

THE COSMOLOGY OF THE FRONTIER

A cosmology, in anthropological terms, is a belief system, an account of the ordering of the universe and the relative places of beings within it. Cosmologies are most often expressed as stories about a sacred time when powerful ancestral beings walked the earth. We call these stories myths, and whether they pertain to Greek gods misbehaving, Adam and Eve being evicted from the Garden of Eden, Coyote or Waynaboozhoo getting into yet another scrape, or George Washington chopping down cherry trees, they express deep, core beliefs—which might be difficult to express in any other way— about how one should behave to be a moral person.

Myths also function to articulate the collective memory of a people and of their world: not a history in the chronological sense, but a cumulative record of experience and knowledge gained. Individuals link their own histories and experiences to these larger ones to make sense of their own lives, doubly so given the idealized values and behavior expressed by myth. All our lives are informed by one myth or another.

One of the myths which has shaped settler countries across the colonial experience has been that of cultural and racial hierarchies, accompanied by beliefs about the technological superiority of Western, settler societies and how, in Wayne Fife's phrase, Europeans "earned" North America through hard work (Fife 2004:69). These myths have been associated with the North American frontier.

Whether one speaks of the frontier of the American West, or the earlier Great Lakes or later northern frontier, what most Americans and Canadians think happened on the frontier lies at the roots of North American identity. It was the very place where the "inevitable progression" from Native to settler society is supposed to have occurred. Its symbols say much about who we think we are today. We associate it with "honest values, good neighbors, hard work, virtue and generosity, the success ideology, and the sense of community" (Bruner 2005:167; see also Lowenthal 1989:120). As Richard White has noted, we have imbued such things as covered wagons and log cabins with "latent narratives" about "migration, primitive beginnings, and ultimate progress" (1994:12–13). The frontier was thought of as a wild place to which European settlers brought the light of civilization, of Christianity, of Western technology and agriculture. For centuries, the frontier has been popularly thought of as "the engine of progress and the domain of real men who dominated other men and nature. . . ." (White 1994:49).

In this narrative, the men (and women) who were dominated were Native, and like the wilderness they lived in, they had to be transformed, or allowed to vanish in the face of progress. The common assumption by settlers during the colonial era that their society was superior to tribal ones; that the frontier had an inevitable plot; that tribal peoples should conform to a certain image of the Noble and Authentic Savage, untainted by adaptation to historical reality and contact, if such peoples wished to maintain a place within North American society—these myths are still woven into our society today. The frontier, where this process occurred, has become, in our collective consciousness, a sort of crucible for the production of North American society, a place and process heated by conflict over access to land and resources. The frontier has become our heritage, and as Robert Hewison (1989:17) reminds us, "heritage is a source and vehicle for myth."

The imagery of the frontier, in this sense, has become an equally coded and ideological "language for signifying the meaning and fate of the Native population of North America" (Jasen 1995:17). Displays of Native people have often used the frontier as a setting to evoke and enact such stories. Buffalo

Bill's Wild West Show, which was advertised as "an exact, complete and entirely genuine historical and equestrian revelation" (Blackstone 1986:53), was the most popular such display, and it had many imitators. In Buffalo Bill's shows, Native people performed within linear narrative scripts that used a series of vignettes of battles to show the ultimate triumph of Civilization over Savagery. In this century, reenactments of the frontier myth remain popular: at Disneyland's Frontierland, visitors are encouraged to shoot at various targets, including Indians, at the entrance. Frontierland works so well, says Patricia Nelson Limerick, because its designers have created

> a scene chock-full of the shapes and forms that . . . say "frontier," with the assumption that any visitor so stimulated visually will fall into step with the mythic patterns of frontier life, pick up a gun, and blast away at whatever is in sight (Limerick 1994:72).

Many other frontier-theme venues (Oregon Trail sites; monuments to pioneers) do not overtly refer to Native people, but tend to reinforce notions about hostile race relations while glamorizing the role of White settlers (see Wilson 1992:206; White 1994:55). That the frontier, and the stories and values associated with it, retains mythic functions for parts of North American society, is also suggested by the furor over the exhibition *The West As America* (Truettner 1997), which dared to suggest less than celebratory interpretations for classics of frontier art.

Many historic sites are reconstructed frontiers: trading posts, explorers' wintering camps, early missions, and military posts that functioned as outposts of empires, literally marking the boundary of the frontier. The fives sites on which this study is based were all frontiers of one kind or another in the past, places of cultural contact, where the copresence of and relations between tribal groups, Métis, and Europeans was crucial to the historical processes in which each site was entangled. As I argue in the chapter on "Encounters," these places still function as sites of cross-cultural encounter, this time between Native staff and non-Native visitors.

To think of these places as "frontier sites" begins to suggest the problematic issues of representation they negotiate, and the ways in which, like all visual culture, the images these places convey work to construct and maintain "a sense of order in a particular place and time" (Morgan 2005:29). Like Buffalo Bill's Wild West Show—also set on the frontier—historic reconstructions have always incorporated elements of entertainment and myth as well as authentic period details. Skansen celebrated imperialist nostalgia, and the myth of the vanishing ethnic Primitive; most "pioneer villages" in North America celebrate the establishment of modern settler society and its assumed triumph over the wilderness and Native peoples.[1] And, like Buffalo Bill's show, many historic sites have portrayed Native-White relations as a dramatic battle between the forces of Good (Europeans) and Evil (Savages). A fascinatingly detailed diorama (finally removed in the late 1990s) and an annual reenactment at CM focused on the 1763 attack and capture of the fort by Native people, without discussing Native motives or context for the attack. The stories that historic sites tell, says Alexander Wilson, "are meant to take visitors back to an earlier day: the years of victory over wilderness and savages" (1992:207). In planning the early interpretation at LFG, Barbara Johnstone referred to life in Red River as "a war against the wilderness and starvation" (Johnstone 1962:5). Similarly, a picture of a 1950s parade-float reconstruction of Fort William shows a popular understanding of the fort: it has Hollywood bastions, gun slits, and palisades (flying the Union Jack, of course); and in front, characters representing Daniel Boone, an RCMP officer, a Wild West cow hand, voyageurs with modern firearms, and Indian chiefs in plains headdress (Jasen 1990:15).

Figure 2.1.   Fort William Float, Jubilee Parade, 1952. Photograph courtesy of Thunder Bay Historical Museum Society, 984.53.880XXX.

For site managers and staff, this conflation of the authentic and the mythic can be horribly frustrating: somehow the daily canoe landings and cannon firings at sites today, for all the archival research and educational intent behind them, can seem like Buffalo Bill's daily attacks on wagon trains.

Historic sites have thus enacted core beliefs of North American culture in the theatrical setting of their reconstructed buildings, wigwams, and palisades. These are sites of cultural performance. Broadly defined, cultural performance involves the public display of crucial beliefs and structures of a society within a special context or frame (Beeman 1993; Manning 1983; Schechner 1985; Snow 1993:183–212; Kapchan 1995). At living history sites, this involves the articulation, within the stage set of the reconstruction, of beliefs about the relative worth of Native peoples and settlers, about the inevitability of settlement and of the displacement of Native peoples, and about the utopian nature of historic communities.[2] Thus, historic sites have functioned, on one level, as a stage on which "Indians" play roles in a settler history of progress.

Tourists are both audience and actors in this performance; the costumed staff are the rest of the cast. These combine to form, in Dening's words, a theatre so permeated with convention, with a certain set of standard expectations, that both audience and actors enact them almost automatically. The script for this play was written long ago, and most of us know the characters, plot, and dialogue by heart. If you put a voyageur, a fur trader, an "Indian," a wigwam, a log building, and a palisade together, you conjure up a story about history and culture contact. It is the story of the conquest of North America, of the winning of the West for settlement, of wagon trains and Mounties and patriotism. Of a similar kind of performance in Africa, Barbara Kirshenblatt-Gimblett and Edward Bruner (1994:467) state that, "the story line of the show, the colonial drama of the primitive Maasai and the genteel British, of resistance and containment, of the wild and the civilized, was in place long before" the production was staged. In North America, "Indians" have always played a central role in the consciousness of settler society, representing the Others conquered in the process of creating that society.[3]

Little wonder, then, as I will discuss in later chapters, that many visitors to these places exhibit automatic, stereotyped responses: children break into Hollywood-Indian war whoops, parents make jokes about scalping, and families earnestly inquire of staff in cottages outside the stone wall at LFG if they feel safe out here with the Indians. Frustratingly for site managers and staff, the specific place and year so carefully reconstructed, and the positive messages they wish to communicate about Native peoples, often translate for visitors into the generic frontier drama of good White guys and savage Indians: as one Native interpreter at LFG expressed it in 2005, "I think they think it's [the period depicted] a lot longer ago than it is."

For members of the dominant society, visiting such a place evokes a pow-erful and empowering origin myth (see Bruner 2005:167). The myths of the frontier have always served to reinforce an idealized social structure: one in which Native peoples were subordinate to settler society. Across North Amer-ica, this structure has been true until very recently. Despite the much greater visibility and agency displayed by Native peoples in the past decade or so, in the popular consciousness, the old beliefs are still present. The myth is there-fore still very much alive for people who come to these reconstructions, which serve as "populist attractions . . . commemorating collective memory, into which visitors' personal memories are slotted" (McIntosh and Prentice 1999:592, citing Connerton 1989). They are literally *lieux de memoire,* sites of collective memory, places "where memory crystallizes" (Nora 1989:7) and is expressed materially. Memory, Nora notes, "insofar as it is affective and magical, only accommodates those facts that suit it" (1989:8), which partially explains why historic reconstructions have so often been "celebratory, and not simply a legacy of habits and artifacts" (McIntosh and Prentice 1999:592). The celebratory aspect of the sites is often seen in their marketing campaigns[4] which emphasize nostalgia, the opportunity to experience "life in simpler days"—which in these situations is also imperialist nostalgia (Rosaldo 1989:60), a way of calling to mind the heroic deeds of White culture heroes on the wild frontier, and how they triumphed over the wily savages and the harsh environment (see Kirshenblatt-Gimblett and Bruner 1994:435, 467). Experiencing nostalgia for such stories is another way of wishing that such dynamics might continue.

Imperialist nostalgia has been the predominant characteristic in the history of displays of ethnic or indigenous peoples. The first reconstructed historic villages were developed in Scandinavia in the late nineteenth century to pre-serve elements of folk cultures that were being destroyed by increasing in-dustrialization. In Michael Wallace's words, these sites—funded by industri-alists—"set out to preserve and celebrate fast-disappearing craft and rural traditions" (Wallace 1981:188; see also Anderson 1991:18–33, Wilson 1992:220).

Such displays were done for the benefit of middle-class people who ad-mired these European equivalents of the Noble—and Vanishing—Indian, but who were not prepared to alter their own lifestyle which was suppressing these traditions. They were strongly related to the ways in which non-Western people were displayed at World's Fairs; one early site founder, Artur Hazelius, sent groups of people to be displayed at these fairs (Anderson 1991:25–26). Within the fairs themselves, some of these people were viewed in tableaux showing the changes from traditional to modern life: Dakota chil-dren at their lessons in a schoolroom, for instance. The main attraction, though, were the living areas on the fair grounds where everyone from Inuit to Hottentots lived, on display, in structures representing their traditional homes. These structures, and the house furnishings and clothing worn by the participants, were intended to be "authentic," like those at living history sites. While the displays were ostensibly educational, the crowds saw these people as exotic curiosities, and their "primitive" ways were contrasted with the scientific technology in the central exhibits, which was promoted as the hallmark of civilization. Tribal peoples were thus exhibited as relics of the past, within categories that marginalized them and thus affirmed dominant-society control over them (Kreamer 1992:368; Harris 1990:122–23).[5] A parallel mode of display involved village or house settings erected at zoos. A group of Sicangu Sioux lived for a season at the Cincinnati Zoo in tipis during the summer of 1896. The zoo's annual report for that year stated that "the exhibition of wild people is in line with zoology, and so, when we exhibit Indians . . . or any wild or strange people now in existence, we are simply keeping within our province as a zoological institution" (Meyn 1992:21).

By the end of the nineteenth century, Native people were perceived as things of the past, especially as the "taming" of the western frontier seemed complete. Frederick Jackson Turner's famous work on the American frontier, published the same year as the Chicago World's Fair, exhorted readers to imagine "the procession of civilization marching single file—the buffalo, . . . the Indian, the fur trader and hunter, the cattle-raiser, the pioneer farmer . . ." (cited in White 1994:13). This perception served a useful purpose, "for it allowed [Whites] to see Native people as 'authentic' and yet ineffectual and unthreatening at the same time" (Jasen 1995:17). By relegating Native people to the past, members of the dominant society refused to take them seriously in the present: another aspect of the colonial control of such performances (Fabian 1983), as was the way in which Native peoples were incorporated into the history of the dominant society (as in the chronologically sequenced acts of Buffalo Bill's show), becoming episodes in the conquest of North America.

In this light, Daniel Francis (1992:102) has claimed that Native people who participated in such performances were, in effect, caged by a dominant culture that controlled both what they performed and how they were perceived:

> The Performing Indian was a tame Indian, one who had lost the power to frighten anyone. Fairs and exhibitions represented a manipulation of nostalgia. They allowed non-Natives to admire aspects of aboriginal culture, safely located in the past, without confronting the problems of contemporary Native people. Frozen as they were in an historical stereotype, Performing Indians invoked a bygone era. By implication, they celebrated the triumph of White civilization.

Such ideas have also been prevalent in the literature on indigenous peoples and cultural tourism. I shall explore that literature in greater depth in the chapter on Native staff, but would note here Dean MacCannell's claim that ethnic tourism does not result in significant benefits for what he refers to as "touristified ethnic groups" who are "often weakened by a history of exploitation" (1984:386). From such perspectives, cultural performances are entirely negative and reinforce colonial relations of inequality. What I wish to examine next are the ways in which such representations of Native peoples have been part of the history of historic reconstructions.

HEGEMONY'S HISTORY

Historic sites are not the only form of public representation to articulate social myths and the beliefs they encode: museums, too, have functioned as "space[s] within which the world is ordered" (Prösler 1996, cited in Hendry 2000:154), articulations of idealized relations of power between peoples displayed, and the dominant society doing the displaying.[6] Both forms have been powerful in part because they are official (or, at least, the versions of these genres examined here; there are privately run historic reconstructions and museums which are not considered here). Like museums, public history sites are state-sponsored and funded by government: Fort William and SMAH, for instance, are part of the province of Ontario's Department of Tourism; LFG is administered by Parks Canada, and CM is part of the government of Michigan. Official sites such as these have promulgated what John Bodnar calls "public memory," the official version of the past:

> a body of beliefs and ideas about the past that help a public or society understand both its past, present, and by implication, its future. . . . The major focus of this communicative and cognitive process is not the past, however, but serious matters in the present such as the . . . structure of power in society. (Bodnar 1992:15)

As sites of cultural performance, then, these places go beyond simply articulating core beliefs, to performance in the sense Judith Butler (1997) might have meant: ritual behavior, words, and physical acts which in fact create, make real, and reinforce the intended effect.

The intended effects that public history sites have traditionally had have been tied up with constructing a shared, national sense of the past. Like monuments and museums, historic sites are part of the "imagining" process on which nations are based (Anderson 2003 [1983]); their officially-agreed-upon past, no matter how mediated or contested, provides a sense of tradition and unity in a multicultural, often fragmented society. It also underpins and presents — and therefore upholds — particular versions of social reality, again, officially approved. If we use the past to understand and legitimate the present, then what we show about the past matters in the present. With these ideas in mind, it becomes clear why prior to the late 1980s, heritage-agency policies in both Canada and the United States favored themes of national importance (military, exploration, and fur trade sites) and discouraged the commemoration of minority, labor, and other "divisive" themes (Norkunas 1993:27, Taylor 1990:44, Taylor 1983:24). Native peoples were presented within this framework, if at all, in ways which emphasized colonial control over them and in the context of historical narratives that celebrated the establishment of that control.

Within this nation-building perspective, the western fur trade was seen as the extension of capitalism into the wilderness and thus a precursor to the founding of modern Canada (missionization was seen as the extension of another element of "civilization" into the wilderness). As A. J. B. Johnston has noted, the Canadian parks system acquired many military and fur trade sites "as examples of the advance of EuroCanadian civilization and sovereignty across the land" (Johnston 1995:4). The fur trade fit perfectly into the "nation-building" concept of historical significance as "a necessary link between savage wilderness and civilization" (Coutts 1993:1). Many fur trade sites were designated as official historic sites within this perspective. LFG was also designated because in addition to having been a fur trade site, it was the location where the first Western treaty was signed in 1871, clearing the way for settlement.

The idea of "nation-building" through historic commemoration also had to do with communicating core values and identity to be shared across society. In Canada, provincial heritage bodies were formed by 1900 in a "spirit of patriotism, or, more precisely, of neo-romantic, British-Canadian nationalism" (Jasen 1990:12; see also Friesen 1990:199). These groups, which were in line with academic and government thinking at the time, wished to celebrate the expansion of the Empire, the extension of British culture to the darkest corners of the globe, and the virtues of British culture during a time of high non-British immigration to Canada in order to maintain their perception of the superiority of British civilization and the natural right of rule of the Empire (Jasen 1990:12, Taylor 1990:47; for American parallels, see Jonaitis 1992:23, 41–45, Wallace 1991:185). A broad spectrum of professional and academic society saw historic sites as places where the masses could be educated, and where national pride, knowledge of national history, and national values could be communicated.[7] In 1960, Barbara Johnstone, the first superintendent at LFG, felt strongly that the site should communicate the value of British laws and society in Red River's past to "problem groups" of society, including adolescents and recent immigrants (Johnstone 1960), and that such education comprised one of the primary reasons that LFG should operate as a national heritage site. Similarly, Colonial Williamsburg's mission statement during the 1950s focused on the desire of the primary funder, Winthrop Rockefeller II, to promote such patriotic ideals as "opportunity, individual liberties, self-government, the integrity of the individual, and responsible leadership" (Wilson 1992:218). Williamsburg has also functioned since the 1950s as a reception center for foreign dignitaries because it is both perceived and promoted as a shrine to such national principles (Greenspan 2002).

As part of the process of making material an idealized view of the past which upheld an idealized version of the present, historic sites have tended to portray a highly selective set of themes, and have typically shown a past which is overly prosperous, overly peaceable, and overly White (Snow 1993:22–36; Wallace 1991:184–87; Schlereth 1990 [1984]:350; Norkunas 1993:24; Leon and Piatt 1989; Horton and Crew 1989; Lowenthal 1985, 1989). In a powerful collective visual and narrative effect which transcended the researched details of individual rooms and sites, these places told a selective story about who "we" are, how our nation came to be, who hindered this process, and who helped. Historic sites have thus often focused on elements of the "civilization" of a region, such as fur trade sites, explorers' lives, or the homes of successful entrepreneurs, bringing to bear on these themes an educational and inspirational tone.

Native people were included within this nation-building perspective, but in patterned and patronizing ways: as exotic and fascinating Others in fringed clothing, as Noble Savages who aided the fur trade and settlement, or as Savages of the Wilderness, suggesting threats to civilization that were overcome in the course of history. They were always presented as sidekicks to non-Native historical stars; their contributions to the fur trade and to exploration were downplayed, and their own perspectives on the past were unvoiced. Thus, a commemorative plaque dedicated to La Verendrye, unveiled by the Canadian Historic Sites and Monuments Board in the 1920s, stated that "his explorations and those of his sons doubled the size of Canada"—a statement which was not only an anachronism, since Canada did not exist in La Verendrye's time, but which failed to recognize the crucial contributions of his Native guides (cited in Taylor 1990:51). Similarly, in Manitoba, Chief Peguis was commemorated by a plaque in 1924 which was dedicated to him as the "whiteman's special assistant in grateful recognition of his good offices to the early settlers" (quoted in Friesen 1990:206). The memorial makes no mention of Peguis' own goals or of his leadership of his people. At historic reconstructions, the true numbers and roles of Native peoples have never been shown, even where Native peoples numerically overwhelmed small groups of Whites or where Whites were dependent on Native peoples for food or for political support. For years, at fur trade and Great Lakes military sites, a token chief would be interpreted, generally only on special occasions when events illustrating colonial control were enacted: treaty signings, ceremonial welcomes of settlers, or the return of an explorer and his Native guide.

Such perspectives informed early interpretation at several of the sites I examined. In the early 1960s, in preparation for the opening of the fort to the public for the first time, LFG site director Barbara Johnstone placed topics such as European fur traders, exploration history, the founding of the Red River Settlement, and the transition from Rupert's Land to Canada well ahead of "Indians" on her list of important themes to be interpreted. When she did mention Native people, it was in superficial categories that suggested they were unimportant in Red River (Johnstone 1962). At FWHP, which was a pioneer in including Native peoples in its interpretation, the first lodge, according to now-retired interpreter Freda McDonald, was built "for dwarves"—unlike the large European structures on site, which were rebuilt to their original proportions. This literal, physical diminution of the presence and roles of Ojibwa people is very much an unconscious expression of the broader way in which the dominant society has perceived Native peoples in history.

As Laurel Thatcher Ulrich has noted, this diminution of Native peoples and their roles in the past, their recasting as sidekicks and quaint friends or savage foes, is one of the ways in which historical narratives (in whatever form) have "transformed the violence of colonial conquest into a frontier pastoral" (2001:250). Native peoples are shown only in certain roles within these stories: as savages resisting that frontier pastoral, or as marginalized, rather leprechaun- or childlike figures who existed within it. Such stories fail to question the processes through which the imposition of such control has taken place, or through which it is reinforced by such stories. Randall McGuire has questioned these processes for the effects of standard national histories, which act in a

> double-edged process whereby Native Americans have become included into the pantheon of national heritage as symbols of premodern, naturalized social beings (i.e., "savage Others") and, at the same time, progressively excluded from the mainstream of American political culture. They have become "vanishing Americans" in proportion to the degree to which they have lost control over their own pasts to archaeologists, historians, and other specialists and to the extent that their present existence has been reduced to a mere reflection of a past over which they have little or no control (described in Hill 1992:810–11).

At historic reconstructions, what is shown or not shown about the past mat-ters for precisely these reasons: "hegemonic culture does not depend on brainwashing the masses but, rather, on making some forms of experience more available than others" (King 1993:264, cited in Mason 2004: 842). While I agree with Ruth Abram that historic sites can be critiqued not only for their processes of " concealment, obfuscation, simplification, and misrep-resentation" but "by ignoring the public's call for a usable past . . . that . . . can be used by the public to make informed choices for themselves" (2002:135–36), I might also argue that in fact the past represented through such skewing has been all too usable by majority society visitors to historic reconstructions, to maintain a political status quo that has kept Native peoples marginalized. Sites make certain stories and ideas about the past appear to be natural by repeating, over and over, the image of the controlling elite, and by not displaying the complex realities of the past, such as the experiences of mi-nority groups (Wallace 1991; Norkunas 1993:24). Perhaps most importantly, they have tended, along with their scholarly textual cousins, to present history "as an inevitable progression from the simplicity of the Native American to the complexity and sophistication of the Anglo-American" (Norkunas 1993:23). Alternatively, they represent the stereotype we might call the "Eco-Savage," and/or the "Egalitarian Savage," a new variant of an old pattern of using Native peoples as foils for European society: the Noble Savage redux. Even these superficially positive images are Othering, though, and fail to dis-place the controlling relations between Native peoples and the dominant so-ciety in historical narratives. Native histories are incorporated into these nar-ratives, but in ways that confirm their subjugation: as elements of the story of the dominant society, a perspective that effaces and denies the very different perspectives on the past that colonized groups acquire.

These sites are not simply value-neutral, "objective," three-dimensional versions of scholarly research or "facts." While they may be intended as such, they are also vehicles by which members of the dominant society tell stories about the past and about today, and about how we should act toward Native people (White 1994:55): they express a belief system and an implicit model of social and political structure that is central to the dominant society from whose perspective they portray the past. This is why I believe that national historical narratives serve cosmological functions, providing an ordered vi-sion of the links (or barriers) between peoples, the basic social and political structure of a society: in this case, between Native peoples and Europeans. The same stories that have justified and upheld settler society have con-strained and damaged Native societies, and maintained their marginalized place in North America.

When I analyze public history sites, then, I am not looking at them simply as facets of the tourism industry, but as reflections of public culture, as sites that reflect and reinforce social structure, the patterns of relations between social groups, and the legitimacy of authority in North American society. I see visitors to these sites not just as tourists, but as participants in enacting core social myths and the structures of power they uphold. It follows, then, that revising the nature of the representation of Native peoples and histories at these places is incredibly challenging at some core levels of society.

Having said all this, I recognize that as articulations of official, public memory, heritage agencies and the places they reconstruct are incredibly political and contested institutions, mediated by differing visions and agendas about what parts of the past should be commemorated and reconstructed, and why.[8] If these sites are hegemonic, imposing a top-down vision of the past in order to create certain effects in the present, it is a very complex and often undermined hegemony.

Only in the 1990s did the presence of Native interpreters at historic sites become significant, and their stories seen as central to the sites. This shift had much to do with the policies of multiculturalism in the present which first Canada and, later, the United States, embraced during the 1990s: historical narratives at public history sites began to shift in order to depict a multicultural past. Even now, however, the nature of the representations of Native peoples and their roles in the past remains fundamentally distorted, sometimes amounting to tokenism: there are too few Native staff and structures to suggest the real size of the historical Native population, the historic balance between Native and non-Native populations is usually reversed, and Native people are depicted in roles which fail to acknowledge their centrality to these places. What has been done at these sites has been tremendous, but across the board, it isn't nearly enough. The place of Native peoples within North American society, and standard definitions of who historic reconstructions are for, will have to change considerably more than it has before we see anything like accurate representations of Native peoples in the past.

OTHER PERSPECTIVES

"We're playing ourselves, the real First Nations people" (Cecilia Littlewolf-Walker, FWHP, 1994).

Things are, of course, a good deal more complicated than they first seem. While there are still processes at work in these cultural performances that marginalize Native peoples, Native peoples are also using these places to affirm and articulate Native identity to themselves and to visitors, and to challenge established social structures. Historic reconstructions are sites of cultural performances, plural.

They also reflect the fact that the cultures performed are constantly changing. The change in global conditions that has led to increased Native self-determination in recent years is now being reflected in our public dramas. Consider, in this context, Corinne Kreamer's thoughts about such performances:

> Expressive events such as tourist encounters and museum exhibitions are stages. . . . The drama enacted in these events is the drama of civil society. . . . Official history, social justice, appropriate norms for behavior, definitions of identity—these are all contested and negotiated in exhibiting contexts. The drama metaphor is appropriate, but this is not a playful drama. . . . Exhibitions can be, and are often taken to be, certifications of self and history. These are no small matters (Kreamer 1992:372).

This is, in part, the basis of my objection to the patterned diminution of the roles depicted of Native peoples at historic reconstructions: if we suggest that Native peoples were unimportant and marginal in the past, we suggest that they are also in the present. The fact that government-sponsored heritage agencies have not taken the representation of Native cultures in the past seriously says much about how Native peoples are viewed by the dominant society in the present as well.

However, historic sites have added Native areas and interpreters, and are now weaving Native themes throughout their reconstructions—and not just at the sites examined in this book, but at hundreds of sites across North America. If these are places where culture is performed, then they are also places where quite different dramas and beliefs may be enacted. Such change has come about through both global forces—the effects of global decolonization; a new attention to issues of power, voice and authority within representative modes such as museums and scholarly texts; the adoption of social history by public historians—and through more local forces, which comprise national, regional, and quite local politics. If the drama enacted at historic sites has been revised with the addition of Native interpreters and perspectives, if these officially sanctioned reconstructions of history have been altered, does this mean that North American society is changing?

Intriguingly, the balance of power implied between societies has shifted in the language that sites use to describe the past: the most common phrases used to describe historic Native-White relations since the early 1990s are "alliance" and "interdependence." This is a far cry from the patronizing "friend of the White man" rhetoric of earlier representations, asserting much greater Native agency and importance. Such shifts are a reflection of revisionist scholarly works on Native history and Native-White relations, and of the realities of multiculturalism. More important than these, however, has been the profound determination of Native peoples to reclaim control over their histories and lives, which they have pursued vigorously across the past few decades at many levels. Gaining control over the representations of their cultures and histories has been a key strand in this movement, and has led to confrontations with museums and public history sites. David Neufeld, a senior historian and project manager with Parks Canada, notes that First Nations people have actively disputed the myths behind most public history commemoration:

> In spite of the national story, aboriginal people and their stories have not disappeared. They remain a dynamic and vital cultural force within the country, rejecting the national story in which they are rendered powerless. First Nations in Canada vigorously contest the story through political and social actions, actions founded and directed by a set of coherent and powerful oral traditions that distribute power and meaning to their lives and forward their vision of the future (Neufeld 2004: n.p.)

The nature of this contestation has sometimes been quite robust. In Canada, it led to the Canadian Museums Association Task Force on Museums and First Peoples (1992), a national consultation exercise which led to a set of recommendations for the museum and public history professions on the involvement of First Nations in heritage representations. This process resulted in Canadian heritage agencies such as Parks Canada being mandated by government to establish partnerships with Native peoples and involve them in reviewing interpretation: "Parks will involve First Peoples in the presentation and interpretation of places, objects and historical information to which they are traditionally related" (Parks Canada 1995:3; see also Parks Canada 1992).

Such initiatives have not all come from "head office"; they have often been developed by site administrators, many of whom are social historians hired during the era of the adoption of social history by heritage agencies (see Gable and Handler 1994:119). Since 1990, most of the sites considered here have commissioned reports or solicited input from Native consultants on the themes, interpretive messages, and operation of the sites. Pine City commissioned a report on the fur trade from an Ojibwa perspective from Sandra Goodsky, a Native interpreter and consultant; LFG put together an oral history project; CM hired Anishinaabe consultant Wes Andrews to provide input for exhibition planning. There are many non-Native administrators at these sites who want to increase Native perspectives in their programming, because they embrace recent revisionist scholarship, understand the need for heritage agencies to be responsive to social developments, and believe the time has come to do this.

It is crucial to remember, however, that in embracing change, heritage agencies have tended to fulfill their own mandates, and have often failed to consult with Native communities about community goals—which are often quite different. David Neufeld's experience in trying to implement Parks Canada's policy of involvement of Aboriginal peoples suggests the problems involved when heritage agencies and individual historic sites attempt to simply add the "Indian side of the story," without understanding that this does not exist in isolation from Aboriginal perspectives on history, or from Aboriginal community goals. Neufeld was assigned the job of obtaining "the Indian side of the story" for the Chilkoot Trail, a site managed by Parks Canada pertaining to the 1890s Gold Rush. It was agreed within Parks that this could best be done through an oral history project with First Nations peoples through whose territories the Trail ran. Parks Canada staff expected that the project would enhance existing interpretation about the Trail. As Neufeld recounts, however:

> The Chilkoot Trail Oral History Project did not fulfil the initial expectations of Parks Canada for the "Indian" side of the Stampede story. The attempt to simply throw light on a previously unexplored facet of the national story was a failure. The Carcross-Tagish [a First Nation consulted on the project] were quick to challenge the project's assumptions of the past. In one instance after an extended set of oral interviews the project anthropologist and an Elder relaxed on a lake shore. The anthropologist found a stone hammer nearby and brought it out to the Elder as proof of the aboriginal presence. The Elder briefly examined the stone and then casually threw it back in the bushes, "What have I been telling you all week?" As the project progressed we watched the First Nation similarly discard the Parks Canada notion of the project objectives. It became clear there was no "Indian" side of the Chilkoot Trail gold rush story, the stampede was simply seen as an annoying but brief interruption of their lives. Community stories instead put forward a parallel historical narrative describing their long use of the area and their connection to it as "home" (Neufeld 2004: n.p.)

Carcross-Tagish objectives and perspectives were completely different from Parks Canada's in this case, and underscore Randall McGuire's statement that, "just because two peoples share a common history does not mean that they shared a common experience" (McGuire 1992:816). Beyond the contestatory aspect of Native perspectives, though, are broader discrepancies about why Native peoples should participate in heritage commemoration. Heritage commemoration has been linked, in the non-Native community, to nation-building; for Native communities, it is linked to what we might think of as nation rebuilding, and issues of postcoloniality and sovereignty. This can be manifested as a desire to convey tribal perspectives on historical experiences;

to have their own voices heard, and to have the authority to speak directly; to assert tribal continuity of occupation and control in a region; to be seen by governments as an equal audience or partner for heritage interpretation. Native partners see interaction with heritage agencies by Native communities as part of a larger package of political action linked to land and resource claims and rights. At Colonial Williamsburg, the nascent American Indian Interpretation Program is seen by some Virginia tribes as potentially an important platform to assert continuity of tribal presence and thus build a case for federal recognition of tribal status (Peers, field notes, 2004).

Neufeld makes the point that Parks Canada's failure in the Chilkoot Trail project lay in its failure to consider the dynamics of adding "the Indian story"—a very different set of perspectives—to the nation-building model still held by Parks, rather than reconsidering the model altogether. Similarly, a Parks Canada conference in 1992 asked delegates to "identify some of the general contributions of Aboriginal Peoples which might lend themselves to the representative commemoration approach. Advice would also be appreciated as to those aspects of shared experience of Aboriginal people which might be associated with important historic places . . . " (Parks Canada 1992): again, trying to fit Native histories and experiences into existing dominant society emphases for commemoration. This is a patronizing level of inclusion that fails to grant real authority to Native peoples, and has resulted in the decision by some Native communities not to work with heritage agencies. In other cases, Native peoples participate only insofar as they can pursue their own goals. Thus, while "The Chilkoot [Trail] itself doesn't appear to be of interest as an Aboriginal national historic site [to Carcross-Tagish people], . . . [because] it is perceived as being too cluttered with other national messages to encourage meaningful community participation (e-mail, Neufeld to Peers, September 6, 2005), other First Nations/Parks collaborations have been successful because they serve Aboriginal goals in a very direct way. Most of these so far have been in northern Canada, where new Aboriginal national parks and historic sites have been created as part of Treaty agreements.[9] These areas are comanaged, some actually owned, by Aboriginal groups, under the Parks Canada umbrella. As Neufeld has pointed out in personal correspondence, such parks "are permanently protected landscapes that allow continuing aboriginal use" for traditional purposes such as hunting: "the national park area is [thus] an effective extension of the [treaty] settlement land quantum, thus adding to the total amount of land that the aboriginal group either owns outright, retains surface rights over or comanages with a constitutionally reliable partner" (e-mail, Neufeld to Peers, September 6, 2005). The new National Historic Sites in the north, which are owned or managed by Aboriginal groups (with Parks providing some professional support for research and planning) appear, Neufeld says, to serve the same function for Aboriginal peoples: they are an extension of territory controlled by Aboriginal groups, and a way to protect important cultural resources related to traditional culture and land-use. They also allow Aboriginal groups to "control the messages and values that they wish to commemorate thus managing their relationship to the national narrative" (e-mail, Neufeld to Peers, September 6, 2005).

This raises the question whether national or regional heritage agencies— Parks Canada, the Ontario Department of Tourism, the Mackinac State Historic Parks Commission, the Minnesota Historical Society—can in fact serve the very different interests of minority groups, or represent their very different versions of history (Neufeld 2004, 2002). Indeed, Neufeld pointed out in concluding his thoughtful note to me that while First Nations appreciate aspects of comanagement and control over new historic sites and parks in the north, this does not mean they are willing to embrace Parks' narrative of nation-building: what First Nations are actually articulating, he says, is "their desire to refrain from absorption into the nation."

This is an important issue, and raises several complexities. We need, firstly, to bear in mind the very real differences between the situation in northern Canada, where tribal people still live on and largely control traditional lands, and that in southern Canada and the United States, where tribal groups often have less power over traditional lands and cultural resources. In considering the relationships between tribal groups and heritage agencies in more central and southerly areas of North America, I see several conflicting trends. While museums and historic sites certainly once functioned (and may still) as shrines or temples to social and racial hierarchies (Duncan 1995 [1989]), this has begun to change. The idea that museums and historic sites should be "forums of discourse" between peoples (Ames 2003), that they should challenge preconceptions about the past and encourage visitors to consider the legacies of the past in the present (Abram 2005)—these have become useful, and quite energetic, models for these places. They link, as well, to an emerging model of museums and heritage sites as sites for social change and social justice (Janes and Conaty 2005), as moral institutions. Within this model, the promotion of social history is part of a set of values which embrace more egalitarian modes of representation and links to a model of the multicultural society: hence the popularity of terms such as "alliance" and "interdependence" for contact-era sites and their staff. Many staff at historic sites whom I interviewed clearly believed in such values. Those who were less enthusiastic about the broader social implications of such perspectives were still keen to make history "more accurate," in their words: again, more representative of the full spectrum of life in the past and its material culture.

On the other hand, in revisiting sites in 2005, it became clear that formal relationships between historic sites and Native communities have failed to develop. In 1994, all five sites were exploring such links, either as partnership agreements with local tribal governments or through formal recruitment procedures for Native staff. Some of these initiatives were mandated by heritage agency policy, such as Parks Canada's 1995 response to the Task Force on Museums and First Peoples, which advocated "partnership with Aboriginal people" (Parks Canada 1995). Despite various efforts by heritage agencies to establish these, by 2005 none had come to fruition. Several site managers felt they had failed in this, and it was clearly a sensitive matter. At other sites, informal relationships had developed of varying strength. Some were formal, annual contacts with local bands; others involved frequent consultation on various matters. Commenting on developments at FWHP since 1994, Ann Magiskan noted that while the fort's Native advisory board had ceased to exist, she has adopted the practice of going to elders in the Aboriginal community and asking for advice to introduce new topics, or for their teaching and contribution to the work she is doing at the fort: in effect, she is serving as the site's liaison with an informal board of advisors (interview, November 15, 2005).

This is quite different from the direction that major museums have taken across North America, where the establishment of Native advisory boards and the appointment of representatives of Native communities to boards of governors has become relatively common.[10] The withering of formal relationships at historic sites has been paralleled by an overall reduction in Native interpretive staff on each site: where in 1994 all sites were actively trying, despite budget cuts, to increase their Native staff, numbers had dwindled by 2005 (along with overall interpreter numbers) and one site has cut its Native interpretation program altogether.

Budget cuts and the struggle to address falling visitor numbers are the obvious causes of such developments, but the difficulties of reconciling opposing interpretations of the past, and different agendas for commemoration, are involved too. I think that the work of Native interpreters, and the implications of adding Native perspectives, has posed more fundamental challenges to historic sites than expected, and I think that some sites have begun to stall in their process of revision because they cannot reconcile different cultural perspectives on the past, cannot meet the very different agendas of tribal communities, and are uncertain how to proceed. Equally challenging has been the question of to what extent sites should communicate the damage caused to Native peoples by the historical eras and processes they represent: showing agency, adaptation, and resilience is a good balance to older messages that Native peoples became either extinct or assimilated as the result of European contact, but such positive messages now tend to veer away almost entirely from the darker aspects of Native-White relations: alcohol abuse, disease, dispossession, and racism are touched on, but seldom incorporated into the central messages of public history sites.

Budget cuts are undoubtedly painful at these places, but may also be providing a convenient reason to put the process of revision and change on hold. Bureaucratic processes also impede revision (see Gable and Handler 1994:120 and ff. for a discussion of this at Colonial Williamsburg). Parks Canada, for instance, has implemented a Commemorative Integrity program, which insists that heritage sites be interpreted according to the reasons they were originally designated as national historic resources—and ignoring more recent scholarship on Native histories and Native-White relations in historic situations (Coutts 2000; Peers and Coutts forthcoming). This policy has certainly not been conducive to the creation of comanagement agreements with First Nations at the more southerly Canadian sites. Lower Fort Garry has done an exemplary job of incorporating revisionist scholarship, and could have branded itself as Canada's original multicultural community with strong links to local First Nations. Instead it could be forced to interpret the signing of Treaty One, an event considered by most local Aboriginal people to be the moment of imposition of external control over them. This does not bode well for either the interpretation of Native perspectives or for the involvement of Native communities with the fort. Other sites face similar tensions: CM, which has had to axe its Native interpretation program for budget reasons, continues to host the reenactment of the 1763 event, to the frustration of local Native people, but hopes to include Native perspectives in future displays. Overall, few sites have appointed Native staff at the managerial level; the vast majority are seasonal workers, with little input into decisions about content for interpretation, or budgets.

The failure of relationships between heritage agencies and Native communities across these and other sites is significant, and a symptom that commitment to this new direction in public history could potentially come to a dead end. Without a real commitment to inclusion, without formal relations with Native communities, and without explicitly tackling the harder issues of the past and their legacies in the present, it is entirely possible to see historic sites still as places of commemoration of dominant society heritage, dressed up with a few Native people, with lip service paid to Native presence and roles in history.

On the other hand, some sites and individuals have taken a fairly radical approach to change. Armin Webber, the former director of FWHP, told me that he "would like to see that people are aware that 50 percent of the Native encampment is to serve the needs of the Native community, and 50 percent is to serve the [site's] needs" (1994: personal communication). Webber was extremely proud of the fact that Native staff showed a sense of ownership of the encampment and were starting to bring friends and family to see it, and that Native people came to the Ojibwa Keeshigan festival to learn about historic cultural practices that they could not see at powwows or other kinds of gatherings. Webber's comment on the encampment is very powerful: it began, he says, as

> a well-researched display, just like any other place [in the fort], and we hired Natives to man the display. And the display was operated, dramatized. And [then] 3 or 4 years ago . . . Natives took ownership of that encampment in a different way than had ever happened before. And they all of a sudden wanted to bring their friends out like the white people do to see the fort when the visitors are in town . . . and share with them their encampment, their heritage. And if that [the encampment] didn't look like it was comfy, like your home would be—do you know the difference between your home and a display? Well, that's what happened. They said, "I don't want a display. I want [it to look like] a home."
>
> And that's what happened. And I stepped back and said, "the Native development in Canada is so important right now, it's [the community] going through so many convulsions, we are not here to fight that trend."

Others can also see the potential for using these sites to support Native cultural healing and self-determination. The Sto:lo First Nation sees Fort Langley National Historic Site in British Columbia as a resource to learn about historic culture before twentieth-century pan-Indian influences, and in the mid-1990s was establishing training workshops at the fort for Sto:lo people (Carlson and McHalsie 1995). Some other historic sites have taken similar approaches. Clearly, though, this is a dramatic shift in intent and operation for these places. This is not the climate that Gable and Handler have accused Colonial Williamsburg of fostering, where managers were "interested mainly in managing an image of openness and debate rather than participating in discussions they could not control (1993:27)." Some managers think quite daringly about these places. Others still find it easier to deal with the politics of heritage agencies than to venture along the unfamiliar road of creating relationships with Native communities.

As well as seeking to change the basic relationship between historic sites and themselves, Native people seek in many cases to change the basic narratives told by these sites, to voice their own perspectives on history and the complex relationship between past and present. Reconstructions which deal with historic interactions between Native peoples and Europeans have been grappling with these issues for years. Older narratives about history as the process of the cultural domination of Native people are being replaced (partly in the form of the Native interpreters themselves) by stories about adaptation, continuity, and mutual cooperation (see Clifford 1991).

Every one of the Native interpreters with whom I have spoken over the past decade has said something to the effect of, "We're playing ourselves, the real First Nations people" (Littlewolf-Walker, interview, 1994). Though called squaws and braves many times daily by site visitors, they are not such in their own minds; their roles and their work mean completely different things to them. Whether they, and historic sites along with them, will be able to revise our understanding of the past and along with it our understanding of Native-White relations in the present, remains to be seen.

The project of adding Native interpreters and themes to historic sites, then, goes against the grain of traditional historical narratives and the ways that the past has been represented at historic sites. In this light, the addition of Native people and voices to historic sites is a critical challenge to notions of present society as well, and raises the question of whether mainstream heritage agencies can in fact serve the agendas and needs of minority communities. I am hopeful that they can; I am certain that the addition of Native staff and perspectives has already set a host of changes in motion. I am reminded of Edward Bruner's citation of Bakhtin, in Bruner's analysis of another "frontier" site and its competing meanings:

> Power, however, is rarely monolithic and is usually contested. Despite the efforts of a nation or an organization to present a monolithic view of itself as integrated and unified, without dissent or internal conflict, . . . [this] is something strived for rather than finalized or achieved. . . . [It] is not just a tension between the official and the heretical or between the establishment view and its resistance; rather it is one of multiple competing voices in dialogic interplay (Bakhtin 1981, cited in Bruner 2005: 127–28).

Some of the most important of these "multiple competing voices" at historic reconstructions are those of visitors, of the sites themselves and the messages they communicate through their physical elements, and of Native interpreters. In the following chapters, I will examine each of these sets of voices and perspectives.

NOTES

1. Barthel 1990:83 and Lowenthal 1989 also discuss the telling of mythic stories by reconstructed historic villages.

2. I am indebted to Garry Marvin of the University of Surrey, whose 2005 ISCA seminar at Oxford on foxhunting and English landscapes encouraged me to develop

the concept of "physical landscape . . . as a performance space" in relation to historic reconstructions. In her review of literature on tourism, Harrison (2003:31) notes several studies which have focused on tourists as "myth-makers" and myth participants; this is part of the larger idea of the "tourist gaze."

3. On the roles of "Indians" in North American society, see Deloria 1998 and Huhndorf 2001.

4. SMAH website, accessed November 16, 2005: "Follow in the footsteps of Ontario's first Europeans . . . features a unique time in Canadian history when French missionaries and their workers lived and worked among the Wendat. A rare chance to see the earliest in Canadian pioneer life. . . ." FWHP website, accessed November 16, 2005: "Tired of technology? Need a break from the rat race? Come to Fort William Historical Park, and experience an authentic 1815 fur trading post. Relax in a wigwam in the Native encampment, bake a loaf of bread with Mrs. Taitt, . . ."

5. There is of course a much longer history of Native cultural performances for non-Native viewers, going back to the early contact period with tribal peoples who were transported to European courts as proof of discovery and later tribal delegations and dance groups. See Dickason 1984:205–12; King 1991.

6. On the relationship between museums, ethnographic display, and colonial regimes of power, see, among others: Stocking 1985; Coombes 1994; Karp 1992; Lidchi 1997.

7. Such perceived functions paralleled those of museums; see Coombes 1994:123–24, 126–27; Bronner 1989; Duncan 1995 (1989).

8. Taylor 1990, Taylor and Payne 1992, Johnston 1995, and McGuire 1992 have written about the politics of creating and revising heritage agencies and their public representations of the past.

9. These include Ivvavik, Vuntut, Aulavik, Tuktuk Nogat in the Yukon and western Arctic.

10. Much of the recent literature on museums has also emphasized the importance of relationships with source communities: Peers and Brown 2003 and essays by Michael Ames, Gerald Conaty, Trudy Nicks, and Ruth Phillips within this; Hanna 1999; Kelly and Gordon 2002:163.

Vignette: Nokie

Audrey Wyman, who is of Ojibwa descent, received awards for her interpretation at the North West Company Fur Post, where she worked until the late 1990s. She wore a leather dress, moccasins, wispy braids, a head scarf full of trade silver brooches, and looked like a grandma. Her first-person tour of the post was done in an accent somewhere between Ojibwa and voyageur French, and went, in part, like this:

"My name is Nokie, it means Grandmother in Ojibwa. You can call me Granny if you like; lots of people do . . . now, if you have any questions, you just ask me; [teasing tone] I'm so old and wise that I have all the answers!

" . . . Now, here is where the voyageurs lived. Now, I know what you are going to say: Nokie, you told us that Mr. Sayer had sixteen men, and some with families—all living in two little rooms?? No, no, no. The men who are lucky are the men who are married, and they will live in a nice Ojibwa wigwam outside of the walls, which the wife will build, and [he] has a better life. Every year as part of his wages he gets two shirts and two pairs of pants—by fall his elbows and knees are coming out of them, but if he has a good wife she'll go to the trader and get good wool cloth and make him new clothes for the winter . . . he won't have to walk around with holes in his moccasins. She's going to make sure that he has everything just fine, because she doesn't want those old women who talk about everybody to say, 'Oh, that poor man—she doesn't take very good care of him!'

"And he will eat better, too, than the voyageur. Everyone goes to the boss every day to get the rations: deer and bear meat that the hired Indian hunters bring in; wild rice, bought from the Indians. The men have to cook it themselves, and most of them are lousy cooks. But the Indian woman, she knows every berry bush within a mile and a half, and she picks them and dries them for winter. She digs the cattail roots, which are like the potato. She raises the garden with corn and beans and squash . . .

"Well, you want to have a wife. You don't just walk down to the Indian encampment and buy a wife the way you buy a dog for pulling the sled. You have to do things the right way, so it's smart to talk to the old people and find out what the proper etiquette is. . . . Now the last thing an Indian mother and father need is a lazy son-in-law lying around the wigwam. If it were a young Indian man, he would have been bringing deer meat and bear meat . . . for months to show what a good provider he is, somebody you would really like to have as a member of your family. But Pierre, he has no time to hunt. But he has credit at the company store. He goes to the boss and the boss says, 'Pierre! Take for the father this fine NWC trade musket. And for the mother, a big kettle for making maple sugar, and blankets for all the relatives . . . ' Pierre says, 'But boss, I can't afford it!' 'Ah, no problem, Pierre; just sign on to work for the NWC for three more years.' . . . Maybe Pierre will never go home to Montreal now; maybe he will stay here and become the ancestor of people who live here in your time. But most of all, now this young voyageur is related to everybody within twenty miles of here, and they'll come to this fur post to trade . . . "

[Moving to Mr. Sayer's room]: "Well, you know, Mr. Sayer is lucky to be married to the wife that he has. She's an Ojibwa woman . . . [who] comes from a very distinguished family. Her father and two brothers did a great deal for their people, and it raised Mr. Sayer's status to become a member of such a respected family. She has been a great help to him. When they are here, they have been married nearly twenty years, they have children . . . and he sends to Montreal and gets her a fine dress such as the ladies wear. . . . When Mr. Sayer leaves here, he goes back to Montreal eventually, and she chooses not to go with him. I don't blame her: I wouldn't go! . . . you know, in Montreal in 1804, the Indian woman and the Métis woman like myself, they are not always accepted among high society. Oh, Mr. Thompson and Mr. Harmon, they take their wives back with them, but they weren't trying to mix with what you might call the upper crust; they had nice little estates in the country. . . . You know, those women from across the ocean, they're treated like dogs! She can't vote, she can't hold property. The Indian woman has a better life. She owns the lodge because she built it . . . "

Chapter Three

Anishinaabeg

This chapter is about Native people who work as interpreters at historic sites, their goals and agendas; about issues of identity, authenticity, and authority within touristic encounters; and about the roles of Native staff in cross-cultural work at historic sites. I have headed the chapter *Anishinaabeg*—"human beings," the word used by Ojibwa people to name themselves—to signal a shift in perspective from the other chapters, away from the visions of site managers and academics and visitors (all of whom are mostly non-Native) and focused more on the experiences and perspectives of Native staff at these places. As a non-Native person, I have found it challenging to begin to see from this other perspective. I am not alone in finding this reorientation of perspective difficult. The majority of the literature on cultural tourism fails to engage with Native perspectives, and is far more influenced by the emphases of academic discourse than by the experiences of Native people working in this sector. In beginning to construct a new set of meanings informed by Native perspectives, then, it seems appropriate to use a Native word.

I use the word *Anishinaabeg*, in the plural, to indicate also the plurality of Native perspectives within and about these places and this kind of work: there is no single, monolithic "Native perspective" on historic sites, and the experiences of Native staff who work at them has been quite diverse. Nor, indeed, were all the Native staff I met Ojibwa; they also included Odawa, northern and plains Cree, Métis, and others. They ranged from the ages of eighteen to elders, and had widely varying relationships with their bands: some had always lived in their birth communities on reservations, some were raised in cities, while others had been raised by non-Native families. They included Christians and traditionalists, those raised within reserve communities and those raised without contact with their communities, those who could and could not speak a tribal language, make bannock, do beadwork, or tan hide. These are not "generic Indians," then.

Anishinaabeg is also used in Ojibwa discourse to mean "Native" as different from "non-Native," though, and I use it in this sense to refer to them as a group distinct from the equally diverse non-Native staff at these sites. Native interpreters described to me a set of perspectives that seem to be common to them and different from those of non-Native staff, a set of motivations, self-investment in aspects of the work, and experiences in interacting with visitors. As a group, Native interpreters also represent certain elements of Native communities: they are interested in history and in knowing tribal traditions, in education and working with the public, in learning period-specific decorative techniques and archivally documented details of life in the past. As a group, Native staff are representative of those parts of their communities which have historically been involved in negotiating face-to-face encounters with outsiders, whether in the context of diplomacy, of trade, or of tourism. Not all tribal members have such interests, and some of those hired to work as interpreters quit because the work is not for them. I will try to explore the commonalities shared by Native interpreters while also bearing the diversity very much in mind.

If the physical reconstructions at historic sites serve as stage sets for the performance of history and culture, it is the interpretive staff in period clothing who serve as key members of the cast, who communicate the official messages of each place, and who answer visitors' questions. Most importantly, at the sites I researched, it was the interpreters who contradicted traditional historical narratives, and visitors' assumptions based on these, by voicing alternative perspectives. Native interpreters infuse their work with highly charged, personal meanings that challenge on several levels the stereotypes expected by visitors. These messages are not always the same as the official ones of the site, or the ones they are supposed to communicate. Many non-Native staff also challenge such stereotypes and support the work of Native interpreters. In this chapter, I examine the work of Native interpreters at historic sites: their goals, the special nature of their work, the ways in which they respond to prejudice and misinformation, and their relations with other staff and managers.

Native staff draw on the same historical information, academic sources, and training material as their non-Native counterparts. As Gable and Handler note (1993:28), "there is an elaborate process for the training of [front-line] personnel" which involves the translation of the site's official themes into characters and information to be used by interpretive staff. This process differs from site to site. At North West Company Fur Post, interpreters are given a crash course on the history of the site, on the function of each building, and on material culture and daily activities of the era, and they research and write the biographies of the characters they play. At LFG, training consists of one week in which health and safety and employment topics are emphasized; there is little training in the history of the site or in interpretive techniques. Instead, staff are given thematic and building-specific binders of information to read and digest: "The Big House," "Women at LFG," "Native Women," "Voyageurs," and so forth. Native interpreters share this training with other staff and are hired to deliver standard messages and information just as non-Native staff are. What Native interpreters do differently, though, is add to their reading of site manuals, building inventories, and scholarly articles a personal perspective to the imparting of this information: "our people," they say; "we did it this way." Ann Magiskan, Native Heritage Program Officer at FWHP, advises Native interpreters to "make it personal: for me it is personal—having Aboriginal and French background, the fur trade *is* personal for me" (interview, November 15, 2005).

"Making it personal" for Native interpreters affects what they say as well as how they say it. They portray history from a very different perspective than that of the dominant society, such as "Nokie's" tour spiel which emphasizes a Native and laboring-class view of the fur trade: this is history as intimately experienced, more than a simple description of events. Their view of history tends to contradict the upbeat, nation-building master narratives within which these sites were all originally commemorated.[1] Thus, the fur trade, from a Native perspective, was not just a presettlement phase of North American history. Nor was it solely a set of relationships that stimulated Native culture through the development of trading and marriage partnerships and the adoption of new material culture. This latter set of ideas has been a popular interpretation in fur trade literature since the 1980s, but tends to downplay the dark side of the trade, the legacies of which Native people are all too aware: the effects of over-hunting; the fur trade as a transportation network for epidemic disease, and the horrendous damage that the use of alcohol in competitive trade situations did to Native communities. Missionary activity tends, similarly, to be viewed by many Native people as an attack on Native culture and sovereignty. If contact-era historical reconstructions have been interpreted largely as triumphs of civilization over savagery, they are often seen within Native perspectives as bitter moments marking the processes through which Native peoples lost control of their lives. Asking Native interpreters to explain standard historical narratives to dominant-society visitors involves them in difficult decisions as to how to reconcile such oppositional perspectives. And since public history sites still do not often communicate these darker aspects of the past, Native interpreters find themselves also in the bind of feeling that they have to do so themselves, unsanctioned by official site messages.

Despite their disparate tribal and personal backgrounds, as a group Native interpreters identify far more closely with their work than non-Native interpreters do: as they told me repeatedly, "we are playing ourselves."[2] Because they represent Native people, and are Native people, and are seen by visitors as Native people, there is a conflation of what they represent and who they are.[3] They do not get to dissociate themselves from their work as neatly as their non-Native colleagues: unlike their non-Native colleagues, they do not get to go home at five o'clock as different people from those they represent all day. This is true, as well, for Native staff who deliver educational programs, an increasingly large part of what these places do: Native staff teaching moccasin-making or talking about the fur trade to a group of Brownies, a sixth-grade social studies class, or a group of local adults are still Native people talking about and demonstrating aspects of their own culture. "We talk about history but we bring it forward to today," says Ann Magiskan of FWHP, and she and her staff are prepared to use their personal lives as examples to reinforce messages when they are teaching (interview November 15, 2005). Such staff are living representatives of the culture on display, and experience a thinner and more porous boundary between self and representation than, say, a cooper displaying an occupational-based set of skills. Because of these dynamics, Native interpreters tend to break frame, and add to their historical information a sense of how their lives are still affected by the events of the past.[4] Compounding the tension this conflation of personal and professional identity can produce, Native interpreters tend to have different goals than their non-Native counterparts. Native interpreters are focused on fighting prejudice, communicating revisionist knowledge about their ancestors, and on learning skills and knowledge which support their personal identities: they have more invested in the work than most non-Native interpreters.

OTHER HISTORIES OF CULTURAL PERFORMANCE

In the chapter on "Cosmologies," I explored a history of cultural performances in which Native peoples were forced to conform to stereotyped expectations. And as I demonstrate in the chapter on "Visitors," the vast majority of visitors to historic reconstructions fit into a category that we might think of as the dominant society. The dynamic of people from this category, in the context of historic sites, looking at costumed Native interpreters, risks repeating the dynamics at World's Fairs. It also risks the continuation of colonial relations which characterize cultural tourism in some Third World settings, something that Native Hawaiian scholar Hanauni-Kay Trask has called a form of "cultural prostitution" (Trask 1999; see also Harrison 2003: 13–14).

This is not what I see happening at historic sites, however. The nature of cultural display at these places is very different from past representations and from other forms of cultural tourism. We need to bear in mind that there are alternative histories of performance, and that cultural performances for non-Native audiences have long served the goals of tribal peoples, some of which have involved creating bridges with non-Native society and counteracting racism. Native interpreters who work at historic sites today are working, as they see it, within a tradition of cultural performance in which the performance serves as a vehicle for Native agendas and creates an intercultural space which can be controlled by Native performers. Understanding this tradition helps us to understand the distinct work of Native interpreters.

While Native people were forced to do certain dances and wear certain costumes in early shows, few of them were literally coerced into performing: most chose to, for pragmatic reasons.[5] Performers themselves noted that the pay and the living conditions were often better than anything on the reserves (Beauvais 1985:136; McClurken 1991:94). In 1881, Ojibwa men who guided tourists through St. Mary's rapids at the Sault were paid two cents a pound for fish, and five dollars each time they guided a tourist down the rapids (Jasen 1995:98). Blanchard (1984:113) similarly notes that "Kahnawake Mohawk were most active in the entertainment business during the Depression" when other work was scarce. Research with Native craftworkers for the exhibition "Across Borders: Beadwork in Iroquois Life"[6] and by Trudy Nicks on the contexts of souvenir production (1999) suggests that performances were often used to bring visitors in to craft sales areas. Shops and performance areas within Native communities were operated by Native men who had worked for Wild West shows (see Beauvais 1985:137; Nicks 1993). Photographs of the Ettawageshik craft sales business in northern Michigan show two generations of proprietors in headdresses and posing (or, in a term used by Native performers, "chiefing") for the camera with bows and drums (illustrated in McClurken 1991:109–10, Ettawageshik 1999).

Performing also offered a chance to escape some of the most restrictive aspects of reserve life. One could wear recognizably Native clothing and perform Native dances, both of which were at times either illegal or discouraged by Indian agents. It was a setting within which traditional skills were valued and could be practiced, at a time when these aspects of Native culture were being actively suppressed. With some shows, one could also travel: Black Elk, the Lakota holy man, joined Buffalo Bill's show because he "wanted to see the great water, the great world and the ways of the white men . . . " (DeMallie 1984:245). In its heyday, Buffalo Bill's show traveled to dozens of venues every year, and its performers toured Europe.

This determination to use to Native advantage the opportunities provided by performance gradually developed into a genre of Native-controlled cultural performance. Despite being shaped to meet the stereotyped expectations of non-Native audiences, these performances have allowed Native people to communicate information about their cultures to foreign audiences, to express pride in their heritage and traditions, to make a living, and to survive emotionally within a colonial context by turning stereotyped images of themselves to their own purposes. These Native-run performances fall roughly into two related categories: theatrical-style performances, such as versions of Wild West shows, traveling "medicine" shows, and community pageants; and Native family craft businesses, in which performance was part of the sales pitch. There were many such performances[7]; the ones I use here are simply intended to suggest the existence of this tradition for Native interpreters working in the same region today at historic reconstructions.

Sioux, Mohawk, and other Native performers who had worked in P. T. Barnum's, Wild Bill Hickok's, and other early "Wild West" shows began organizing their own such shows in the last quarter of the nineteenth century (Beauvais 1985:136; Blanchard 1984:104–106). After the success of Buffalo Bill's show during the 1893 Columbian Exposition, many imitators sprang up, some of which were created by seasoned Native performers who had worked for one of the older shows. One such show was begun by Howard Sky, a respected Six Nations elder, who created a performing and dance troupe in 1946 that toured widely. Sky's nephew Jim Sky purchased the show's regalia when Howard retired in the 1960s, and from then until the mid-1990s, Jim Sky and his extended family performed for audiences around the world (Heth 1992: figures 33, 35).[8] Having grown up in the business, Sky understood what non-Native audiences expected to see from Native performers, and he gave it to them as a hook so that they listened while he achieved his goal, which was to educate non-Native people about real Native cultures, lives, and histories (Sky, personal communication 1993). The men's costumes and many of the acts were Wild West in style, so that if the audience wanted a "real Indian," Sky gave them one; but having thus gotten the audience's attention, he had a nephew recite the Haudenosaunee Thanksgiving Address (a key text in traditional Iroquois culture), and would talk about the Iroquois ceremonial cycle, as well as political and cultural problems facing Native people today. The costumes acted as instantly recognizable symbols to draw non-Native audiences, leaving Sky free to transmit his own messages. "Some people don't like to hear what I tell them," he said (interview, 1993).

Similar dynamics can be seen in pageants organized by Native communities. These were most often given to tourists, such as the Hiawatha pageants at Conway, Michigan, which began in 1905 and continued until the 1950s

(McClurken 1991:94). Others also attracted Native audiences, such as the festival begun in 1935 by the Michigan Indian Defense Association at Harbor Springs, some thirty-five miles from the Colonial Michilimackinac site. Both the festival and the association were founded "to continue Odawa customs and cultural knowledge (and) to promote the growth of their political association" in the wider, non-Native local community. The festival included the lighting of a ceremonial fire, traditional dances, and the giving of Indian names to young Odawa people (McClurken 1991:94–95). Heirloom clothing was brought out for this festival; drums and pipes were used; people camped together and spoke Odawa. Other events involved public naming ceremonies for non-Native people, and one of these had to be held in a stadium to house the large audiences (McClurken 1991:95, 98). Some of the props for these performances were Wild West in nature, but the scripts were written by Odawa people, the dances were traditional, and the events were clearly important to the Odawa community. A similar set of performances at Lac du Flambeau in Wisconsin in the 1950s has been discussed by Larry Nesper (2003). Like Jim Sky's performances, these were intended to assert pride in heritage and identity, to educate non-Native audiences about Native culture, and to combat the prejudice that Native people faced (Nesper 2003a:415).

While such events were based on bitter economic and political necessity and made use of stereotyped elements (the pageant at Conway enacted Longfellow's poem "Hiawatha," which is based on tropes about Noble Savages), they also addressed issues of Native sovereignty. They did this by using these performances as spaces between cultures to communicate human commonalities, to assert identity and dignity, and to claim the right to speak for themselves. Touristic spaces have thus long been appropriated by Native performers to create "new spaces for defining new parameters of identity, livelihood, and meaning" (Adams 2003:571; see also Swain 1977, Stronza 2001:272). Clearly, they did not always manage to communicate these things. There was always the danger, as Fred Gleach notes about a Powhatan performance in Jamestown in 1907, that

> They were visible, and some people were certainly affected, but the ways they were presented were not ones that would contribute to improved recognition and social standing in the modern world—they may have existed but were allowed only to be entertaining icons from the past. The dominant view was undisturbed by the counterhegemonic effort (Gleach 2003:440).

Countering this is Ruth Phillip's declaration that each and every one of the countless sales of souvenir goods by Native peoples to non-Native purchasers (and, by extension, cultural performances) constituted "innumerable small meetings across cultural boundaries" (Phillips 1995:99): repeated contact across cultures in spaces which breached the usual boundaries between them.

All of these performances and events dealt with the relationship between history and identity; all made use of symbols of Native identity to assert self-determination; all were public proclamations of pride in a Native heritage at times when Native people were being pressured to acculturate; all brought Native communities together to plan, profit, and socialize. These dynamics have been true as well in other settings for cultural tourism around the world, ranging from touristic experiences provided by Australian Aborigines and Mayan Indians to those provided by the "Others" of Europe, such as the Welsh.[9] In these examples—which are but a few among many—we can see the need to look beyond the surface of such representations, and the problems posed by theoretical literature on cultural tourism which in general fails to consider the perspectives of peoples who provide such experiences (Stronza 2001:262; Burns 2004:14).

The dynamics of such performances differ greatly from those expressed by Buffalo Bill's Native performers, who also "played themselves," but in shows in which their image, actions, and messages were controlled by Cody to support a dominant-society version of history (White 1994:35). This is not the case for Native interpreters at historic sites today, who communicate messages that they themselves determine, in addition to the official themes of the sites, and who use their work to pursue their own agendas.[10]

I emphasize the distinctive perspectives that Native peoples have brought to touristic performances, and the agency within such work, because these are the people whom scholars of cultural tourism have dubbed "tourees" (e.g., van den Berghe and Keyes 1984:347): a word suggesting passivity, lack of agency, and victimization which has become a central assumption in the literature on cultural tourism.[11] As described by van den Berghe and Keyes (1984:346), "The touree . . . makes it his business to preserve a credible illusion of authenticity. He fakes his art, his dress, his music, his dancing, his religion, . . . to satisfy the ethnic tourist's thirst for authenticity. . . . " Not only does "he" begin to modify his behavior in response to the presence of Whites, but his culture is supposed to become "museumized," "frozen," and lose its authenticity.[12] MacCannell (1984:388) has claimed that "when an ethnic group begins to sell itself, or is forced to sell itself, as an ethnic attraction, it ceases to evolve naturally," and van den Berghe and Keyes warn that, "The first signs of 'spoilage' are clearly evident: requests for payment in exchange for posing for pictures" (1984:346).

Such arguments parallel the arguments about "primitive" peoples that stem from an old Western cultural paradigm. "Primitive" peoples are supposed to be everything that Western people are not: not civilized, not urban, without his-

tory, without market economy, without contact with contaminating cultural influences (i.e., Western society), and without individualism. Such stereotypes
are part of the way in which Western peoples have controlled non-Western
peoples. Clearly, within such a paradigm, "primitive" people cannot demand
cash for photos and remain "authentic" in Western eyes.[13] In the same vein,
scholars who claim that Native peoples are incapable of distinguishing between performances for outsiders and rituals for community members, or that
Native cultures are rendered inauthentic by touristic performance (Medina
2003:354), or that tourism causes indigenous groups to cease to "evolve naturally," suggests that they are seeing Native peoples not as real human beings
in real historical contexts, but as "primitives" for whom tourism leads to a fall
from primeval grace. I would counter the arguments about the purely negative
effects of cultural tourism by pointing out that much cultural performance is
developed in response to Native experiences of loss of sovereignty, loss of
land, and racism, in which contexts the creation of new spaces for communication may be one of the few ways past cross-cultural barriers.[14]

Cultural performers have always been perfectly capable of distinguishing
between overtly constructed cultural representations for tourists and the culture of everyday lived experience. Native performers and their communities
engage in serious and often heated discussion of these issues: performances
are deliberately choreographed, and the selection of cultural elements to be
shown to the non-Native public is debated.

Overall, I would agree with van den Berghe (1994:17), Medina (2003),
Nesper (2003b), Hammond (2001:16) and others that while there are many
difficulties with cultural tourism, it can also renew indigenous cultures. Gamper notes that "by reviving ethnic pride and by prompting a search for authenticity, tourism [has] had the effect of reestablishing traditional culture
even though the 'fake' ethnic markers of the earlier period had worked quite
well as a tourist attraction" (Gamper 1985:251). This has been an important
dynamic in Native communities, as craft techniques, dances, and music have
in some cases been kept alive within touristic performance until recently,
when they have been reclaimed for community use. Cultural performances
have had a range of positive effects on Native communities for centuries.

Indeed, as Native scholars and activists have voiced, *not* participating in
the representation of culture, allowing dominant-society institutions to represent Native peoples in their absence, is far more problematic than cultural
tourism. Native peoples have been campaigning for increased inclusion and
authority within museum- and museum-related representations of their histories and cultures for several decades, and have achieved acceptance of the
need for this change in the production of knowledge. Cultural performances
for tourists have been spaces where Native peoples have endeavored to do

this for centuries, and historic reconstructions have become spaces for Native peoples to speak in their own voices. Native peoples have indicated a strong desire to participate in the creation and delivery of representations about their peoples, and there are important reasons that they should do so. I am reminded of Martha Norkunas: "But what happens when you don't resist? . . . You allow others to control the present through their interpretations of the past" (2004:115).

NATIVE INTERPRETERS AND HISTORIC SITES

Native people who become historic interpreters do so because they share interest in the past. When they become interpreters, they also find that they share with other Native interpreters a distinctive set of challenges in this work.

These challenges begin with the conflation of person and role noted earlier. As the Native interpreters explained, they do not get to "dress up and play history," and then take off their costumes at the end of the day and go home as different people. They are themselves in historic costume, and still themselves when they take off that costume: as Del Taylor, a Native staff member at SMAH, told me, "What a great job—a chance to dress up and be ourselves!" Cecilia Littlewolf-Walker at FWHP similarly stated, "We're playing ourselves, the real First Nations people." The "playing" they do, however, is not of such a ludic nature as that by non-Native interpreters. These people are ambassadors, not actors; they represent their communities, past and present. Keith Knecht expressed the complicated nature of this kind of representation by initially denying that was what he did: "We don't represent Native people; we are Native people! and we want our public to know that we're still alive and living here." The kind of representation that these interpreters do involves both "acting for," as in on behalf of; making present again; and "standing for" (Mitchell 1990:11; Prendergast 2000); at the same time, it also involves being themselves, as well as representing people of the past.

A further complication is the way that Native peoples are entangled in the legacies of the pasts they represent. One might say that they are haunted by their histories, in ways that non-Native people seldom feel. Interpreters who are Status Indians, or on tribal rolls (or not: from a tribe which is not federally recognized, or Métis in the United States where this is not recognized as an official category), whose families were acculturated through residential schools, people who grew up off-reservation because of the political forces that affected Native peoples in the past, interpreters who grew up being told their ancestors were Spanish because their grandparents thought it would be easier on them to deny their Aboriginal heritage—such people exist within

Figure 3.1.   Cecilia Littlewolf-Walker, Fort William Historical Park, 1994. Photograph by Drew Davey in collaboration with Cecilia Little-wolf-Walker.

layers of historical legacies which continue to influence them.[15] The non-Native university students who make up the majority of interpreters seldom feel the past interfering in their lives in this way. Furthermore, Native interpreters who portray historic Native ways of life do so in embodied knowledge of what happened to the people who lived that way, and to their descendants. Like many of the ancestors they portray, Native interpreters have first-hand knowledge of the effects of colonialism on Native lives. "Playing ourselves" gives a whole new meaning to the idea of "living history."

Portraying ancestors has also a double meaning for Native interpreters. For cultural reasons, some Native interpreters with whom I spoke were very uncomfortable when asked to portray specific historic individuals, especially in first-person techniques (i.e., acting as, claiming to be, a specific deceased individual). In contrast, non-Native interpreters commonly represent historical characters: Simon McGillivray, Bishop Anderson, a specific Jesuit priest, for instance. There is also another burden for Native interpreters in representing the dead, for ancestors are held in high esteem as role models: those who lived through difficult times, those who passed the culture on to their grandchildren and kept it going. They are also mourned as those who were sometimes lost to the forces of history. To represent one's people as they existed in the past is thus weighted with both the esteem and the sorrow one associates with ancestors: it is not done lightly.

A few Native interpreters have chosen to portray specific ancestors, or composites based on these, because they feel a connection to that individual. Ruth Christie at LFG portrayed her great-grandmother, Isabella Monkman, and says, "Having the experience of portraying a Native elder at LFG has really been positive for me. Because I'm not only able to be myself there, I get to be an ancestor." A young Ojibwa man who worked at the Pine City site stated that he felt comfortable with the composite character that he had created, because the character had the same ancestry as him, including a European grandfather. Composite characters also suit the fragmentary evidence available for Native peoples in the historic era (Magiskan, interview, November 15, 2005). FWHP has moved to composite first-person interpretation in the Native encampment, modified when necessary to address visitors' questions about the interpreter's life or about Native life in the present. The composite character technique has other attractive aspects: Audrey Wyman advised me that interpreters should base their characters on people they admire "because you will become those people"; she based "Nokie" on all the wise old Ojibwa she could think of. Depending on the site's policy on interpretation, some interpreters choose not to portray specific characters (composite or not) at all, but are simply themselves. These people communicate information to visitors in the second person plural ("oh yes, you'd see us here in the summertime, come to trade" or "our people never did that").

These feelings of entanglement in the past, and the importance in which ancestors are held within tribal communities, increase the conflation of person and role within Native interpretation. These dynamics make this work far more personal and emotionally draining than it is for most non-Native staff. This is compounded by the fact that many visitors' questions are very personal, not about the past. A few examples of the kinds of questions that visitors ask Native interpreters make it clear that these staff members do far more than the usual "emotional work" (Urry 1990:70) of being friendly with visitors that tourism normally demands:[16]

- Marie Brunelle, who helped to initiate and lead the Native interpretation program at SMAH, once had a White tourist ask her, "Are you an alcoholic?"; the visitor assumed that all Native people were.
- "Smoking the old peace pipe around here last night?" (visitor comment to Native interpreters, LFG summer 2005)
- "There was this family visiting and the kids were running ahead, and the dad said, 'Careful, the Indians will get you. . . .'" (Leah, interpreter, LFG, summer 2005)
- Annette Naganashe, who comes from a respected Odawa family and formerly worked at an Odawa museum, came to CM with her public school class as a child. She was one of the few Native students in the class. The class viewed a diorama about the capture of the fort by Native people in 1763, which featured painted warriors bloodily scalping British officers. As her class left the building, one of Annette's classmates turned to her and said, "So you're an Indian"—with all the negative connotations that word could imply. In 1994, Annette worked as an interpreter at CM; the diorama was still there. The exhibit has since been closed.
- comments heard daily at every encampment:

  - "Go stand with the squaws and I'll take your picture."
  - "Are you an Indian Princess?"; "Are you Pocahantas?"; "Are you a Chief?"
  - "Watch out, they'll scalp you!"
  - "Whose scalp is that?" (pointing to a fur or a bison tail)
  - "Woo-woo-woo-woo-woo. . . ."
  - "Do you speak your language?" (most Native interpreters were raised speaking English)
  - "Are you a real Indian?" "Are there any real Indians anymore?"

In 2005, interviewing Native interpreters at LFG, I asked if visitors assumed "there's some sort of a hostile relationship between the Natives and the people in the fort?" and they answered:

Ashley: Yes. And the Pocahantas stuff.

LP: Really! What do they say about Pocahantas?

Ashley: They often call us Pocahantas.

Amanda [imitating visitors]: "Oh, you're so beautiful, Pocahantas!!"

Ashley: Yep, or they take our picture and they ask if the chief will get mad.

Amanda: They like to sing songs in front of the tipi, with random words, and then ask if it's going to rain. . . .

Not only do visitors say these things, they say them over and over again, making the irritatingly repetitive monotony of interpretation described by Valene Smith into a potentially degrading situation for the interpreters:

> Catering to guests is a repetitive, monotonous business, and although questions posed by each visitor are "new" to him, hosts can come to feel that they have simply turned on a cassette. Especially late in "the season," it becomes progressively harder to rekindle the spontaneity and enthusiasm that bids guests truly welcome. . . . Guests become dehumanized objects to be tolerated for economic gain, and tourists are left with little alternative other than to look upon their hosts with curiosity, as objects (Smith 1977:6).

Few of these sites provide standard preseason training for interpreters to assist them in dealing with such comments by visitors; none of the sites acknowledges in job descriptions that the work of Native interpreters involves dealing with

Figure 3.2.   Native interpreter and visitors, Colonial Michilimackinac, 1994. Photograph by Drew Davey.

such comments. At large sites where interpreters average hundreds of contacts with visitors each day, Native staff can find their work very difficult indeed.

Such stress contributes to the difficulties of recruiting and keeping Native interpreters. Herb Clevenger, who interprets Native histories for the National Parks Service, commented trenchantly on how, after correcting racist stereotypes all day with visitors, he then had to beg management for new moccasins for his outfit, and thought hard about quitting (personal communication, 2001).

In response to these pressures, Native interpreters make use of a shared set of attitudes and emphases. Whatever their differences in age or tribal background, every Native interpreter with whom I have spoken over the past decade has been motivated by a commitment to removing discrimination against Native people by educating non-Native visitors. Freda McDonald, the now-retired elder who worked in the FWHP encampment, said to me in 1994 that she was able to forgive a great deal by reminding herself that the tourists she sees have been raised on the wrong version of history; she took great satisfaction in teaching them. Marie Brunelle, who had worked at SMAH, similarly said that "If we can just reach one person, teach one person that we are real human beings, then it's all worth it." For most interpreters, it's "dispelling myths, one visitor at a time."[17] For these people, the educational function of historic sites is primary, but the messages they wish to communicate go beyond the site's official ones: these interpreters are not simply "enlivening . . . meanings already established by their superiors" (Gable and Handler 1994:120). Indeed, they often deliver messages never approved by their superiors. Native staff know that tourists come to have fun, but one of the primary reasons they work as interpreters is because it gives them an opportunity to reach so many non-Native people.

ACROSS THE CULTURAL DIVIDE

Reaching these audiences is not as straightforward as it might seem. For many visitors who have never spoken with a Native person before, the encampment and its staff are terra incognita. Visitors are sometimes uneasy in this area, either looking uncomfortable or verbally hesitant in speaking with Native staff, and some choose not to enter the encampment. Others express curiosity but are constrained by the boundaries created by ignorance. I will explore the encounters between visitors and Native staff further in a chapter on "Encounters," but wish to note here the work that Native interpreters do to establish bridges between themselves and visitors. Thus, walking toward the encampment, the visitor is often hailed by interpreters before entering the space. Visitors are greeted with an orienting statement to give them basic information and to enable the Native staff to take control of the conversation. At LFG, interpreters say, "Hi! Welcome to the Native encampment! You would have found us here in the summer, working for the fort." Native staff also greet visitors with big smiles, "Welcome to our camp! Have you paddled far today?" and often an immediate introduction to life in the camp ("Can you clean fish? If you help us with the fish maybe you can stay for dinner! You see, we are catching fish and trading it to the HBC for goods that our families need . . ."). Such techniques are an extension of the playful approaches and greetings made by interpreters elsewhere on site (see Bruner 2005:166), but are especially needed in this setting to engage visitors who may be uncomfortable speaking to Native people.

Native staff at several sites have sometimes been headed by older women (Freda Mcdonald, Audrey Wyman, Mary Vanderpoel, Ruth Christie, Marie Brunelle), who used a grandmotherly persona to create trust and respect in conversations with non-Native visitors. Nokie's "You can call me Granny, lots of people do" is echoed in Ruth Christie's statement that "One family came to visit me four times this year! The kids would say, 'Let's go visit Kookum' ('grandmother')!" Younger women interpreters sometimes make jokes about their "husbands" or "sweethearts" with visitors. In the all-woman fishing encampment at LFG in 1994, questions by visitors about "Where are your husbands?" are answered first with jokes ("Are you kidding? The fish are being brought in just now—they left so they wouldn't have to clean them!") and then with serious comments on gender roles in Ojibwa and northern Cree society ("Actually, at this time of year, they'd be off up the lake working as tripmen for the Company"). While such playful approaches are used at virtually every historic site in North America (Bruner 2005:166–67), their use in the Native areas of these sites is intended both in the usual way, to begin an interaction with visitors, but also to begin pulling down the barriers that stereotypes erect. More serious approaches are also used in dramas, such as one at FWHP in which Native women interpreters express their concerns about the arrival of white women to the region, and the implications this might have for Native wives and kin of Europeans. In this case, their concern for the effects of racism on their loved ones would work very well to engage visitors' empathy.

Native interpreters' initial statements also deliberately serve to establish themselves as authority figures who speak on behalf of real tribal groups. They frequently say "my people" or "we would . . . ," and to visitors' frequent question, "What tribe do you represent?" they reply, "I *am* Ojibwa/Ottawa/ Cree." At other times, cultural information confidently imparted establishes interpreters' status as teachers. At LFG, visitors entering the tipi are instructed to "turn to your left and follow the circle of the sun and the path of life."

School groups coming to FWHP for a "Life in the Wigwam" field trip may be given a pre-trip briefing in their classrooms by FWHP staff which includes a talk about the importance of elders and about proper behavior in the wigwam; the experience in the wigwam may also begin with a smudge ceremony (Magiskan, interview, November 15, 2005). Native interpreters demonstrate a breadth and depth of knowledge about Native peoples in the past that allows them to address visitors' interests that are often "more about the culture than history," in Freda MacDonald's words.[18]

Much of the discussion about culture begins with responses to visitors' questions about specific objects, followed by links to information about broader aspects of culture or history. The extraordinary materiality of historic reconstructions prompts certain questions from visitors, and visitors who may be concerned that they might inadvertently offend Native staff also tend to focus on object-questions as "safe" entries to conversations. A skilled interpreter can use this as a way into teaching: visitor questions about objects such as ricing sticks, *tikinagans* (baby carriers), fishing nets, carrots of tobacco, pelt stretchers, and various furs can lead to information on spiritual beliefs, gender roles, subsistence patterns, or the logistics of the fur trade. A question about an interpreter's face paint turned into a discussion of Odawa-European relations ("No, it's not war paint, actually; that would have been inappropriate, because my people were allies of the British . . ."); a question about a *tikinagan* turned into information about women's roles, birth control, family structures, and child rearing.[19] Interpreters work hard to supply information that visitors lack, both about props and about culture and history.

Such teaching is also a way of asserting the worth and dignity of Native cultures to prejudiced non-Native tourists. Much of the object-oriented discussion addresses a key set of assumptions that visitors bring with them, which is that Native peoples were "primitive" and technologically inferior to Europeans. This is a variant on the common pattern of visitor responses to historic sites noted by Edward Bruner: a tendency to use historic reconstructions to allow visitors to celebrate progress (2005:167). However, as applied to the Native elements of historic sites, visitor assumptions also reference a widespread notion that indigenous peoples are somehow frozen in time and unable to adapt (Fabian 1983, Price 1989). Thus, Steve Greyeyes, commenting at LFG in 2005, noted that visitors tend to "say things like 'well, you wouldn't have had metal pots and pans back then,' or 'you wouldn't have had matches.' There's a real surprise that we're not cooking with hot rocks in bison stomachs out here." Every Native interpreter to whom I have spoken in the past decade has commented on these assumptions, which I have heard articulated hundreds of times in interactions between visitors and interpreters. In one incident at SMAH, a Native interpreter making a bark container was asked if Native people had scissors in the seventeenth century. The interpreter said yes, that scissors were a popular trade item. On being asked the question for the third time in twenty minutes, however, the interpreter responded to what the visitors expected: he reached around to his knife sheath and pulled out an antler-handled stone blade, to which the visitor responded with a satisfied, "Ah!" Scissors, mirrors, and tin lanterns seem to provoke consistent remarks from visitors on this theme ("Did Indians *really* have scissors/cloth/beads back then?"). When one is representing one's culture, to be thought incapable of adapting must be galling: essentially, what visitors are articulating is the idea that the ancestors of these Native interpreters were stupid.

In response to such assumptions, Native interpreters assert the technological competence and adaptability of their ancestors. To a frequent visitor comment that the lodge "must have been cold in winter," interpreters reply that the lodge is actually warmer than the European buildings, and explain why. The following is a typical exchange on this topic, here between Keith Knecht ("K") at CM and a middle-aged female visitor ("FV"):

K: You know, the soldiers don't like me to say this, but this is the warmest building in the fort in winter.

FV: Really?

K: Well, it's got a low ceiling, and it's pretty small. And the thing is, the house is the chimney. The heat as well as the smoke has to pass through the house, and it warms everything up. With a fireplace, you're sending all the good stuff up the chimney: the smoke goes up, but it takes [woman joins in] all the heat with it. So you actually got to get the hearth hot, and then it radiates the heat.

FV: Yeah, but aren't you breathin' in all that smoke?

K: No, it's not too bad—not too bad.

FV: You gotta be smelling pretty good by the time you leave here!

K: Oh, yeah—I smell like a smoked ham! But once the fire's going good, I can usually control and regulate the smoke by using the smoke flap up top and regulating the height of the door off the ground. So you're actually making the house into a flue.

FV: Yeah, I see!

Native interpreters also provoke conversations about the adoption of European material culture by deliberately adding mirrors, scissors, cloth and other goods to the encampment. As part of these conversations, interpreters emphasize that their people carefully chose certain items but rejected others, and that far from being "primitive," Native knowledge of hunting and geography meant that during much of the early contact period Europeans were dependent on Native peoples, rather than the reverse. Such messages also address the widespread assumption that Native peoples were victims of the fur trade or of missionization. An outstanding trading session held at the Ojibwa encampment at FWHP in 1994 addressed these ideas:

"EN DEROUINE" TRADING SESSION, FORT WILLIAM HISTORICAL PARK

[Featuring the TRADER, in top hat and green velvet cutaway coat; his assistant, a VOYAGEUR with sash, carrying trade items; a TOURIST CHILD who helps the trader to decide on prices; KOOKUM, an older Ojibwa woman in chemise, strap dress, leggings, and moccasins; and a YOUNG OJIBWA MAN (YM) in gartered trousers and voyageur shirt who translates for KOOKUM. Action takes place in the Ojibwa encampment.]

Trader: [greetings and bowings and doffings of hat] . . .the Northwest Company does indeed spare no expenses in providing trade goods for our trade. Now, Kookum, as a sign of trust and respect, I offer to you a gift—a gift of beads, and a gift of tobacco, as I know how important tobacco is to you.

Freda: MIIGWETCH! miigwetch! [Thank you, thank you]

YM: Kookum says thank you for the gift you have given us.

Trader: You are quite welcome, quite welcome indeed! Now I brought with me today, as I have mentioned, quite a number of trade goods, goods from all over the world . . .

Freda: [puts beads on, in paying no attention to trader: MIIGWETCH!]

YM: Kookum says thank you for these nice beads!

[Freda speaks in Ojibwa as she pokes at goods]

Trader: . . . fine ribbons, ribbons from England, excellent for decorating clothing . . .

[Freda points out something on a piece of cloth and talks in Ojibwa]

YM: She says it's dark on that side. [points out large stain]

Trader: Well, it's a rather long journey some of these trade goods take from Montreal to Fort William, six weeks by canoe . . .

[Freda says something emphatically in Ojibwa]

YM: She says these [furs] come from far away, too [i.e., and they're not stained!].

Trader: Yes, I know, gathering the peltries of the animals is no easy task.

[Freda says something, rather wheedling, in Ojibwa]

YM: She says, I work more than you people do, I trap and skin these furs—it's a lot harder.

Trader: Your hard work and toils are very much appreciated indeed!

[Freda pokes goods and talks in Ojibwa]

YM: How much for this?

Trader: A pitcher like that, valued at two beaver pelts. [YM translates]

[Freda exclaims in Ojibwa]

YM: She says that's a little too much!

Trader: Two is too much. Well, what do you think would be reasonable?

Freda/YM: One beaver pelt.

Trader: One beaver pelt for the tin pitcher. [asks tourist child: What do you think? One beaver pelt? she says YES] DONE!

Freda holds up ribbon and one finger: BEHZHIG?

Trader: One? [checks with child: One beaver pelt for that? She nods] Yes, one beaver pelt for that as well.

Freda/YM: One beaver pelt for BOTH! [audience laughs]

Trader: Ohh . . . [to girl: What do you think?]

Freda/YM: These are very fine furs!

Trader: Yes, yes . . . these are quality pelts here . . .

[Freda in Ojibwa, gestures]

Trader: How many beaver are equal to one otter pelt? [Consults with girl] Each otter will be equal in value to one beaver pelt!

Freda: Kaawin! [Young man: Kookum says No.]

[Freda holds up three fingers]

Trader: [watching Freda] Each pelt worth three beaver?! Oh, no!

[Freda stomps over to trader and snatches back her furs, starts walking away, says something in disgusted tone in Ojibwa.]

Trader: Upon further consideration, these are excellent quality otter pelts. I think we could settle upon a value of two beaver pelts for each otter. Does that sound reasonable?

[Consultation; they come to an agreement]

Trader: Are there any other wares here you would be interested in?

[Further bartering ensues over a blanket. Trader asks twelve beaver for it initially, received with amazement and an offer of six from Freda]

Trader: Oh, no. Eight!

Freda: [Sharp "Kaawin!"; long sentence with "Hudson's Bay Company" in English; moves to reclaim her furs again; crowd laughs]

YM: She says she's going to trade with those other people up-river.

Trader: Well, now, let's not be hasty . . . how about seven?

[Freda gets it for six in the end.]

This drama kept a crowd of about seventy-five transfixed for nearly twenty minutes, and conveyed a great deal about the autonomy of Native people in the trade, about their sense of self-worth, about their competence, about European dependence on Native people, about Native ability to manipulate fur trade competition, and about human relationships in the trade. Its messages were based on recent historical research, filtered through a set of outcomes desired by Native interpreters as well as by many non-Native staff, who wish not only to communicate "authentic" period life and history, but to use facts as "historical 'ammunition' . . . to destroy [visitors'] preconceptions" (Gable and Handler 1993:29). If visitors assume that Native technology was primitive, Native interpreters assert that it worked better than European technology of the time in the North American environment. If visitors assume that Native people always live in the past, Native interpreters stress adaptation as well as the idea of heritage as a living tradition that extends into the present. If visitors assume that Native people played unimportant roles in history, Native interpreters emphasize alliance and interdependence as the foundation for North American history. If visitors assume that Native people were passive victims in the fur trade, Freda's sharp trading counters that notion. The same trading drama is held frequently at FWHP to this day, because its messages are still valid.

Finally, interpreters make statements that are intended to counter other prejudices that visitors commonly express. Sandra Goodsky, an Anishinaabe interpreter who has worked at NWCFP, included in her report for the site a list of points that should be made in all tours at the post. These included: the fact that Europeans were a minority at the site; the fact that Native people still exist; the fact that the palisade was not for defense; statements about the role of Native women in the fur trade (and that they were not prostitutes); information about the use of alcohol in the fur trade; and the perspective that the

fur trade was just one aspect of Ojibwa life (Goodsky 1993:121). These
points seem important to interpreters to make because they are so often raised
by visitors, who are working from a script about the frontier as a Wild West
movie. Leah Still, in her sixth year as an Aboriginal interpreter at LFG in
2005, said that visitors tend to come to the fort with

> lots of Hollywood type of information. Some people especially from the States,
> I've had them come and ask where are the scalps or are we the squaws, and
> things like that. . . . Other times they just think that we didn't really get along
> with the Europeans, and they [visitors] often say something about the walls, be-
> cause of the way that they're built, like "this is from when they had all the bat-
> tles here," or attacks, and it also shocks them when we say, no, nothing like that
> happened here. . . . I guess people have an idea of an Indian in their head (in-
> terview, July 2005).

Non-Native women interpreters portraying mixed-blood laborers at cottages
outside the walls at LFG also reported a constant stream of questions such
as "do you feel safe here outside the walls?" They expressed frustration at
the constant need to assert to visitors that the Native people at the site were
relatives of the local mixed-blood people, that they were valued laborers,
and that they were as trustworthy as anyone else in the fort. Visitors seemed
to express assumptions about the inferiority of Native peoples more readily
to non-Native interpreters, but these lurk behind many visitor encounters
with Native staff.

Just as visitors' questions about objects are tinged by moral bias, interpreters' responses often assert a sense of moral superiority.[20] This is most frequently expressed as claims that Native people used only what is needed from
nature and never wasted what nature provided (for a recent argument against
this claim, see Krech 1999). It is also expressed in statements about the relative freedoms of Native and European women, as in Nokie's comment,
"Those women from across the ocean, they're treated like dogs! She can't
vote, she can't hold property. The Indian woman has a better life. She owns
the lodge because she built it. . . ." Quite often these interpretations are supported by revisionist scholarship; at other times information from such
sources is combined with feminist and Native critiques of historic European
culture, making this discourse both parallel to and slightly different from that
recorded at Colonial Williamsburg regarding miscegenation, where different
messages were given about the topic by interpreters of different racial backgrounds (Gable 1996). Perhaps most importantly, such morally tinged responses are supported by more interpreters across the sites I worked at than
Gable encountered at Williamsburg: visitors asking non-Native staff whether
something a Native interpreter said is true are most likely to be told, yes.

There are some disputes about moral interpretations of the past, which I will discuss in the chapter on "Authenticities and Materialities," but on the whole these sites are willing to implement Native perspectives on the past as much as possible: "Don't you feel sorry for those weedy, pale White women up at the fort? They couldn't pick up a decent-sized stick of wood if they tried. They're *supposed* to be useless! And you should *see* the airs they give themselves. . . ."

Gable and Handler criticize the use of such "historical ammunition" as producing discourse that was "a surreal pastiche rather than a sustained discussion," and because the narratives underlying the information were not discussed with visitors (1993:28). I would argue that since visitors experience these sites in an uncontrolled and multisensory way, fragments of information are a useful form of communication; furthermore, I have seen many conversations in the Native encampments that qualify as "sustained discussion." These sites do not lend themselves to text- or lecture-based scholarly forms of communication, although they draw on these. Historical interpretation at its essence is about getting visitors both to learn and to rethink: Freeman Tilden, whose 1957 work on interpretation is still the definitive text for this genre, stated that "the chief aim of interpretation is not instruction, but provocation" (Tilden 1977 [1957]:9). Interpreters, especially Native interpreters, need "ammunition" in the battle against the racist assumptions they face every day in visitors' questions. Given the depth to which these assumptions are embedded within mainstream historical narratives, it is no wonder that there are conflicts between tourist and Native discourses, or that interpreters should attempt to provoke visitors to rethink things.

I will examine the actual confrontations between Native interpreters and visitors in the chapter on "Encounters," but wish to underline here the importance of such contested messages, of being able to tell one's own perspective in one's own voice, of being able to assert tribal perspectives on history, and of being able to counter misinformation and prejudice: this is what keeps Native interpreters going. Such work goes well beyond what Native interpreters are hired to communicate. It is necessary, though: Native interpreters face, on a daily basis, the kind of prejudice that has haunted their ancestors for centuries. For many of them, their commitment is such that they are also prepared to face such attitudes off-site. At CM, Keith Knecht shaved his head except for his scalplock in the interest of historical authenticity, knowing full well that he would be subject to harassment in his off-duty life. He was motivated by pride in his heritage and identity, and a sense that fighting prejudice is part of the larger battle for self-determination.

Figure 3.3. Keith Knecht in eighteenth-century guise, 1995, Colonial Michilimackinac. Photograph by Drew Davey.

KNOWING THE PAST TO UNDERSTAND THE PRESENT: IDENTITY CONSTRUCTION AND RECONSTRUCTION.

Such personal commitment is a key to understanding, in part, what motivates Native interpreters to do this work. Knecht was committed to portraying a documented, eighteenth-century Great Lakes historical reality because this work meant a great deal to him personally. This is especially true of older, long-term interpreters, although younger people who work for only a single summer often incorporate their learning from that time into their identities. For Native staff, being on site, learning, and interacting involves an active process of identity construction—something to which, as Fife (2004:62) notes, scholars have paid little attention.[21]

These processes can be terribly important to the individuals involved. Some of the interpreters with whom I spoke were adopted and raised in non-Native families, or spent much of their lives off-reserve. Working at historic sites and doing research on their tribal and family histories has been crucial to these individuals in the process of regaining their Native identities.[22] Freda McDonald, who had lost her Native status and been forced to leave the reserve when she married a white man, "took one look at [the FWHP encampment] and knew that this was where I wanted to work. It was as if, after all those years in exile, I'd come home. A few days later, I started work as an Indian" (quoted in Wilkins 1994:70). For many of these interpreters, the messages given by Pine Ridge Sioux respondents to Rosenzweig and Thelen's study—that the past was "essential to group and individual survival"—has taken a new form in their work at historic reconstructions (1998:174).

There are other facets to the personal investments that Native interpreters make in their work. In the LFG area, many Aboriginal and mixed-blood families tried to escape prejudice in the late nineteenth and early twentieth centuries by denying their ancestry. When I taught a course on Aboriginal history at the University of Winnipeg, students came to me after lectures every year saying that they had the same surnames as the local Aboriginal people I had been lecturing about, but that their grandparents had always insisted that their ancestry was Spanish—or French, a common euphemism in western Canada for Métis heritage. In July 2005, Leah Still, an Aboriginal interpreter at LFG, said, "my grandparents think it's really neat [that I work here] because they didn't even know lots of these things [about local history and culture] when they were growing up." Residential schools, having to hide one's ancestry because of prejudice, and the disruption faced by Native communities since the late nineteenth century mean that Still's grandparents are not alone in not knowing much about their own history. Ruth Christie, who is extremely knowledgeable about Aboriginal history in the LFG area, had lost the name of her great-grandmother whom she was portraying: it simply hadn't been recorded in her family. One Native interpreter, in her first season at LFG in 2005, expressed great trepidation at having to represent Aboriginal people when she hadn't been raised with many traditional practices. These insecurities were especially acute when other Aboriginal people visited the camp, whom she felt must know more than she did:

> They generally know what things are [in the camp] a lot of the time, and then they'll tell stories, like, "My grandpa, . . . he stretched his beaver [pelts] this way too." And that's when I'm afraid they're going to know all the processes, and they'll ask [something], and I'll be like, "I'm not sure." Because they generally know the answers, a lot of them still practice traditional things (Anonymous, Native interpreter interview, LFG, summer 2005).[23]

Prejudice exists within Native communities as well, and those who did not grow up on a trapline in the bush are sometimes looked down on for their lack of knowledge. On the other hand, while this interpreter was nervous about encountering this kind of situation, she could see the potential of her work for strengthening her knowledge of tribal culture and history and thus feeling more confident about her own identity. All Native interpreters, whatever their personal backgrounds, enjoy learning more about their histories while working at historic reconstructions.

These processes of identity development are rather different from Mac-Cannell's (1984:377) proposition that cultural tourism creates new, less authentic, forms of ethnicity. While MacCannell also proposed in the same paper that "tourism promotes the restoration, preservation, and fictional recreation of ethnic attributes" (ibid.), he then went on to propose that such "reconstructed ethnicity" is *for* "the entertainment of ethnically different others" (1984:385, emphasis added). I take the point that the reflexivity produced when indigenous peoples create touristic representations causes them to think deeply about culture, and about what is appropriate to show to outsiders. Rather than maintaining traditional knowledge or cultural expressions for the education of others, however, Native performers—including interpreters—have engaged in such work for themselves. These performance spaces are, as Adams has noted, "new spaces for defining new parameters of identity, livelihood, and meaning" (Adams 2003: 571). We might join to this Kirshenblatt-Gimblett's observation that while the discourse of heritage is all about resurrecting the dead, the effect it produces is to vitalize the living:

> Despite a discourse of conservation, preservation, restoration, reclamation, recovery, recreation, recuperation, revitalization, and regeneration, heritage produces something new in the present that has recourse to the past. . . . By production, I do not mean that the result is not authentic or that it is invented out of whole cloth. Rather, I wish to underscore that heritage is . . . a mode of cultural production in the present that has recourse to the past (Kirshenblatt-Gimblett 1995:369–70).

Participating in these recreations of the past, and teaching one's own version of one's history to others, has everything to do with the present—and, for Native interpreters, for their future.

I would also argue that the work of Native staff at historic reconstructions needs to be seen in a broader context of the reclamation of cultural knowledge, the strengthening of cultural identity, and the healing of Native communities across North America by beginning to reclaim Native interpretations of history, and to articulate these. One crucial component of this work has involved reclaiming knowledge from historic artifacts, including the linguistic and spiritual knowledge which is tied to material forms and their complex processes of production, for use within tribal communities (see, for instance, Thompson and Kritsch 2005). One of the main interpretive activities that Native interpreters do at historic reconstructions involves historically documented craft activities. At FWHP, staff have made birchbark canoes and routinely make leather bags, birchbark mokuks, paddles, and snowshoes. At the NWCFP, interpreters have to make moccasins as part of their training, and make mokuks, birch-bark bitten patterns, bags, fishing nets, and other objects. A recent project there has been Mary Vanderpoel's attempt to make a Great Lakes twined bag entirely from *wigoob*, the inner fiber of poplar or basswood bark—a material form that is nearly extinct. Keith Knecht also made *wigoob* twine. Porcupine quillwork, beadwork, hide tanning, and the making of finger-woven sashes all occur at these sites, which have functioned as regional centers for the revitalization of traditional crafts. Few Native interpreters begin their work with such skills, but they have the opportunity to learn many of them. Knowledge of and competence in traditional skills are still greatly admired within Native communities and are associated with cultural identity.[24] I will discuss this point further in the chapter "Authenticities and Materialities," but wish to point out here that historic artifacts function for many Native people as anchors for identity, material forms of information and values from the past which through study can be resurrected for use in the present.[25] I am also reminded of Kirshenblatt-Gimblett's important article on heritage and the point she makes about the role of heritage objects in affirming identity:

> What is at stake is the restoration of living links to taonga [Maori treasures] that never died. . . . The life force of taonga depends not on techniques of animation, but on the living transmission of cultural knowledge and values. What is at stake is not the vividness of a museum experience, but the vitality, the survival, of those for whom these objects are taonga. And that depends on intangible cultural property, which lives in performance. (1995:378)

The things that Native interpreters make as part of their work are crucial, not only in demonstrating these processes to visitors, but in strengthening aspects of identity. The process of making while at the same time teaching visitors is also about teaching oneself. At historic reconstructions, the "commodification of culture" so despised by anthropologists may actually create "new channels to access cultural traditions" (Medina 2003:354), and strengthen individual and tribal cultural identity.

CONCLUSION

At historic reconstructions, Native interpreters draw on a long tradition of performing elements of their cultures for tourists; of understanding tourist expectations of "Indians," and responding to these; of imbuing such performances with deep meanings about identity. Their work resonates with Mason's analysis of a Native-run tourism program near Ottawa, in which the performers reclaim signifiers of Native identity (drumming, music, dance) from the realm of stereotypes to educate non-Native tourists about certain realities of Native culture (Mason 2004). At long last, a literature that examines Native agency in cultural performance is emerging, and I would place the present study within it. When Native interpreters tell me, "We're playing ourselves, the real First Nations people" (Littlewolf-Walker, interview, 1994), they mean that they are expressing their contemporary identity as persons rooted in their heritage. Native interpreters are using their own versions of personal, family, and community histories to challenge too simple, exclusive, national histories; they are struggling to replace popular narratives about primitive and vanishing Indians with "stories of revival, remembrance, and struggle" (Clifford 1991:214): ideas about competence, adaptability, dignity, even superiority. "We are playing ourselves," they tell us: "we are still here."

The work that Native interpreters do at historic reconstructions in communicating a more inclusive view of the past, and in challenging stereotypes, is extremely important in this process. But how are these new perspectives received by visitors? Who comes to these sites, and what happens during encounters between Native interpreters and visitors? I will explore these questions in the next chapters.

NOTES

1. In addition to my conversations with Native interpreters, I am drawing here on experiences of teaching courses on the history of Native peoples of Canada at the University of Winnipeg, in which a substantial number of my students were Aboriginal, and in which they tended to challenge standard historical interpretations in the ways I describe. Rosenzweig and Thelen (1998:165–66) encountered similar perspectives amongst Oglala Lakota, who expressed their view of the past as "pretty much opposite" the textbook one. I also draw on a research project with members of the Kainai Nation in Alberta, which taught me how much standard and tribal historical narratives can differ even when they are related to the same historical photograph (Brown, Peers et al. 2006). There is a large literature on "contested pasts" and Indigenous peoples; see especially Hill 1992, Friedman 1992, McGuire 1992, Schmidt and Patterson 1995.

2. Studying Viking reenactors in Newfoundland, Wayne Fife has noted that reenactors distinguish between colleagues who are said to be "'real' while others 'play a role'" (Fife 2004:63). I take his point, and the reenactors', that some participants in this work feel a strong connection with those whom they portray, but would argue, as I do here, that Native interpreters experience a deeper and more multilayered entanglement and conflation between role and person than do reenactors.

3. And see van den Berghe and Keyes 1984:345, "In ethnic tourism, the native is not simply 'there' to serve the needs of the tourist: he is himself 'on show,' a living spectacle to be scrutinized, photographed, tape recorded, and interacted with . . . "

4. Fife (2004:75) notes similar role-switching by Newfoundlanders who represent Vikings, and there may be a similar dynamic of visitor curiosity in encountering "primitive" peoples behind this.

5. The exception would be those Lakota who were interned at Fort Sheridan after Wounded Knee and then offered contracts with Buffalo Bill's Wild West Show; following a two-year European tour, they were permitted to return home. See Maddra 2006; Moses 1996.

6. I am grateful to Trudy Nicks, Jolene Rickard, and Ruth Phillips (personal communication) for information about the research findings for this exhibition.

7. Blanchard 1984 and West 1998 describe others, as does Nick Stanley (1998) for a broader range of indigenous cultural performance. Hill 1999 outlines cultural performance among Haudenosaunee (Iroquois) peoples.

8. The Jim Sky Dance Group still performs Iroquoian dances at festivals, including Native-organized events.

9. Medina 2003; de Azeredo Grünewald 2002; van den Berghe and Ochoa 2000; Stanley 1998, among others. Moscardo and Pearce 1999:417 cite Pitchford (1995) who wishes to include ethnic groups such as the Welsh within the definition of cultural tourism: "This group's striving for identity and independence is linked to the tourism presentation of their culture."

10. This is of course very different from Gable and Handler's data that note that "the main task of interpreters is not to construct meaning out of evidence, but to enliven and embody meanings already established by their superiors" (1994:120).

11. Rossell 1988 and Nash 1978 give an especially bleak picture. The position and literature is discussed in Burns 2004:9.

12. See, for instance, MacCannell 1976, 1984; see also Hitchcock 1997:95 on negative assumptions about the effects of tourism. Medina 2003:354 provides a very useful overview of this literature in reference to indigenous cultural tourism and the stance I am taking on it. Stronza 2001:268 also notes the negative tone in the literature.

13. This argument has also been applied to objects made by "primitive" peoples, and involves extensive scholarly discourse about "tourist art"; see Phillips 1995, 1998; Price 1989.

14. MacCannell 1984:388 credits van den Berghe with the concept of tourism as an intercultural space; Bruner and others have used this concept as well.

15. Rosenzweig and Thelen (1998:170–71) also noted an extraordinarily strong connection with a collective past for Oglala Lakota people they surveyed.

16. Most of these questions and comments appear on the previsit preparation part of the website for Plimoth Plantation (www.plimoth.org/visit/plan/cultsensitivity.asp, accessed March 4, 2006) and are referred to in Sandra Goodsky's 1993 report for NWCFP.

17. Asked why he performed for tourists, Native dancer Dennis Zotai replied that he was "dispelling myths, one venue at a time" (presentation, British Museum conference, 2005). MacCannell (1984:387) also acknowledges that what he calls "ethnic

attractions" stress "the need to correct the historical record insofar as it undervalues the contribution of the minority, and it reminds the visitors of past discrimination against the minority." Margaret Bruchac, who interprets Molly Geet, an "Indian Doctress" at Old Sturbridge Village, has similarly emphasized the importance of countering prejudice in her work (Bruchac to Peers, Clark, and Clevenger, e-mail August 25, 2001).

18. Freda McDonald and Marie Brunelle pointed this out to me in 1994, and many Native interpreters since have made the same observation, including—independently—the entire staff of the encampment at LFG in the summer of 2005.

19. Tikinagans prompted similar conversations on similar topics, with similar visitor responses, both in 2005 and 1994 at CM, LFG, and NWCFP.

20. Deutschlander and Miller 2003:38 also note similar moralizing discourse and inversions of expected stereotypes by Native staff at other cultural tourism sites in Canada.

21. Backhouse 2005 examines English reenactors (hobbyists) and their processes of identity development and personal investment.

22. Rosenzweig and Thelen 1998:176 also touch on issues of identity and engagement with history among American Indian peoples.

23. Another young, first-season, urban Aboriginal interpreter at LFG in 2005 panicked one day when her more experienced colleague was not present to make bannock over a fire, as she herself had never done this before.

24. At historic reconstructions, this produces an odd parallel with non-Native reenactors, whom Handler and Saxton described (1988:243) as locating authenticity in the past, a dynamic they see as essentially postmodern.

25. John Urry has picked up on the link between craft and other performances of culture, and heritage, in touristic representations worldwide: "Questions of heritage . . . make 'history' central to the nature of given cultures and demonstrates that heritage cannot be divorced from the various 'techniques of remembering'" (2002 [1989]:159).

Vignette: What's This?

Lower Fort Garry, Aboriginal Encampment, summer 2005: a family chatting with a Native interpreter:

Interpreter: You can sit over here [to children] and I can show you things.

Child visitors: Is that a real fire?

Interpreter: Yes, it's a real fire, it's very very hot.

Child: It doesn't look real!

Interpreter: This is the Aboriginal camp, so there's lots of different Aboriginal people here: the Cree, the Ojibwa.

Parent: You kids come here and listen!

Interpreter: Do you know why we're here?

Child: Why?

Father: Trading.

Child: Will that fire blow away?

Interpreter: No, the wind actually helps the fire . . . [discussion about cooking with the fire pit]

Child: He's making something— [sound of blacksmith]

Interpreter: Yes, he's making something, and that's some of the things that we trade for. We'll trade things like the fish we catch with our nets over there, or these moccasins that we make, we trade these to the company over there, and in exchange we'll trade for things we can't make on our own, 'cos we can't make things out of metal—can you make things out of metal?

Child: No, not unless you're a blacksmith.

Interpreter: But I'm not a blacksmith, so I have to trade for those things. That's why we're here. We have a good relation with the HBC, we're like friends, we'll do work for each other, we help each other out. That's how it works. So we come here only in the summer. . . . You guys want to take a look around and see if you find anything interesting that you might want to look at?

Child [pointing at beaded bag]: I made a bag! But it wasn't like that. It was made of leather, and string.

Interpreter: Sinew? [shows artificial sinew]

Child: Yeah!

Interpreter: And beads like this?

Child: Yeah!!

Interpreter: This thing here is our sewing kit, see our needles and everything in it. . . . Beads come from Italy then they go to England to here. You guys can touch this if you want. It's called loom beading.

Child: What's this?

Interpreter: This is just string, like thread.

Child: What are these?

Interpreter: We use these when we're taking the coals out of the fire because they're super hot—we can't use our hands, and we can't use our clothes because we'd burn holes through them. [demonstrates moving coals, cooking with spider pan]

Child: What are those horns?

Interpreter: They come from different animals like elk or deer. We can carve things from them. We try to use as much of the animal as possible.

Child: You can use all the animal! You can use the fur for clothes, the bones for tools and the meat for eating.

Interpreter: Take a look at this. What do you guys think this is?

Child: A knife holder?

Interpreter: Yes, but what's the decoration on this knife holder?

Child: Skin?

Interpreter: Close! It comes from a little animal, very round and spiky.

Child: Porcupine!

Interpreter: Yes, these are porcupine quills. And so before we traded with the Company and we wanted to decorate things, we used quills and they're hollow just like a drinking straw so . . . we flatten them and dye them and [sew them on] . . .

Chapter Four

Authenticities and Materialities

> Both [museums and tourism] are in the business of representing the culture of others, usually those who have lived in another time or in another place. Both must construct and hence invent what they display. Both have to select from a vast array of potential objects and events to valorize some as worthy of exhibition. . . . Both museums and touristic sites have themselves been constructed in a particular social context and historical period, and are embedded in the politics of their settings. (Bruner 1993:6)

A wooden palisade, dubiously claiming to be a "fort"; a clearing in the forest. Outside the walls, a few bark wigwams, their bent-pole frames tied together. Inside the lodge, a cradleboard; pine boughs and hides on the floor; a few birch-bark mokuks holding dried corn, wild rice, maple sugar. Beaver skins on sapling stretchers outside the door; a trade gun, bow, and quiver of arrows inside. Knives, tin lantern, metal scissors, glass beads, flashy trade silver brooches. A painted drum, swinging gently in the corner of the lodge.

Walk away from the wigwams, through the sturdy log gate of the fort. Timber buildings, multipane windows, a church steeple, kitchen gardens. Laundry hanging from lines. Fireplaces, bake ovens, herbs drying; smells of stew and bread. Four-poster beds, upholstered chairs, fine turnings on table-legs; pewter dishes, blue-edged china. A ruffled linen shirt being mended. A fur-press; bales of furs; the trading-shop, with its cloth and powder, shot and muskrat spears, tin mugs, and strings of beads.

Historic reconstructions are extraordinarily material entities that communicate with visitors through sensory stimulation. The details of their physical recreations of buildings and furnishings are crucial to showing "life" in the past: somehow, the physicality of these places is believed to have the capacity to reanimate the people of the past. It certainly animates people in the present. Staff have varying, but always powerful, investments and engagements with the physical reconstruction, its furnishings, its clothing, and its props. Historians have spent months combing archival documents for mentions of objects on which to base reconstructions. Site managers emphasize the documented, "authentic" nature of the reconstructions they manage. Curators for costumes, furnishings, and props spend ages, and small fortunes, sourcing and purchasing reproduction items. Craftspeople are hired to create items, sewing stitch-by-stitch or making pot-by-pot the things that "bring the past to life" and encoding their years of learning into every thing they make. Interpreters do up the buttons, sit in the chairs, shift the heavy cast iron pots onto the blacksmith-forged tripod over the fire, and explain these things to visitors. Many interpreters also do historical research, and some are skilled craftspeople who are thirsty for comparative examples and documentation. All staff members feel they walk a line between "real" and "fake," and staying on the "real" side of the material reconstruction matters to them. And visitors respond very strongly to the physical stimuli offered by these places: touching, tasting, smelling, hearing, drinking in the view. More than anything else, historic reconstructions are distinctive forms of communication and experience because of their rich materiality.

Recent theory in material anthropology has focused on several ideas that are useful in thinking about historic reconstructions. Alfred Gell's notion (1998) that artifacts have agency in their own right, that they have effects on human perception and behavior, and that they are simultaneously indices of human thought and behavior, is helpful in considering the role of material culture within these sites. Chris Gosden has built on these ideas to propose that artifacts can be seen not just as physical objects, but as nexuses of social, economic, and political relations involved in their production, collection, transfer, use, and reinterpretation across time: in this case, the relationships involved in producing, maintaining, and interpreting the buildings and props involved in these reconstructions (in Gosden and Knowles 2001:18–24). Artifacts can thus be used to tell about these relationships, to retrace, reinvigorate or change them. Just as recent histories of the colonial contact zone aim to capture "the texture of cultural hybridity in everyday life, capturing the simultaneous affection, ambivalence, and antagonism that whites and Indians . . . felt for each other" (Smolenski 2003), the buildings, clothing, and props do similar work at living history sites, embodying and communicating cultural identity, relationships, hybridity, boundaries, and tensions. There is, as well, an added set of meanings for Native interpreters for the replica tribal artifacts they work with, for historic material culture has come to embody ancestral knowledge and traditional identity: what Clifford (2004:16) has called heritage objects, "specially valued material sites of remembrance and communication" which are crucial in the transmission and strengthening of cul-

Figure 4.4. Native items in European spaces: Big House interior. Image courtesy Parks Canada/E. Kennedy.

tural knowledge and identity. At historic reconstructions, things matter, for many reasons.

The agency and sociality of objects is demonstrated in the way they are vehicles for many things at historic sites. They are used to communicate certain information to visitors. The questions "What is that?" "What's it made from?" and "What was it for?" are the most common beginning point for conversations between interpreters and visitors. Objects also embody knowledge, skill, and professional standing within the public history community and among staff on site. They can represent elements of personal identity of the makers and interpreters, and details of authentic manufacture are used as boundaries between staff who consider themselves good historians and those others who are just doing this as a job. Material details are used by public relations officers to advertise the site and by scholars to evaluate it. They are the proof of historical narratives as enacted at historic sites. When the narratives are revised, the buildings and props and furnishings and costumes are as well. Or, sometimes, the narratives will change but the objects stay the same because someone powerful at the site has too much invested in them to allow them to change (clothing, especially upper-class women's dresses, has often been a contested category of object at many of these sites for this reason). Infuriatingly, authenticity, which ought to be verifiable and fixed, proves to be elastic and the product of power as much as of historical fact. As Bruner notes, authenticity is also authority in disguise, and studying it can reveal structures of power in the present as much as historical facts. I would add to this that even the most historically accurate details of reconstructions can communicate narratives and ideas which are quite untrue. While this is frustrating for me as an historian, as an anthropologist I find the capacity of objects and buildings to embody such disparate meanings fascinating: this is what makes historic reconstructions such lively arenas for cross-cultural communication (see Mason 2004:838). What I want to do in this chapter is explore how Native objects and buildings make meanings for different groups at historic sites, and how they are bound up in systems of power.

"WHAT'S THAT?": VISITORS, OBJECTS, AND COMMUNICATION

Most importantly, artifacts, costumes, and reconstructed buildings at historic sites act as points of connection between the site, its staff, and visitors. The very first questions visitors ask are almost always about the things they see, especially about unfamiliar objects they encounter in the Native encampments. The conversation between child visitors and an Aboriginal interpreter at LFG that prefaces this chapter is a typical object-centered exchange with visiting public. Many of these conversations spiral out from the objects to discuss social history, more ephemeral aspects of Native culture, and cross-cultural relations. They almost always start with the question, "What's that?" however, and I have heard such questions asked of turtle shells, a feather fan, ricing sticks, a twining loom, pitch on bark cracks ("did Indians have glue?"), the scent in the lodge, pelt stretchers, a "partridge" (actually a Cornish hen) roasting over the fire, glass trade beads, porcupine quills, baskets, the corn pounder, a carrot of tobacco, a drum, furs, a fish smoking rack, and a *tikinagan* (baby carrier).

These objects have been added to historic reconstructions as part of the process of adding Native themes. Not only have wigwams been built and furnished, but across each site, Native objects have been inserted into existing buildings as evidence of cross-cultural relationships: moccasins by bedsides, wall pockets over tables, mokuks of rice or corn in the "European" spaces. In some cases, props rendered inappropriate by new themes have been removed.

Such changes are constrained by many things. Handmade Native replica objects can be extremely expensive, as are wigwams and their maintenance which require specialist consultants. In some regions, traditional skills such as porcupine quill embroidery are no longer practiced by local Native communities, and it is virtually impossible to find anyone who can embroider with quills with the same skill as seen on early nineteenth-century objects. Virginia Lockett, Interpretive Curator at LFG, wrote to me describing some reproduction objects that had been commissioned for the Native encampment:

> Some of the reproduction artifacts are better than others. Two of the beaded pieces (shot bag and fire bag) are copied from pieces in the HBC collection. Very few people are doing quill work now so it was difficult to find someone to make the awl case and the knife sheaths—the reproductions are not as fine as the historic pieces in our collection, but do provide examples of that type of work (Lockett to Peers, September 29, 2000).

At LFG, the Native encampment was initially added on a shoestring, with props pilfered from other parts of the site. To keep costs manageable, commercially made canvas tipis were used: they are inaccurate but much less expensive than paying someone to build a bark lodge.

This raises the question of authenticity. Clearly, what the visitor sees, and a site claims, as "authentic" is the product of extensive negotiation and compromise by administrators, researchers, curators, and interpreters. Bruner is right that authenticity is closely linked to authority at these institutions (2005:163), in that what is shown as authentic has much to do with which individuals have the power to insist on having certain things implemented—or not. However, one needs to delve into the politics of budget approval and administrative hierarchies at these sites to fully appreciate the trade-offs involved in formulating "authentic" reconstructions. Site staff may have research reports detailing the kind of china used in a specific building, but be unable to afford to purchase the china; adding a new wigwam will almost certainly absorb the budget for maintaining another part of the reconstruction. Other practicalities concern staffing issues. In some years far fewer men have applied for interpretive work than women, so that dairying, baking, and laundering may suddenly assume a new prominence, and men's roles may be downplayed. For several years in the 1990s, no Native men applied for summer positions at LFG, so the women who staffed the encampment told visitors that their absent "husbands" were all off fishing or working. In other years, when a site is unable to hire Native staff, non-Native staff may have to

Figure 4.2.   Shot bag reproduced from historic artifact. Image courtesy Parks Canada.

represent them. Very practical factors affect authenticity, as well as competing authorities of historical researchers, Native staff, budget-minded administrators, and Native and non-Native local communities which, as Bruner
says, make authenticity into "a struggle, a social process, in which competing
interests argue for their own interpretation of history" (2005:163).

These are some of the common factors that have affected the addition of Native interpretation programs to historic sites. Each site, of course, portrays a
different moment in history, a different kind of European presence, a different
Native presence, and different Native-White relations. Despite these differences, Native areas and programming have taken remarkably similar forms,
and these sites communicate similar messages about Native peoples and
Native-White relations in the past. In the next part of this chapter, I wish to explore these messages as they are suggested by physical elements of reconstructed historic sites.

SITE MESSAGES: WHAT DOES A WIGWAM MEAN?

Historic reconstructions are creations which evoke the past, but which do not
reproduce it exactly. Despite the painstaking research that goes into ensuring
that buildings and furnishings are accurate, ideological biases about the nature

of the past and the lessons it should teach as well as practical considerations in the present make these places very different in their second incarnations than they were historically. In their portrayal of Native life and Native-White relations, all of the sites I examined showed patterned, consistent differences between the historical roles and presence of Native people, and those portrayed now. And while the Native areas of these sites were added to counter Eurocentric perspectives on history, they can still communicate messages that can reinforce old prejudices: what site administrators intend to communicate may not be what visitors actually learn.

Wigwams and palisades may not speak, but they communicate nonetheless. The relative size and complexity of different parts of historic reconstructions, and their relation to one another, imply certain messages, and undermine others. When sites "select from a vast array of potential objects and events to valorize some as worthy of exhibition" (Bruner 1993:6) they initially tended to select buildings and artifacts that depicted the everyday life of Europeans at the sites. Today, the palisades and European buildings still dominate the site; the Native areas tend to be much smaller and less fully developed; and the Native and non-Native areas are separated. These factors tend to minimize the roles of Native people in the past, and mute intended messages about the existence of cross-cultural relations.

Despite the fact that all of these sites were, in their respective historic incarnations, small islands of a European presence surrounded and visited by larger Native populations, the Native areas at these sites are all very small compared with the reconstructed European areas. SMAH is the exception here, with its two imposing longhouses taking up about a third of the total area inside the palisades. FWHP has the next largest area, with three wigwams, a traditional kitchen space, and a contemporary "Learning Wigwam." LFG has one tipi and an outdoor kitchen area; CM one waginogan (a dome-shaped winter lodge), a summer shelter, and several incomplete pole frames; NWCFP a single furnished winter lodge. Historically, these sites were visited seasonally by Native populations ranging from several dozen to hundreds of people. At CM, several hundred Native people from around the Great Lakes camped every summer, creating a temporary village of lodges on the beach. The European areas of these sites, on the other hand, are reconstructed as completely as possible based on archaeological evidence: FWHP, NWCFP, SMAH, and CM were rebuilt on the original foundations.

Native interpreters at these sites tend to be stationed outside the walls of the European compound. The Native encampments are further distanced from the rest of the site by being located on the margins: at LFG, the encampment was initially on the riverbank, and has now been moved to a small wooded area away from most of the reconstruction; at FWHP, in dense woods along the path leading to the fort; at NWCFP, on the edge of the woods near one of the main paths to the fort. The exception to this is SMAH, where the Native areas are located inside the palisade. Staff at other sites do enter the palisaded areas: at NWCFP, all staff give tours of all areas of the site; at LFG, Native interpreters also play a second character who could be found in the stone buildings (Steve Greyeyes made a fine Judge Thom in a 2005 drama), and FWHP sometimes has Native staff drumming in the main square, or leading tours which enter the palisade. Apart from SMAH, however, the encampment areas are all outside the walls.

The Native encampments tend to be located outside the palisades for good reasons: other than wives of fur traders, Native people seldom lived inside the walls when visiting trading sites (they did at SMAH), but camped nearby. At some sites, such as CM, there was a seasonal Native encampment outside the walls. Elsewhere, such as LFG, the encampment is historically inaccurate, as Native peoples tended to live in settlements elsewhere in the area and come in to work or trade. The encampment here has been added to make a statement about a Native presence in the area. Only the NWCFP and FWHP strongly suggest the presence of Native wives within the walls. Without information on why the camps are outside the walls, this placement can be misinterpreted by visitors, who may approach the site with the dynamics of the mythologized Frontier in mind. From this perspective, the physical separation between peoples, and the marginalization of the encampments, reinforces ideas about the assumed hostility between Native and European societies. The depiction of very limited numbers of Native people, and of their physical separation from other peoples, suggests the absence of strong relationships between them. Although much of the revision of themes at sites such as these has focused on the existence of alliance, marriage, and interdependence between Native peoples and Europeans, these ideas are seldom actually shown. The woman's dress in the NWCFP is one of the few strong hints that there were Native wives in these places, kin who visited, social and political networks which crossed the palisade. A few sites have dramas about trade, but these are some of the few actual depictions of any cross-cultural interaction, and they seldom stray beyond the boundaries of trade to explore broader aspects of historic relations. This is a pattern noted early in the social history movement by Wallace, who observed that while historic sites were creating more pluralistic representations of the past, they were not showing relations between the groups depicted (Wallace 1991:196; see also Blakey 1990:42).

The other patterned distortion shown at these reconstructions is the minimization of the roles and importance of Native and Métis peoples. In Native encampments, this is introduced by the insistent use of furs (and especially by the use of individual furs as pelts or on stretchers) as props in the encamp-ments. Although several of the sites considered here had important roles in the fur trade, only one (NWCFP) was an actual trading post. At LFG, CM, and OFW, warehouse and transshipment functions were primary, and rela-tively little fur trading was done locally. The trading of local foods and coun-try goods at these sites—meat, wild rice, grease, corn, fish, pitch, tumplines, and snowshoes—was far more important than the furs actually traded, as was Native and Métis labor to hunt, fish, paddle, make canoes, guide, translate, mend snowshoes, and perform other skilled tasks. Even at NWCFP, a typical wintering post in the fur trade, furs were traded along with food, roots and pitch for repairing canoes, maple sugar, and other vital goods. However, food items tend to be seen as props only in sufficient quantities to suggest family use (usually a single mokuk of wild rice or dried corn), and not nearly in the quantities which would suggest the real levels of trading of foodstuffs to Eu-ropeans which actually occurred, or even the actual quantities of food pre-served for winter use domestically by Native families (the one exception is SMAH where in 1994, rows of dried corn in several buildings suggested large-scale horticultural activity). What we see instead is fur, which suggests that Europeans were only commercially reliant on Native people, and did not depend on them for their very existence. Where this distortion is combined with a relatively small number of interpreters depicting Native and Métis peo-ple, it becomes very difficult to convey to visitors revisionist messages about the reliance of Europeans on these peoples.

Such disparities are largely a product of the time lag between the "era of the big project" (Taylor 1990:169–90)—and big budgets—from 1950–1980, when most of these sites were reconstructed, and the era of cutbacks, begin-ning in the mid-1980s, during which the Native areas were added. Site ad-ministrators are dismayed that their representation of the Native presence is so limited, and budgets—always contested at these places—have been stretched by every manager I have spoken to since 1993 for funds to improve Native ar-eas and increase Native staff.

The problem is that nowhere are such processes communicated to the vis-itor. Like museum exhibits, historic reconstructions are silent about the curatorial decisions that affect their production. The implication is that the reconstruction is a transparent representation of "the way it really was"—except, of course, that it isn't: "the call for 'realness' requires that the in-terface, the means by which the representation is staged, be muted or con-cealed" (Kirshenblatt-Gimblett 1995:375). By allowing the visitor to be-lieve that the reconstruction is an exact replica of what the site really looked like, sites give visitors free rein to interpret what they actually see. Visitors do this in light of popular discourses about the past and especially about the frontier, rather than those about the politics of representing the past. As McIntosh and Prentice (1999:607) have noted,

> tourists at heritage attractions assist in the production of their own experiences through their imaginations . . . and imbue objects in the setting provided with their own personal meanings. Consequently, individual tourists may interpret the context provided at cultural attractions in an entirely different way from what was intended, such as through memory prompts rather than educational insight.

While interpreters, orientation displays, and brochures do their best to communicate the actual size of Native and European populations, and the nature of the relationships between them, it is hard to contradict the compelling messages suggested by the physical elements of reconstructions. Edward Bruner has also commented that interpreters' words can be "less effective than the more physical and visual way that New Salem is experienced" (2005: 142, 132). The nature of reconstructions invites tourists to play with stories: just as one begins to tell a story about what is going on in a dollhouse, these sites come across as fascinatingly detailed full-size playhouses, demanding that we engage with them as would-be resident or as latter-day narrator. The densely furnished rooms at NWCFP, with different kinds of clothes and furnishings in each room to suggest people of different backgrounds and statuses, and women's clothing and toys suggesting the presence of families, spark all sorts of responses from visitors who often "read" the rooms to each other ("My goodness, look at that old blue-edged china. And a hobby horse! I guess the man in charge and his family lived here . . ."). Without prompting by interpreters to realize that the dress belonged to an Ojibwa wife, though, or understand her crucial political and social roles, visitors are also likely to "read" the palisades and the placement of the Native areas as mostly outside the walls, as indicative of the racially antagonistic, mythical American Wild West. At NWCFP, interpreter Mary Vanderpoel notes that, "Out of every four persons I take through in a tour group, there's at least one person who asks, "What is the wall for? To keep out Indians?" (cited in Goodsky 1993:122.) Such narratives hold a secure place in popular culture and in the minds of most visitors, and visitors indicate by their comments when they are in the encampments that they are drawing on them.[1]

MATERIALITY, MIMETIC REALISM, AND DEFLECTION

If visitors' interpretation of historic reconstructions can frustrate the communication of intended messages about the past, so can sites themselves. One of the fundamental contradictions of historic reconstruction also occurs in the relationship between materiality and message, but in another way: the rich detail of these sites functions to keep the stories they tell (and visitors' involvement with them) at the surface level and to prevent visitors from asking deeper questions about the role of the site and its inhabitants in history (see Lutz and Collins 1993:276, Canizzo 1987:1). The fascinating details of room interiors, the iconic qualities of spinning wheels and blacksmith's shops (and the opportunity to try both), the ability to touch homespun, period clothing, or furniture, can all focus visitors' attention on these things to the extent that it never goes any further. When crowds gather to watch musket drills or cannons being fired, they do not ask why the military was at the site, who it was serving, who it was there to control, or what its relationship was to local Native populations. When room settings are recreated in meticulous detail, one does not ask what the effects of the European presence was on local Native people, or whether Europeans were welcomed, or were kin to Native people. In my observation, such broader questions are seldom articulated by visitors: they may come up in the course of talking about the site if interpreters prompt them, but the site easily leads visitors away from such thoughts. It takes a certain amount of skill by interpreters to "bounce" visitors' questions and observations about the material surface of these places to the social and political histories in which materiality is embedded, and this doesn't always happen.

This is unfortunate at sites involving several distinct populations within a colonial setting, which provide opportunities for considering issues such as the development of racism, or the effects of contact on Native peoples. Martha Norkunas (2004:116) has discussed this problem, noting that visitors "are able to describe very well how a candle is dipped, yet as Christy Matthews, director of African American Interpretation at Colonial Williamsburg in the late 1990s, noted, it's not about dipping the candle. It's about who's dipping the candle, why they do it, and what's affecting them." Historic reconstructions offer material history masterfully, but can strip away social and political and cross-cultural histories in the process. If visitors understand only how to dip a candle and not the dynamics of social or racial hierarchies in which candles are made, real histories are rendered into quaint nostalgic fantasies.[2] Such focus on surface processes can also obscure the legacies of the past that still exist in the present (Handler and Gable 1997:225).

While this is clear as a theoretical issue, dealing with it in the material world of reconstructions poses real difficulties. Candles, spinning wheels, and tipis may raise narratives in visitors' minds that staff do not want to reinforce, but if they were there historically, any accurate depiction of the past needs to include them. More thought needs to be given to interrupting the narratives such things evoke, and to how to communicate alternative information through such objects. By and large, if an object is documented for the site and period, and if a replica of it is available and affordable, it will be acquired, without consideration of how (or whether) it contributes to the communication of the site's intended messages. As A. J. B. Johnston has noted in his review of Native representation at Heritage Canada sites, "if enough appropriate items can be presented—so the thinking goes—visitors will be convinced of the veracity of a given site. History is seen, essentially, as an objectifying process" (1994:6–7).

The problem of providing authentic artifacts without sufficient contextual information for them is exemplified by the reconstruction of the war post in the encampment at CM. The post has been removed since I first saw it in 1994; I should like to make it clear that I use this as an example not to be critical of CM, but to demonstrate the communicative problems that can be posed by material elements of reconstructions. The decision to include a war post was made by site administrators before the Native encampment was opened; it was seen as appropriate given the site's overall emphasis on military operations. The interpreters' manual for the encampment stated that war posts were used by Great Lakes warriors in predeparture ceremonies, but did not say whether there actually was one at the fort (Porter 1992:38–39). The manual stated that the war post was meant to symbolize "the participation of the upper Great Lakes Indians in the American Revolution . . . [and] to explain how Michilimackinac functioned as a recruitment and staging center for Indian warriors in the 1770s" (Porter 1992:38). With the appropriate background knowledge about Native American participation in the American Revolution, such a prop would be fine. Most visitors did not have this knowledge, however, and often made comments indicating that they associated it with stereotypes about savages, scalping, and the warpath, as well as with the much-emphasized 1763 Ojibwa attack on the fort. Given that the war post raised these assumptions, the Native interpreters often found themselves having to persuade visitors that Native peoples were generally allies of the Europeans at the fort, in order to deliver the site's official messages.

If the main message of the encampment at CM is supposed to be alliance and cross-cultural support, it might have been more appropriate to have a hundred filled sacks representing corn ready to be traded, or an area prepared for formal inter-group political councils, rather than the war post. I am reminded of Alexander Wilson's (1992:212) caveat that "while authenticity is often a goal for the designers of historical museums, it is a notion irrelevant to a discussion of cultural history. Contemporary culture and ideologies always intervene between people and historical objects." Site staff need to take this on board when choosing from a myriad of things they might possibly represent. Despite their attempts at, and claims of, authenticity, historic sites are constructed, often haphazardly so, within the constraints of the present. More attention needs to be paid to the messages that objects actually suggest to visitors rather than the ones we hope they will. I am not suggesting that staff avoid issues by not representing them, but that historians and managers assist interpreters by providing guidance about interpretation of problematic objects and by also including equally authentic artifacts that lead conversation in other directions, toward the messages that interpreters are supposed to deliver (see Handler and Gable 1997:232, who note a general lack of communication between researchers and front-line staff).

OBJECTS AND COMMUNICATIVE POTENTIAL

There is another side to the problems caused by the materiality of historic reconstructions: the extraordinary opportunities opened up through interaction between visitors, staff, and objects. As Laurel Thatcher Ulrich has written, artifacts from the past have been woven into power-laden nostalgic fantasies about colonial relations, but can also be used to unravel these, to put real people and accommodations and relationships back into history. Describing a twined and imbricated wallet, she states that such items preserve

> a different story, a story of intercultural exchange rather than war. The weave structure is Algonkian, the form European. Combining native hemp and moose hair with a commercially woven wool lining, it shows the complex intertwining of cultures in this period (2001:259).

We can use the physical elements of historic reconstructions to explore political dynamics and cross-cultural issues: the fascinating material details can be used as a bridge to teach. Done well, this is precisely the strength of historic interpretation. Within this kind of performance, furnishings and costumes—like theatrical props—fulfill the critical function of keeping "all parties engaged with each other during communication" (Beeman 1993:386).

This can often be seen in the reactions of visitors in the Native encampments. Whether they express assumptions about Native hostility and primitivism or not, many visitors are fascinated by the material culture in the encampment. Their admiration of the ingenuity of Native technology often produces very positive comments about other aspects of Native culture. At FHPW, one woman visitor expressed this fascination when I asked her to describe what she had seen in the encampment that was new to her: " . . . a birch [bark] container, and I would have stayed all day to learn how to make that. I was just enchanted with it—what the process was—they were very, very advanced in many things." Children, especially, will stand for ages watching Native interpreters make things, and beg to be allowed to try their own hands at activities.

Figure 4.3.   Children scraping hide, Northwest Company Fur Post, 1994. Photograph by Drew Davey.

Objects are also used to bridge cross-cultural divides by stressing commonalities between visitors' lives and those of Native people in the past: discussions of what was used for diapering infants, for instance. At present these messages of shared humanity outweigh discussions of real cultural differences, but this is a symptom of a particular historical moment in which these discussions are occurring.

Objects are also used to communicate with visitors by being placed so as to introduce unexpected ideas. As noted in *Anishinaabeg*, visitors are provoked to ask questions by the sight of European trade goods in Native living spaces, because this violates assumptions that Native peoples were always precontact Primitives. Managers, curators, and interpreters (often independently of each other) place artifacts in rooms and encampments to make certain points, or opportunities to do so. Virginia Lockett, Interpretive Curator at

LFG, stated that they had "a number of reproduction trade items (copper kettle, knife blades, beads, blankets, etc.) at the camp so that visitors will have the impression that First Nations peoples selectively chose some European goods, while still using traditional pieces" (Lockett to Peers, September 29, 2000). Elsewhere, Native-made splint baskets have been added to European and Métis rooms to suggest interaction with local Native people; articles of women's clothing or jewelry, or beadwork supplies, are placed to suggest the presence of Native or Métis wives; tin lanterns are introduced to wigwams to suggest Native adaptability to new technology; dried corn is hung from the ceiling or stored in mokuks to suggest European reliance on Native-produced local foods.

Chief's coats and wampum strings given in alliance rituals open lines of discussion about agency by tribal and settler groups; placing glazed European china in wigwams initiates conversation about kinship and the nature of cultural change. Objects here become voices, things representing certain peoples and perspectives. I am reminded here of David Morgan's useful discussion of visual culture, the study of which, he says, "concentrates on the cultural work that images do in constructing and maintaining (as well as challenging, destroying, and replacing) a sense of order in a particular place and time" (Morgan 2005:29). I would substitute "objects" for "images" in

Figure 4.4.   Tin lantern in wigwam, Colonial Michilimackinac. Photograph by Drew Davey.

the context of historic reconstructions, but clearly the analysis of objects and the work they do—and can be made to do—is crucial to communicating revisionist history.

The real voices that matter, though, are those of the interpreters themselves. While the stories suggested by artifacts are crucial, it is dangerous to let them remain implicit, for—as with the war post—they can be "read" by visitors as easily within misinformed narratives as they can within intended ones. Neither sites nor their furnishings speak for themselves: they are spoken about, by interpreters and visitors. Opportunities for talking about the past can be prompted, but need then to be acted on. If the interpreter is not there or lacks the skill to steer the conversation about the scissors in a wigwam, visitors may maintain older assumptions that Native material technology was inferior to manufactured goods, or that in adopting European technology, Native people became acculturated. They may not see the scissors, or may decide that their placement is an error. Interpreters are crucial in the process of ensuring that the messages suggested by the physical elements of the site are accurately received.

OBJECTS AND IDENTITIES IN NATIVE ENCAMPMENTS

As discussed in the chapter *Anishinaabeg*, historic artifacts constitute important sites of cultural memory and identity for Native peoples. Interpreters who acquire now-rare skills to produce such objects (making and using sinew thread, for instance) also learn considerable cultural and spiritual knowledge. For them, issues of technical authenticity go hand in hand with respect for the ancestors who produced such objects using little or no European technology: many makers try, at least once, to produce an artifact using awl and sinew or spruce root, and "getting it right" is an act of homage. Within contemporary Native communities, those who strive to acquire such skills and knowledge are highly respected. It is also often known in Native communities that an interpreter at a local site has managed to learn a specific technique, bringing it back into use after lying dormant for decades, and interpreters sometimes go to elders and ask to be taught particular techniques: objects are indeed a nexus for social relations.

Making traditional artifacts thus involves the strengthening of cultural identity for Native interpreters and their communities, and can be an important catalyst for personal growth. James Clifford (2004:8) has also noted that "the work of cultural retrieval, display and performance plays a necessary role in current movements around identity and recognition" for indigenous peoples. Such retrieval and the performance of retrieved knowledge, in knowledge of the context of "historical experiences of loss" of such knowledge and of so much more (Clifford 2004:6) is empowering work that heartens those who do it and those who look on. Some tribal groups also consider historic reconstructions as opportunities for learning about details of history and material culture, which often get lost in today's more recent traditions of dress and belief (Carlson and McHalsie 1995). Interpreters are often highly motivated to do this work. I was once privileged to witness, at CM, two Native interpreters discussing archival research that one of them had done on her day off, which she spent working in the archives, and then came back onto site to show her colleague the evidence she had unearthed. And when, as a thank-you gift for spending their time with me, I provided interpreters at two sites in 2005 with images of local, early nineteenth-century artifacts in museum collections, I was astounded at their enthusiastic questions: were the ribbons silk? Was the sewing in linen or sinew? Why hadn't I photographed the lining of that bag? Could I send a close-up shot of how the tassels were attached? The detail of the questions, and the level of dedication to learning, underscored the importance of artifacts and of historical knowledge for cultural and professional identity. The materiality of historic reconstructions leads to education in many directions.

AUTHENTICITY AND AUTHORITY

Issues of authenticity and authority surface in another way at these sites, in the sometimes differing stories told by Native and non-Native interpreters about the same objects or events, and in what is deemed—and by whom—as being authentic and permitted to use, and what is excluded from display. Such disputes over authenticity reveal structures of power and processes of legitimation (Bruner 2005: 163; Gable and Handler 1994).

Intriguingly, one might view the process of the material and intellectual revision of these sites to reflect Native themes as equally reflecting shifting relations of power within heritage agencies. The addition of encampment areas, the use of scarce financial resources to build wigwams or furnish them, the removal of inappropriate objects from buildings and the insertion of items deemed suitable to communicate new messages: these changes have involved a lot of money and a lot of work. They reflect bureaucratic processes of decision-making from the top levels of heritage agencies down to the individual site, as well as political pressure on heritage agencies to acknowledge the historical experiences of Native peoples, and to involve them in the management of heritage resources.

Decisions about what historical themes should be interpreted still tend come from the top down: as Taylor and Payne state, within heritage organizations, "master plans identify a range of historical themes and subthemes and then slot existing sites into the appropriate category" (1992:2). Thus, LFG's interpretation has shifted in response to Parks Canada's policy revisions emphasizing particular themes across certain regions, and the decision to increase Aboriginal elements. It has also responded to the agency's Commemorative Intent policy, which reasons that resources should be expended to implement the original criteria for designation as a national historic site, however thinking about the site may have changed since. At LFG, this means a greater emphasis on transportation networks and could, in the future, lead to the reduction of Aboriginal themes at the site with the exception of Treaty One, which is the only mention of Aboriginal peoples in the original designation text. What is "authentic" and legitimated at LFG clearly reflects structures of power within the national heritage system and hierarchies, and layers of decision-making above that of the individual site. Elsewhere, senior managers and researchers determine what will be said about the past without consulting lower-level, seasonal employees such as Native interpreters.

This helps to explain why some "authentic untruths" are accepted without question, while others cause contention. In sites involving cross-cultural interpretation, many of the disputes tend to focus on the "facts" and interpretation of these surrounding cross-cultural relations, especially where interpretations suggest less than flattering things about Whites (see Gable 1996, Gable and Handler 2000 on such problems surrounding racial issues at Colonial Williamsburg). These tensions are heightened when staff and managers directly represent different groups from the past, as in the Native/Métis interpreters and non-Native managers at most of these sites. There are also significant differences in the perspectives of Native and non-Native interpreters. At several sites, I heard radically different explanations of the amount of alcohol made available to tribal peoples in the fur trade, accompanied by different degrees of condemnation of the traders who supplied alcohol, delivered by Native and non-Native interpreters. Native interpreters often attach moral judgments to their descriptions of life in the past, whether it be of traditional Native life (judged positively, as in more egalitarian) or historic European culture (judged negatively). Such moral judgments were either not used by non-Native interpreters, or were disputed by them. Native interpreters were also more likely, and more willing, to discuss the negative aspects of historical relationships with visitors—problems caused by alcohol, disease, racism, and the legacies of the past—topics which non-Native researchers and managers often muted in training materials for interpreters.

In this vein, some of the disputes I have had with site managers over issues of historical fact become quite interesting. At LFG, the administrators who began the Native encampment joked about my "meddling with our Indians" after I suggested that the staff in the camp could legitimately knit as an interpretive activity, as well as work with hide or do beadwork. Knitting, of course, is associated with settlers. The Cree and Ojibwa who lived around LFG, however, had Métis relatives, and women of all three groups did fine needlework with silk thread, glass beads, and porcupine quills. Knitting was certainly possible within their range of skills, and there was nothing to prevent this skill from being passed from one family member to another across cultural boundaries. Some of the northern Cree women had been schooled by Anglican missionaries, who included training in European women's roles; spinning and knitting are documented as having been part of such training.[3] The LFG managers, not having done any specific historical research when they began the encampment, had an image of less "acculturated" tribal peoples in mind. Knitting, to them, was a European activity, not part of their image of Native society. By insisting that the site portray the complex historical reality of tribal peoples, non-Christian and Christian, missionary-schooled and not, I was indeed "meddling" with their "Indians."

As Bruner has identified (Bruner 2005:12), one of the key issues at historic reconstructions has to do with who has the right to tell the story, and whose stories are suppressed. Suppressing the stories of northern Cree who migrated to Red River to farm and were trained by missionaries to knit in favor of the stories of "traditional" Ojibwa says much about the uncertainty attached to the changing narratives that are being told at these sites. It also says a good deal about the relationship between power and authenticity. Had I not intervened as a scholarly consultant with historical evidence, the Native interpreters would have been told that knitting was not a legitimate activity for them (and it seemed to have faded as a desirable activity in the encampment by 2005).

The moral shadings given certain descriptions of cultural features by Native interpreters, the different sets of expectations about authentic activities for Native interpreters, the sometimes differing emphases or explanations of objects and historical processes that one finds across a historic site—all of these disparities can give rise to a level of contention far beyond that due to historical inaccuracy, which is always a problem with staff who are given only a few days' training at the beginning of a season (and who are mostly expected to learn the site's history on their own). Staff debate these things heatedly on site. The heat arises not just from commitment to period correctness, but from the tensions between Native and non-Native historical narratives, from recent scholarly debates over the problems of representation inherent in Native histories written by non-Native scholars, and from friction in society generally between Native peoples and the dominant society. In discussing tensions over the interpretation of Elmina Castle by locals and tourists,

Bruner (1996:293) notes the central dilemma the site faces: "Which story shall be told? Vested interests and strong feelings are involved." The feelings can be very strong indeed when cultural "Others" attack cherished historical myths or when official training material denies one set of historical experiences. Who has the right to settle disputes of historical fact and perspective: the site manager? The heritage agency curator? An elder? A scholarly consultant? A further complication in such sensitive situations is that these competing authorities seldom speak to each other directly about such differences.[4]

Scholars' (and site managers') first response to such disputes over the meanings or authenticity of objects is often that they are unsupported by archival documentation, or driven by political or moral agendas.[5] I would repeat Handler and Gable's (1997:92; Gable and Handler 1994:121) caveat, though, that the insistent emphasis on "facts" (and especially on a set of facts determined by non-Native scholars) works to deflect emphasis away from discussions "of the moral or political significance" of cross-cultural issues. Such insistence is also a good way of refusing to introduce revisionist information and perspectives, or of limiting change. I am not simply condoning presentism here, or the use of unsupported or simplistic narratives about Native people in the past. Rather, I think we need to acknowledge that the goals of non-Native staff at historic sites differ from those of Native staff, just as the historical experiences of Native people still differ from official historical narratives. The importance I place upon documentation and the fine, changing details of material culture is not always shared by those who are waging rather larger battles against ignorance and racism. A. J. B. Johnston, who interviewed First Nations scholars as part of his research on Parks Canada's portrayal of their histories, concludes that language, customs, and values are the stuff of First Nations history, not the particular changing details over time of clothing, housing, or weaponry. The implication for sites that wish to interpret the history of a particular Native group is that the group may well want to talk more about their worldview and less about the "things" to which its culture has often been reduced. "'We are more than arrowheads,' is how Marie Battiste (Mi'kmaq) put it" (Johnston 1995:7). After being appalled by visitors' misinformed questions and astounded at the uniformly stereotyped goggles through which visitors view Native interpreters, my quibbles with costume details and house forms began to seem like arrogance. They are not; but there are other realities in operation at these sites, and other things going on than the transmission of information about the past. As David Neufeld commented on historic sites, "Perhaps the focus on the material is the problem. What is the point of remembering the past? What services do we wish it to perform and in our representations who controls the services it does perform?" (personal communication 2004). Objects become the focus of great contestation at historic reconstructions precisely because they are nexuses for such broader debates.

Such skirmishes are not only "about" the past, but also relate to Native-White relations in the present. Sometimes staff members need to sit down with each other and engage with the different perspectives and "facts" they bring to this work. This rarely happens. Historic sites also need to acknowledge that Native interpreters are educating visitors to respect Native people. Their work involves challenging stereotypes that affect them in the present. From this perspective, the use of elements of the lived experiences of Native cultures seems quite justified. It also suggests that the "policing" of information through recourse to archival documentation is as much about an attempt to control the overall narrative being communicated, and to maintain a dominant-society perspective on this narrative, as it is an attempt to agree on facts. Disputes over artifacts serve as lenses to observe such larger battles in action.

The underlying problem here stems from the way in which objects function as icons to raise certain narratives in the minds of dominant society visitors: especially mythological narratives about the frontier, the founding of North American society, and the roles of Native peoples within this. Foregrounding the material culture without disrupting older assumptions simply reinforces those assumptions. Nostalgia, one of the predominant narratives evoked for visitors by the materialities of these reconstructions, can be a mask which effaces the importance of the roles of Native peoples, the true nature of Native-White relations, or the establishment of European dominance over Native peoples. The deliberate evocation of nostalgia without challenging such assumptions continues them in the present, perpetuating the marginalization of Native peoples within North American society. As Ivan Karp states, the ideas and artifacts chosen for display are selected within systems of power that uphold the hierarchies of civil society. Exhibitions, he goes on to say, are "political arenas in which definitions of identity and culture are asserted and contested" (1992:1). Representations of the past at historic sites are equally arenas for broader national politics, and using officially sanctioned educational sites to reinforce myths about the past and about Native peoples that support the dominance of settler society is unacceptable.

Visitors are, of course, quite likely to attribute different meanings to objects than site managers intend, and they have very different criteria for authenticity. Baxandall has explained the complexity of such attempts to communicate through objects, and how their meanings can be "hijacked":

First, there are the ideas, values, and purposes of the culture from which the object comes. Second, there are the ideas, values, and certainly, purposes of the arrangers of the exhibition. These are likely to be laden with theory and otherwise contaminated by a concept of culture that the viewer does not necessarily possess or share. Third, there is the viewer himself, with all his own cultural baggage of unsystematic ideas, values . . . (Baxandall 1991:34)

For most visitors, authenticity is not tied to historical documentation or to struggles over power, but to the relation between what they see and what they expect to see (Moscardo and Pearce 1999:418; Kelleher 2004:10; Stronza 2001:271)—or what they want to see. As Richard Handler has noted, authenticity has much to do with Western longing for "the unspoiled, pristine, genuine, untouched and traditional" (Handler 1986:2). Partly because of this, visitors do not generally care whether an artifact is old or a reproduction. For the vast majority of dominant-society visitors, so long as what they see conforms to nostalgic ideas they bring with them ("Oh, look, John, your grandmother had one of those!") and to visual stereotypes such as quilts or rough blankets on beds (the "primitive" and traditional), they are satisfied that things are authentic.

This is, again, very different from the value placed on authenticity by many historic site staff. These disputes over objects and authenticity also become heated because of the peculiar value of knowledge at historic reconstructions, where the amount of historical research one has done is a measure of worth. Managers and interpreters alike value historical knowledge and research. The hunger for the images of historic artifacts I gave, the many questions of historical fact I was asked by staff, and the respect shown to me as an historian are all manifestations of this value system. This commitment to learning and to accuracy is crucial for this system of communication, of course: it is part of the experience of these places to be treated to a lecture on why this particular size or color of beads was used in the period portrayed, or on the reasons for the different sorts of dinner plates in the rooms of different ranks within the fort. This brings us back to Bruner's notion that authenticity and authority are the same thing, for within this system of value, objects and information about them become controlled, policed, as part of a process of establishing authority. The legitimation of objects and knowledge about them equally reveals patterns of authority.[6] Thus, at LFG in the summer of 2005, interpreters in the Native encampment felt that some of the activities they were asked to do with the public were of questionable authenticity and historically inaccurate (one involved an activity called "Mother Earth's Dress," with four colors of plastic beads), but these activities had been given to them by site management—so they did them. At the same time, the knowledge of mid-nineteenth century skills such as the loom weaving of panels for panel bags had not been transmitted to the encampment staff: they had a loom which had clearly been made for panel production, but were only (here is the historian saying "only"!) making modern-style narrow bracelets. Contrasted with staff at the NWCFP, who make period-specific items such as birchbark mokuks, the LFG situation demonstrated problematic relations between layers of staff in a complex organization (interpreters seem to be estranged from curators; managers have the power to sanction inauthentic activities) as well as the relative disempowerment of the encampment staff.

The authenticity of the material elements of historic reconstructions, then, reveals lines of power and dispute within these institutions, but specifically shows where the authority to legitimate lies (Bruner 2005:151). Such authority has an extra dimension for Native interpreters. As Hastrup and Elsass observe (1990:306), cultural survival "implies not the conservation of a preconceived identity anchored once and for all in an objectively existing (reified) culture but continuing control by the agents of a particular culture over the shaping of local history." Who has control of cultural representations, and who has the authority to make and enforce decisions about what is authentic and permitted and what is not, matters in this context. That Native interpreters have developed a distinctive style of interpretation and give sometimes oppositional versions of their sites' histories suggests that they have claimed the authority to do so. That they are relatively often involved in skirmishes over authenticity suggests that this authority is being disputed.

CONCLUSION

These problems of communication are inherent in the medium of historic reconstructions, in which the details are so compelling, and often suggest different narratives than those intended by managers. One needs to be careful that the desired messages are communicated through the physical elements of sites, as well as by staff, and that visitors actually receive them and integrate them with their existing knowledge. Staff play a crucial role in balancing information received by visitors, but need support from props, the placement of areas of the site in relation to each other, and training to convey the most accurate view of the past.

Historic sites are, above all, constantly constructing, producing, and (re)inventing the past, imbuing it with new meanings, and participating in "the processual, active nature of culture, history, tradition, and heritage" as it has existed past and present (Bruner 2005:127). The communication of such alternative information depends on staff to interpret the physical fabric of reconstructions. Palisades, trading shops, and encampments are stage sets for interaction between visitors and interpreters, and it is in this interaction that staff voice other ideas and ways of seeing the past.

NOTES

1. McIntosh and Prentice (1999:591) also note that "without . . . interpretations, and often without even labeling, period theme parks require cultural competence on the part of their visitors. For many, this is the stimulation of selective memory or nostalgia, often for anachronisms found in the childhood days of older visitors." Edward Bruner (2005:128) also states: "despite the efforts of museum professionals, historians, and the scholarly community to present an ever more 'accurate' perspective of Abraham Lincoln and life in the 1830s in the village of New Salem, their scientific views are contradicted and suppressed by the way in which the reconstructed village is produced and by how it is interpreted and experienced by the visitors." The contest, he says, "is between the museum professionals and scholars who seek historical accuracy and authenticity on the one hand, and the people's own popular interpretation. . . ."

2. Wallace (1991:192) similarly critiqued museums that "focused relentlessly on objects and work processes rather than social relations or politics." Joy Hendry (2000:133, 139), cites parallel critiques of Ironbridge Gorge, a British mining reconstruction, as making quaint and (in the words of a former miner at the site) "mummifying" the political history and labor exploitation of the era, quite possibly in a deliberate strategy to erase or deny certain memories.

3. See, for instance, Church Missionary Society papers, microfilm reel A77, Rev. Cockran to Secretaries, July 25, 1833.

4. Handler and Gable (1997:88) claim a similar situation about the African American and White staff at Colonial Williamsburg regarding the interpretation of miscegenation.

5. Handler and Gable 1997:84, and Gable 1996, similarly describe a situation at Williamsburg where attempts to work slavery into interpretation were frustrated by (White) interpreters' perception that black history was "undocumented" or poorly documented.

6. And see Garner 2004:92, 95 about tree pollards (and knowledge of creating these) being used as "material representations of authority."

Vignette: Bob and Betty
Visit Fort William

Bob and Betty, a couple in their early sixties, are visiting FWHP. They are American, retired, and relatively affluent. They are on a month-long vacation (driving their own car and staying at motels) and have stopped because Bob is interested in colonial history—he has watched television documentaries, and read some popular works of history—and she reads historical romance novels set on the frontier. They have been to Williamsburg a few years ago, and to other historic sites.

Our visitors enter the orientation building, and find the gift shop on one hand as they enter and the admission desk on the other; facing them as they walk through the main door is an enormous carved wooden mural depicting fur traders, canoes, Native people, animals, and trees. They pay their admission fee and go into the introductory display. Video screens and displays with artifacts convey information about the fur trade and Native life as they walk through.

Bob and Betty leave the orientation building and take the site's minivan into the woods. When they get out, they catch glimpses of a river and smell smoke. They walk along the pathway, and find—almost hidden off the path—several bark structures, and some Native people working in smaller shelters. Betty stops in her tracks: it's so much like the descriptions she has read of Native villages! Smiling, she enters the camp area, and is greeted by one of the Native staff ("Boozhoo! Welcome to our home! Have you traveled far to visit us?"). She engages in a brief conversation with the woman, and is invited to sample some fresh bannock. They go into the lodges, pick up the cradleboard and paddles leaning against them, stroke the furs hanging from trees.

Bob talks to an older man who is carving a burl bowl, and Betty is invited to sit on some deer hides with a young woman who is sewing a leather dress.

Betty asks her how long it takes to sew such a garment, and how the hides are processed; the woman answers, and adds that the people in the fort are always buying moccasins from her: if it weren't for her they'd be barefoot, and come to think of it, if it weren't for her husband's hunting and fishing, those White people would be hungry! The woman has her young daughter with her, also wearing period costume. After some further conversation about the historic Native presence at the fort, Betty asks about contemporary Native people in Thunder Bay. She asks Bob to take her picture with the woman and her daughter, and then they thank the interpreters, leave the camp and walk towards the main fort.

They now see the large palisade, and reading from the site brochure, Bob says, "This place is the largest reconstructed fur trade post in the world, it says here that it's got 2780 feet of ten-foot high wooden palisade!" The imposing main gate faces the river. Betty notices the bastions at each corner of the fort, and wonders aloud if they ever fought with the Indians. Bob says, "Well, I guess they had to be able to protect their trade goods in case of attack." Betty takes a picture of Bob standing in the main gate.

Just inside the gate, a young woman—not Native, but wearing the same ribbon-decorated strap dress as the women in the encampment—greets our visitors and suggests that they might want to stay nearby for a few minutes, because the Governor would be arriving by canoe soon and there would be a welcome ceremony for him. They go into the nearest building, which turns out to be the apothecary's shop, and greet "Dr. McLoughlin" and his wife. Mrs. McLoughlin sits sewing, wearing European clothes, and Betty asks where she is from. It turns out that the historic Mrs. McLoughlin was Métis, and married the doctor in 1811, after being abandoned by her first husband when he left the fur trade. The doctor, meanwhile, seems to have a bee in his top hat about Native herbs and sweat lodges. He dubs these "primitive and unscientific," showing Bob the frightening-looking tools he uses on his own patients.

At the sound of bagpipes approaching, the doctor invites his visitors to come with him to welcome the Governor, and they go out to the wharf. Several other gentlemen in top hats and frock coats are there, and a servant is placing a jug of lemonade on a fancy little table. An older Native woman also waits with them, a little apart from the gentlemen. As the big canoe comes in sight, the visitors are enthralled by the sight of voyageurs paddling in unison and the Governor seated, smoking his pipe, in the center of the canoe. One of the "voyageurs" is a young woman in very fancy Native dress; the older Native woman on shore waves enthusiastically to her. A cannon salute is fired from the wharf, and the Governor is carried ashore. Doctor McLaughlin formally welcomes the Governor, and the men all drink toasts ("to the King," "to the Company"). Bob thinks there's something a bit funny about the response to these toasts, which is "Live long and prosper," but it is a lively and entertaining scene. Several hundred tourists are gathered on the wharf to watch.

Betty sees the two Native women are greeting each other emotionally: this is obviously a reunion. A young man in voyageur dress approaches them, carrying a pile of blankets and trade goods, and he lays these at the older woman's feet. She looks at him very sternly, and then nods and smiles at the young woman, who beams. The voyageurs are offered a regale, a ceremonial dram (of lemonade), and then another toast is offered: "to Jacques and Nancy, on the occasion of their betrothal!" The young Native woman is handed forward to the handsome voyageur, who takes her hand and grins from ear to ear.

The crowd is invited to the betrothal festivities, which will soon begin in the main square. The voyageurs hoist the canoe and head into the fort, waving Jacques and Nancy away. The gentlemen stride away, led by the piper, and already have their heads together, gossiping and discussing business. Jacques, Nancy, and Nancy's mother head toward the Native encampment, with Jacques making great proclamations of his prowess as a trader and hunter, and Nancy interpreting.

As the crowd disperses, Betty and Bob have a snack in the "Cantine," which offers period fare: today it is bread just out of the fort's stone ovens and thick pea soup, with tea. Then they tour the buildings inside the fort: the trading store, the voyageurs' quarters (filthy clothes of the recently-arrived voyageurs strewn about), and the cooper's shed. They touch the chairs, photograph staff at their work, and "overhear" costumed interpreters gossiping excitedly about the Company's feud with the Hudson's Bay Company. The Fort William inhabitants declare their trading methods to be much superior to those of the HBC and vow to break up the HBC's colony at Red River: Bob, at one point, finds himself listening to an impassioned lecture on the affrontery of their rivals' attempt to prevent dried buffalo meat and pemmican—the staple diet of the voyageurs!—from being taken out of Red River.

Our visitors also ask about the women in Native dresses inside the fort (mixed-blood, they are told, and a discussion of fur trade marriage and the roles of women in the fur trade ensues). Bob asks about the boundary line between British and American territory, especially interesting as the fort is reconstructed to 1815, and the staff are well versed on the War of 1812. They both examine documents being copied in the elegant Great Hall (which they compare to colonial buildings in New England), and sign them as witnesses, using quill pens. Betty takes Bob's picture as he signs, with the top-hatted clerk beside him. Hearing fiddles outside the Great Hall, they realize that the betrothal celebration has begun, and they first watch (and take pictures) and then participate in several dances. Eventually, feeling quite tired, they go back out the main gate, past the Native encampment (only the older man is there now; everyone else is at the dance), climb in the van, and go back to the orientation center. Bob sits in the cafeteria and has a beer, and Betty buys her own quill pen, some beaded earrings, and a dream catcher as well as some postcards showing the fort. They leave, well satisfied with their visit.

Chapter Five

Visitors

There are three images that stand out when I recall my fieldwork for this project. The first is of a young child, about five years old, leaning out of the window at a historic site. It was an upstairs window, with a shutter; the child looked like a puppet in a puppet theatre. He was wearing a dyed-turkey-feather headdress and waving a plastic tomahawk. Angelic blonde hair, cute features—and already steeped in the stereotypes that pervade North American society about "Indians." He was playing Indian. All of the reconstructed buildings, all of the costumed interpreters who enact history, became stage set and supporting cast for this child, who was quite confident of his lines, his role, and the play.

The second image is of an older, preteen boy, in the waginogan at the Native encampment of another historic site. The boy was in T-shirt, jeans, and sneakers, and eagerly questioning the Native interpreter, who was in period clothing. The boy asked question after question, and seemed to be seeking something. His questions were misinformed, as if he had had access only to second-rate information, or Hollywood movies. As the interpreter corrected him, point by point, the boy didn't back off or retreat into defensive hostility at being told he was wrong. He kept asking questions; he really wanted to know. Shards of stereotypes piled up around their feet. The boy stayed for at least twenty minutes; it was an amazing encounter. When he finally thanked the interpreter and left, the interpreter turned to me and said, "*That* is why I keep working here!"

The final image is of a group of Mennonite visitors walking through the gates of a palisade and staring at a Native interpreter. The Mennonites were in plain dress, the men with long beards and hats, the women in bonnets and hand-made dresses. They themselves were being stared at by non-Mennonite

Figure 5.1. Boy with headdress framed in window, Sainte Marie among the Hurons, 1994. Photograph by Drew Davey.

families visiting the site. The Mennonites were staring—as at a Martian—at an Odawa interpreter who sported a shaven head and scalplock, nose-ring, multiple earrings, breechclout, ruffled eighteenth-century shirt, moccasins, and face paint. The Mennonites literally stopped in their tracks to take in this sight; as they looked, mothers unconsciously reached down and grabbed their children's hands. Finally, as a group, they walked on, the adults' faces pointedly turned to the next part of the site, the children all with their heads turned toward the interpreter as their mothers dragged them along.

I have suggested in earlier chapters that living history sites have traditionally acted as stage sets for the performance of dominant-society myths, and that Native staff challenge such narratives by asserting their own and their ancestors' humanity and importance. What happens when they challenge myths in this way can be powerful. In this chapter, I set the stage for understanding those encounters by exploring the demographics, motivations, and actions of visitors. Who visits these places, and why? What do they want and expect? What do their experiences at historic sites mean to them?

Bob and Betty's visit to Fort William, in the vignette preceding this chapter, outlines some of the ways in which visitors interact with historic sites. Interpreters would describe Bob and Betty as "good" visitors: they have at least minimal background knowledge, however skewed it may be; they are interested; they stay for several hours; they speak with interpreters; they purchase food and souvenirs on site. We know a fair bit about certain aspects of the background and behavior of such visitors because of industry research on tourism, which has generated a huge mass of data from the average distance visitors travel to get to a site to the amount they spend while there. We know much less about other aspects of visitor behavior, especially about how visitors engage existing knowledge with what is presented on site, and how they respond in both the short and long term to new information. The dynamics of visitor responses at historic sites to Native interpreters seem to fall between much of the existing literature, and I accordingly draw on a broad range of studies covering cultural and heritage tourism to understand why visitors come to these sites, and how they respond to them.

Understanding the motivations and behaviors of "guests" has been a primary goal of the anthropology of tourism. All of the places examined here are tourist sites, marketing themselves as purveyors of authenticity, heritage, nostalgia, and educational value. With the addition of Native staff they are also involved in ethnic or cultural tourism, defined as when the goal of the tourist's experience is an encounter with members of other cultures, who are believed to be exotic in some way (Smith 1977; see also van den Berghe 1994; Boniface and Fowler 1993; Stanley 1998). I am aware that much cultural tourism has not been educational or transformative for tourists, but has simply reinforced relations of power between peoples of different social classes and races (e.g., Horne 1984; Bruner and Kirshenblatt-Gimblett 1994; Trask 1999). This has been the case not only in much modern tourism, but also across the long history of touristic and voyeuristic activity involving dominant-society members looking at Native peoples. In many of these appearances, Native people were framed either physically or by narration within the context of "a race in decline":

> Tourists might idealize or condemn them, but the belief that Native people belonged to the past . . . supplied a powerful, unifying theme. Confining "Indians" to the past had a particular advantage for tourists, for it allowed them to see Native people as "authentic" and yet ineffectual and unthreatening at the same time. (Jasen 1995:17)

Viewing Native peoples was thus pleasurable for middle- and upper-class non-Native tourists, providing as it did the thrill of an encounter with the exotic (noble/savage) Primitive, while at the same time confirming the tourist's own identity and idealized social and political relationship between them. This is powerful work, and I suggest that historic reconstructions face a danger of providing similar experiences for visitors. For tourists, visiting historic reconstructions involves active participation in and, often, confirmation of, narratives about their place in society. "Nostalgia," a major commodity at these places, is not purely a longing for the past, but a longing that elements of the past should continue to exist in the present. Where this applies to visitors' notions of Native people and Native-White relations, nostalgia is both a problem and an opportunity for challenge.

AUDIENCES

I take this rather wary approach to the dynamics of tourism involving publicly funded historic reconstructions knowing that the vast majority of visitors to historic sites are White, middle- and upper-middle-class individuals with more education and higher pay than the North American average: members of the Western elite. In a 1995 visitor study done at CM, 94.3 percent of the visitors were White (Korn 1995). This figure is backed up by figures from Colonial Williamsburg (Gable, Handler, and Lawson 1992:792, 803), which suggested that visitors there were "overwhelmingly white." My own field observations also support this. Furthermore, these visitors are more highly educated than the average person (CM: 34 percent have some post-secondary education, 24.5 percent have postsecondary degree; Williamsburg: 60 percent had college degree). They are also wealthier than most people. At Williamsburg in the early 1990s, 58 percent had a household income of $50,000 or more, and in surveys done within the British heritage tourism industry, researchers found that "heritage users are almost always disproportionately likely to be from nonmanual worker households than from manual households, and within the nonmanuals, to be from professional or senior managerial households" (Prentice 1993:227, 54–58; similar demographics also reported for cultural tourism by Bruner and Kirshenblatt-Gimblett 1994:436, Laxson 1991:366–67, Harrison 2003:8). The British study concluded that "heritage users" were distinguished by the uniformity of their social class (1993:227).

Minority groups do visit these sites, but in relatively small numbers. This is part of a long-established pattern in traditional tourism (see, for instance, Meeker 1984 [1973]:131). Although the gay travel market has developed strongly over recent decades, ads featuring Hispanic, Black, Native, and other minority peoples enjoying themselves in standard tourist situations remain rare, as do tourists from these groups at mainstream historical tourist sites (Urry 1990:142–43 also comments on this). In this context, it is interesting to note which minority groups visit historical sites, and why. Mennonites are among the largest group of minority visitors to historic sites in North America, which appeal to such religious groups because they are perceived as wholesome family entertainment and because they suggest some of the religious, cohesive communities of the frontier past that resonate with these people and their chosen way of life. Middle-class African Americans sometimes visit these and other historic sites; one such family I spoke with at CM indicated that they wished their children to see a site of national historic importance and that they felt it was an appropriate family activity. Most minority visitors, however, come on special tours and programs created specifically for "nontraditional audiences." LFG has hosted a swearing-in ceremony for new Canadian citizens because of the fort's importance as a national historic site, and people who participate in this ceremony often bring their families and visitors to the site afterwards. Foreign visitors and recent immigrants are often taken to historic sites; I once encountered a saffron-robed group of Buddhist monks at LFG who were being shown a "national history" site by local hosts (see Bruner 2005:164, Greenspan 2002).

Native people seldom visit these sites as members of the general public, something I noticed during fieldwork in 1994 and again in 2005, and which Native interpreters confirmed on both occasions. As with other minority groups, Native people sometimes visit the sites on special tours (such as Native school children on class trips). In a few cases, they visit because they are related to a Native interpreter and have been invited to visit the interpreter at work, or because they want to see what the site is portraying about Native people. These visitors are rare, however.

These patterns of Native visitation do not mean that history is unimportant to Native peoples; just the opposite. The Oglala Lakota surveyed by Rosenzweig and Thelen defined the past "as not simply 'usable' but essential to group and individual survival" (1998:175). However, mainstream, government-funded museums and historic sites have always been intended to reinforce or inculcate the values, beliefs, and norms of the dominant society (see Meeker 1984 [1973]:132–33). Why should Native people visit these places if the message they receive is that their people were savage, or unimportant in history? As Lakota respondents to Rosenzweig and Thelen's study articulated very strongly, Native peoples have a set of historical narratives which are, in the words of one interviewee, "pretty much opposite" mainstream narratives: "the Sioux seemed to reject the traditional narrative structure altogether, defining themselves as a separate nation with a history that followed a dramatically different trajectory" (Rosenzweig and Thelen 1998:165). Given that the genre of historical reconstruction arose out of a desire to celebrate the victory of non-Native, dominant society in achieving control over the continent, why would it appeal to the descendants of those who were dispossessed as the result of the events depicted at these sites? And having communicated rather blinkered views of history for decades, sites have not won over Native audiences simply by revising historical messages. Even where they are praised by Aboriginal leaders for more inclusive portrayals of history, reconstructions are still often seen by Aboriginal people as linked to government and dominant society, and they tend to be distrustful of such associations.

One of the main reasons for this is that elements of the history depicted at these places remain very painful for Native people (Larry Young, personal communication, CM, 1994). Notwithstanding all of the positive cross-cultural relationships they now interpret, most of the sites discussed here are set in the broader contexts of moments of shifting power that disadvantaged Native people. Mission sites are especially sensitive, raising issues of cultural change and loss. Every summer at SMAH, a few Huron/Wendat—whose ancestors fled their homelands with the Jesuits in 1649, ending up as refugees—visit the site "as a sort of pilgrimage," in the words of one Native interpreter. They tend to identify themselves as Huron/Wendat to the Native interpreters, and it is clearly important to them to be there, but it is a distressing site to them. What would have been their fate had they not accepted the presence of the Jesuits in order to gain access to French trade goods? Would the epidemics have been as devastating? Would they have been able to resist the Iroquois? Would they still be living in their homeland? "You can often tell they're Huron before they tell you," said one interpreter; "they just have this look in their eyes." Rather like visitors to Holocaust museums who have personal ties to the history being represented, Native visitors have a difficult relationship to some historic sites.

Intriguingly, while Native people make up a tiny fraction of public visitors during the tourist season, some sites are attracting significant numbers of Native visitors to educational programs and special activities held on site. Fort William continues to host seasonal events such as Ojibway Keeshigan, and in 2004 hosted a National Aboriginal day event for the region and a regional Aboriginal youth conference. It has also partnered with Aboriginal organizations for promotion and to host these events, and has seen a significant increase in Aboriginal participation in booked education programs and conferences/retreats. At Fort William, classes on moccasin making, mitten making, quillwork, beadwork, and capote making attract local Native, Métis, and non-Native community members. LFG has experimented with special programs for Métis seniors that use fiddling music, stories, and the historic site to prompt visitors' memories. At Mackinac Island, part of the heritage complex of which CM is part, a Native Women's Gathering has used facilities for a retreat each autumn (Brisson to Peers, e-mail October 27, 2005).

Educational programs suggest the diversity of audiences these sites deal with: NWCFP offers enthusiastic sessions for Scout groups who pass through the site on their way to canoe in the Boundary Waters area of northern Minnesota, an area linked strongly with the historic fur trade and Ojibwe culture. At Fort William, Brownies and Scouts, elementary and secondary school children, adult and senior education audiences participate in one-day and multi-week classes on arts and crafts, science, and social history. All of these sites are actively working to develop programs for school children, linking with the established curriculum and using the sites to teach everything from natural history to physics to social history. These are all diverse audiences, with very different goals and needs, and the specific histories of each of these sites are used (sometimes more closely than others) to base each program around and create an engaging learning environment. A small sample of the FWHP programs includes: Aboriginal Cultural Expedition; Between Two Worlds; Methods of Historical Inquiry (all for grades 9–12); Life in a Wigwam; Fur Trade Natural History; Amazing Inventions (for elementary school children); Heritage; and Cultural Awareness (for Guides and Scouts). Artisan workshops open to the public include moccasin making, quillwork, and knitting for beginners. The site also offers March Break camps for children (FWHP Program Guide 2005). People attend these programs for many reasons, including the selection of a program by a troop leader or classroom teacher as suitable because it meshes well with educational needs or to learn skills which require specialist teachers: these audiences are seeing, and finding, very different things in these sites.

Along with educational groups, probably the largest visitor groups at these sites are families. Interestingly, families as consumers are seldom addressed in the literature on cultural tourism, which takes the responses of the educated, middle-class (and usually White) adult individual as the basis for analysis. Working at historic reconstructions, however, it quickly becomes clear that visitors during the summer tourist season are largely in family groups and that the family has chosen to visit the site for both educational and social reasons. For blended and multigenerational families, historic sites and museums provide a neutral space that is valued positively because of its educational associations: a good place for walking around with family members. These are also tourist destinations, well marketed and easy to get to, with good support facilities that increase their attraction to family audiences. Family groups alter the dynamics of communication at these places. As Bruner (2005:164) has noted for New Salem, they become the basic unit for processing information given to them by the site, so that parents or other adults explain the site to the children or guests. One of the special skills that interpreters need to acquire is that of quickly "reading" guests to ascertain their interests and background, and of speaking to several generational and educational levels simultaneously. In her fourth season as an interpreter at NWCFP, Sandy Gimple noted in 2005 that,

> there are a lot of families who come, so often a lot of what we have to do is being able to reach different age levels, so I'm conscious of having to reach small

children, so they can understand, but at the same time not insulting their parents or grandparents. Or people on the [same] tour who don't have children with them. . . . You have to try to read the group when they first come to see what they're interested in.

Family dynamics lead to very fact-based conversations that may or may not broaden to discuss social or political dynamics, as this excerpt from a family visit to the Native encampment at LFG demonstrates:

Summer 2005, LFG, interaction between parent (P), child (CV), and Native interpreter (I):

CV: What are those horns?

I: They come from different animals like elk or deer. We can carve things from them. We try to use as much of the animal as possible.

CV: You can use all the animal! You can use the fur for clothes, the bones for tools and the meat for eating. I know one thing they don't use: the eyes.

P: They used to use fish eyes for candy. Inuit.

I: Oh, that's way way far up north, I haven't been there yet. Do you know we use brains? What do you think we could use brains for?

P: Tanning leather.

I: (joking tone) Hey, you're supposed to let the children answer! But you're right, we use brains for tanning leather. Oh! Look at this. What do you guys think this is?

CV: A knife holder?

I: Yes, but what's the decoration on this knife holder?

CV: Skin?

I: Close! It comes from a little animal, very round and spiky.

CV: Porcupine!

I: Yes, these are porcupine quills. And so before we traded with the Company and we wanted to decorate things, we used quills and they're hollow just like a drinking straw so we flatten them and dye them and [sew them on].

This was an educational conversation, reinforcing visitors' existing information and beginning to transmit new information to a child visitor and his family. The different interests of the three people in the conversation never quite merged with the site's official themes, though, and it was a far cry from the set monologues which are sometimes delivered in various rooms of historic houses at other sites. In such situations—further disrupted by children's attention spans, lack of contextual knowledge, and needs for public toilets and refreshments—what visitors learn is determined by a matrix involving their existing knowledge, family dynamics and physical needs, and interpretive skill and experience. Revising site messages and adding Native components and staff may not be enough to get across desired themes and ideas, although it is remarkable how well experienced staff manage to do so.

Finally, there is a special group of visitors who come to historic reconstructions often. Dubbed "heritage enthusiasts" by Prentice (1993:9), these visitors are "significantly more likely than the nonenthusiasts to want to use their holiday to learn about local customs and culture." Some are reenactors (hobbyists), others are collectors, others engage in a range of heritage-related activities. Clearly, they have a great deal invested personally in such contacts with the past and find visiting historic reconstructions not only satisfying but necessary. There are many reasons for this, as I will explore below. This group exemplifies Rosenzweig and Thelen's conclusion (1998) that a large segment of middle-class North Americans care passionately about the past and engage in activities such as visiting historic sites to learn about the past and construct their own identities in the present.

WHAT VISITORS DO

Regardless of the diversity of visitor backgrounds, visitors share many experiences at historic reconstructions. The visitor's journey through the site begins as they pay admission, pick up the site brochure, and move through the introductory exhibit area. Decoration and architecture immediately give nonverbal clues to the period and people depicted on site. At some sites there are museum displays placing the site in thematic and regional context, as with the fur trade displays at Fort William and NWCFP. At most sites the majority of visitors do not view orientation videos, though a slightly larger group will look at displays. This nonviewer figure was as high as 94.6 percent at CM during one study (Korn 1995:11), although this did not seem to be typical when I observed at various sites; I would guess 50 percent of visitors on the average day might see part of a video or display, especially if waiting for a formal tour to begin. The content of these introductory displays and films can be controversial, especially where new site themes mean that these introductory messages must be expensively revised (in 2005, LFG seemed to have dealt with this problem by removing all orientation displays and videos). At SMAH, where the introductory video was reshot in the mid-1980s to reflect new thinking (the old video featured screams of hapless victims of Iroquois torture over the crackling of the burning fort), some visitors complained that the new video leaned too far in the direction of political correctness and was, in the words of one visitor, "watered down." The video's incorporation of new perspectives seems to challenge some visitors' preconceptions. Some visitors object to the lack of emphasis on figures whom they see as heroic; at SMAH, this complaint focuses on what is seen as the "neglect" of the Jesuit martyrs, in honor of whom many people come to the site (SMAH visitor survey cards, August 1–7, 1994). Most introductory displays now include, with varying emphases, material on the ways of life of local Native people and some information on how Native people were affected by the presence of Europeans. A few sites (SMAH, FWHP, and NWCFP) place great emphasis on these themes and communicate them very well. The NWCFP exhibits drew on MHS's experience in interpreting fur trade society, and represent a state-of-the-art articulation of current thinking on the operation and impacts of the fur trade for Whites, Métis, and Ojibwe people in the region. Visitors who spend a few minutes in such areas at the start of their tour begin their visit with considerably more information about the period than those who simply go from the admissions desk to the palisade.

After passing through the gateway, visitors typically make a number of short stops throughout the site: the encampment, a house, perhaps a work area or barn, and usually the trading shop or blacksmith's shop. Few visitors go into every building, so what people see depends on what areas are staffed that day, and what catches visitors' eyes. Some sites make use of this selectivity: at FWHP and LFG, for instance, the Native encampment has been moved so that visitors would have to choose whether they wanted to enter that area, in hopes that those who did so would be predisposed to learn from the encampment and its staff.

As they move through the site, visitors experience it in a multisensory way. They look at the room furnishings, ask questions of and listen to interpreters, and touch reproduction artifacts made available for that purpose. They may taste period cooking, smell woodsmoke or the reek of rotting hair being slipped from deer hides, put stitches in a quilt or string beads, sit on buffalo hides or trade blankets or rough wooden benches. In the trader's store, visitors "shop": they ask how much things cost, what it took to earn that much money, what things are, how they got there.

In my observation, visitors constantly touched everything they could. This is an important part of visitors' experience, and what sets historic reconstructions apart from other forms of display. Furs and hides hung out for them to stroke have to be replaced each season or so because they wear out. Visitors picked up tikinagans, handled bark baskets, ran their hands through dried corn and rice; sat down with interpreters to get a closer look at beading and leather sewing techniques; tried their hands at stoking fires, stirring stew, flipping bannock, scraping hide. The corn pounders at CM and SMAH were in constant use. Anything not tied down in or around a lodge gets picked up, poked at, or looked inside. This is a very different experience from that of the average museum, and NWCFP staff sometimes have to reassure visitors that "it's ok to touch things!" In fact, the site deliberately uses only reproduction artifacts to encourage visitors to touch:

Interpreters Carolyn and Stella, clerks quarters, summer 2005:

Stella: Part of bringing people into history is letting them touch and feel the things, and try the things on . . .

Carolyn: We encourage people to take photos here at the end of my tour, you are invited to take photographs, . . .

Stella: I think people get a lot more out of it, being able to do a hands-on, especially the children.

This sensory part of the experience gives these places a way to attract visitor audiences that are not usually part of the standard demographics for museum audiences. One group of visitors I saw at CM—who at first seemed to me unlikely to appreciate the site, given their biker-gang attire—stayed for at least three hours, and I saw them all over the site, touching things and talking with interpreters. It is quite normal for children to have to be dragged off the site, protesting, when their parents are ready to leave. People enjoy these places, and experience them thoroughly. The questions and conversations between visitors and interpreters are an important part of this experience, embedded in the total multisensory engagement between visitor and site.

The site's messages are reiterated one last time as visitors leave, in the objects they find and purchase in the gift shop. Postcards of "Native Chiefs" (one of these, found all over Ontario, features Jim Sky in his Wild West gear, but he is not named), voyageurs, black-robed priests, the palisaded fort, cannons being fired, and Native people holding furs, appeal to stereotyped expectations. Beaded jewelry, moccasins, dream catchers, and braided leather headbands feature prominently in the shops, as do objects with the site's logo (key chains, T-shirts, pens). Some shops have tried to get away from the more stereotyped merchandise, focusing on (more expensive) reproductions of stoneware, textiles, and metalwork from the European areas along with a few items such as are used in the Native areas (bark containers, trade silver jewelry). Most of these shops make a real effort to stock recent academic publications as well as historical novels and other related literature such as local history works. As Edward Bruner has noted, the gift shop is one of the places on site, like the brochure and the orientation area, where key messages and themes are presented quite forcefully (2005:129). If visitors "consume" history and nostalgia at these places, they do so most literally in the shops, and the images they take home with them are crucial to either reinforcing stereotypes, or challenging them.

AUTHENTICITY, A DESIRE FOR THE
IMAGINED PAST, AND OTHER MOTIVATIONS

Visitors respond in many different ways to these sites; as Bruner has observed, "their reactions to the site shift historically over the life span and even within the time frame of a single visit" (Bruner 2005:142). There are, however, many commonalities among visitors, especially in the reasons they come to these places. Stephen Snow's (1993:162) description of three basic kinds of visitors to historic sites rings true with my experiences. Most, he suggests, come for entertainment; they express a sense of "fun, pleasure, play, relaxation, joking." The ludic element of historic interpretation, the sense that these people are acting as if they might really be from 1804, is very appealing.

> I love these places. I really like the way that it's done here, going into Ross Cottage, for example, the way that the interpreters present the information—"we are the cleaners, and we are cleaning for the Rosses"—as if they really and truly are those people. . . . I really enjoy the way that everyone is putting their information across! (LFG, summer 2005, visitor from Nova Scotia)

This ludic element, combined with an educational one, motivates many family visitors. Others come for a range of reasons: an interest in local history; because they are interested in the place, lifestyle, or material culture; or because they have a general interest in historic sites (see Prentice 1993:78–83). I would add to this a large number of visitors who become interested in a place or period through novels and movies: hundreds of Europeans visit North American historic sites every summer expecting to see the characters of Karl May's novels, and many North American visitors read romances or Westerns, and watch movies, which are set on various frontiers and involve Native-European contact. There are, as well, visitors who are brought to the site for educational purposes. Not all visitors have the same level of interest. The "best" visitors (from an interpreter's perspective) are what Snow (1993:162) calls experiential, motivated by a desire to learn and by aesthetic appreciation of the reconstruction. A few visitors fall into a third category that Snow calls "modern Pilgrims": visiting the site is a pilgrimage for them, and they feel a profound sense of personal, religious, and cultural identification with the lives of the people represented at the site.

Many visitors are fascinated by the physical and sensory details they encounter in historic reconstructions. Wood smoke, hand sewing, the ring of hammer on anvil, the feel of furs and bark, people wearing clothing of linen and homespun wool, the speech and mannerisms of the time portrayed: these are all emotionally and intellectually compelling for many visitors. For an increasing number of visitors from urban centers, the very rural way of life shown at these reconstructions, the textures and smells and daily routines, is foreign and exotic: not many people cook on a wood fire any more.

For many people there is a strong nostalgic element to historic sites. Although Prentice has dismissed the notion that general nostalgia is an important hook for "heritage users," saying that this is too broad a category (1993:81), North American historic reconstructions do attract visitors for this reason, and nostalgia is a central plank in site marketing campaigns. Edward Bruner's work on New Salem has led him to conclude that most visitors there "consume nostalgia for a simpler bygone era"; reaffirm their sense of progress by comparing past ways of life with their own; and celebrate what they see as the virtues of small-town life: "honest values, good neighbors, hard work, virtue and generosity, the success ideology, and the sense of community"(2005:167). I found these dynamics to be true for many visitors. Visitors expressed the nostalgic attraction of these sites to me quite directly:

LP (at CM): Did you stop at the Native encampment? What did you see there that was particularly interesting?

MV: I liked the skins and that, that they slept on, I found that interesting.

FV: I just liked it all, I liked the fireplaces, I just like the old-fashioned fires burning, smells good, nature. . . .

LP (at LFG): Can you tell me what this place was?

MV (older European couple, heavy Italian? or Spanish? accent): Museo! I like!

FV: I like because I remember something. . .

MV: Old-fashioned. . .

FV: Old, old, old—I think of grandma, my great-grandma, all the times, you know—that's why I like it!

FV, fur loft LFG, summer 2005: . . .I like going through these places because you can hear the stories and feel back two hundred years.

Some literature on tourism claims that tourists desire authenticity from their activities, that they attempt "to overcome the discontinuity of modernity" (MacCannell 1976:13; see also MacCannell 1984) by viewing historic sites that seem storied, coherent, and whole (Handler and Saxton 1988). The "pioneer" details of historic reconstructions are associated by visitors with a very different, positively valued way of life for which they express nostalgia. "Authenticity" in this context means physical cues signaling the qualities of strong, self-sufficient family and community, which many people associate with historic eras, along with the cleaner air and lower crime rates which are assumed to be part of this way of life—in Handler's phrase, "for the unspoiled, pristine, genuine, untouched and traditional" which is at the core of the authentic experience (Handler 1986:2). This is the coherent story often told by visitors to themselves about historic sites; it does not mean that visitors are all looking for authenticity in the sense of carefully documented details of historic furnishings and buildings (nor, indeed, was life ever as it is longed for in visitors' nostalgic vision). By and large, visitors are content with what Bruner and Kirshenblatt-Gimblett (1994:449) call "tourist realism," which is simply what satisfies their expectations of the authentic, including elements of Native cultures.

In this nostalgic gaze, log cabins are cozy symbols of our ancestors' determination, piety, and family values; blacksmiths and spinning wheels represent a society in which the work ethic was strong as well as one in which the rural, home-based artisan thrived before control of production passed to industrialized factories. So popular are these symbols that you will find a log cabin, a blacksmith, and someone using a spinning wheel at virtually every North American historic reconstruction—even, in some cases, where there was historically no blacksmith shop. These are the objects we feel it important to commemorate, even if we have to build them from scratch where none existed. Of "spectacle" generally and the fact that it is often deeply symbolic and meaningful to the public, William Beeman states: "It is almost as if the mere event of displaying these symbolic representative elements in a special framed context is enough to elicit strong positive emotional responses from the observing public" (Beeman 1993:380). The selective and realistic representation involved in historic reconstructions is, I would argue, a kind of spectacle, and certain elements of these reconstructions do evoke "strong positive emotional responses from the observing public."

Such cues also evoke narratives about the past, about the relation between past and present, about Native-White relations in the past and about Native peoples, past and present. Wood fires, log cabins, spinning wheels and long skirts are problematic icons of nostalgia because the narratives in which they feature are very often the older ones that portray Native peoples in shallow and constrained roles. Nostalgia can be a real problem when historic site staff are trying to revise the stories they tell about the past, and it is even more of a problem for Native interpreters who often run up against its implications.

THE PAST, THE PRESENT, AND IDENTITY: VISITOR WORK AT HISTORIC SITES

Choosing to visit historic reconstructions and moving through them, making sense of their multisensory representations of the past, involves identity work for visitors: the confirmation or challenging of narratives about the past which inform one's identity and place in the social cosmos. Relatively few works exist which explore "the construction of social identities through the study of recreational participation in sites involving highly symbolic land-scapes" (Fife 2004:62, citing Darby 2000:1). We do, however, have studies such as Bruner's (1996) thoughtful piece on contested narratives and identity work at Elmina, where African Americans and local Ghanians understand the historic castle very differently, so that it plays different roles in the construction of their different identities.

We also have Rosenzweig and Thelen's intriguing study (1998) of American attitudes to the past, which demonstrated quite conclusively that a large segment of American society feels the need to explore the past in order to understand themselves in the present. *The Presence of the Past* showed that Americans "yearn for history that actively assists them in making connections between the past and the present," a history that "can be used to answer pressing current-day questions about relationships, identity, immortality and agency" (178). It also noted the emphatic rejection by many Americans of simplistically patriotic history, the desire for narratives which explain the complexity of lives lived, and because of this, the turning away from academically based history to historically based hobbies such as genealogy in order to explore identity and the legacies of the past (179). Visiting historic reconstructions is part of such searching. This search for identity and continuity with the past, of course, may be seen more broadly as a search for tradition during a time of rapid social change and challenges to community stability and social cohesion: nostalgia is not only a popular expression of discontent with present realities, but underscores the importance of historic reconstructions as public articulations of an officially agreed-upon past, a way for nations to imagine and represent particular versions of social reality which lend them cohesion. Revising the messages of public history sites, and in particular the messages about Native peoples and Native-White relations, challenges what these sites do and the roles they play in the most fundamental ways, because it challenges the assumptions buried within visitors' nostalgia about the unimportance and inferiority of Native peoples.

The way visitors interpret historic reconstructions within the framework of nostalgia and in relation to self evokes the concept of the "tourist gaze" (Urry 1990), a manner of looking at sights by a privileged and powerful tourist class. The concept is helpful for its explication of the ways that tourists read (their own) cultural meanings into the places they go to see. The tourists that I interviewed certainly read palisades and Native camps in ways that were "socially organised and systematised," as Urry suggests the "tourist gaze" is (1990:3). The "gaze" thus uses commonly understood signs: the thatched cottage as "olde England," for instance, one object standing for a constellation of ideas about village life. The idea of the gaze can readily be extended to the Western gaze on non-Western people in touristic situations.[1] When a White tourist looks at a Native interpreter, a member of the dominant class looks at a member of a less powerful minority, and what the White tourist sees is not just a Native person but "an Indian," a very old European construct. This process invokes not only older concepts, but established relations of power between gazer and gazed-upon as well: one side of this equation has the power to define and thus in some ways control the other through this set of readings (see also Lutz and Collins 1993, Morgan 2005:4).

This aspect of the gaze has implications for change at historic reconstructions. What the administrator sees when looking at a revised site may be "labor history," "women in the fur trade," "cultural differences," "LFG as fur trade support site," "Native-Métis-European relations." On the other hand, what the average visitor sees is often more superficial: "woman baking bread," "man with long braid and top hat," "Native women sitting at tipis with fishing net." The gaze may also mean that visitors look past revisionist messages at these places and see nostalgic enactments of pioneer society, with all the colonial implications of that era.

The "tourist gaze" is also deployed in another act in which visitors engage: taking photographs. The use of the camera is an interpretive act in which the visitor participates in the site and literally puts himself or family "in the picture." It also has much to do with assumptions—widely held, and deeply internalized—about what things mean, another articulation of the tourist gaze. In composing pictures, scenes are "read" in terms of "a traditional stock of signs" (Lutz and Collins 1993:195, citing Barthes; see also Urry 1990:138–39) which refer to standard narratives about the world, and especially about the relationship between White tourists and non-White Others: "the imaginative spaces that non-Western peoples occupy and the tropes and stories that organize their existence in Western minds" (Lutz and Collins

1993:2, see also 196). What is seen as a "photo op" has everything to do with the mental baggage that visitors bring to these places. It is a controlling process, making the unfamiliar fit into established thought, as well as by extending the unequal relations of power between photographer and those photographed (see Hammond 2001:4).

Within the Native encampments, visitors tend to photograph the house structures, the costumed interpreters, and, to a lesser extent, specific objects that look Native (furs, cradleboards). Interpreters who have long hair or braids, distinctively Native facial features, or are wearing face paint tend to be photographed most often: one Native interpreter who has braids once counted over 450 pictures taken of him in a day. The tropes are pretty thick here: what visitors see and often comment on as they photograph are "braves," "warriors," "squaws," "papooses," and "tipis." In isolating these images and signs, tourists signal—as they do with their comments to Native interpreters—the stories that these people feature in for them. They are photographing what they so often say as they enter the encampment: "Look!" they say: "Real Indians!"—meaning, of course, *not* real Native people, but people who fit the stereotypes they have brought to the encounter. This may also explain the poses in which visitors photograph each other. One of the most frequent photo compositions involves a group of tourists posing in the doorway of a Native house structure. Sometimes they hold artifacts found around the doorway: a paddle or cradleboard. Sometimes they actually wrap themselves in the hides or blankets that cover the beds, and adopt stereotypical Hollywood Indian stances: arms folded across the chest, or one folded and the other raised in a "How!" gesture. They seem to be playing with stereotypes by pretending to become those images, and mimicking colonial possession by standing as if they lived in the lodges. As many scholars have noted, photography reproduces relations of power involved in colonial situations worldwide.[2]

Even more than photography, direct comments to Native interpreters show very strongly the extent to which visitors' gaze is socially predetermined. The comments noted below occurred during my fieldwork, and interpreters assured me that they are relatively common:

- a child wearing a fringed vest and beaded belt peered in to the lodge and said, "Hey, this is neat!" to which his mom replied, "Just like in the movies!"
- statements expressing the assumption of hostile relations between Natives and Europeans at the site (visitor comment, semi-joking tone: "Aren't you afraid of those Indians?" or "You don't let them in here, I hope?"; most ask what the walls were for, or if the company "had a fight with the Indians") (See Goodsky 1993:122)

- interpreter dresses visitor in a capote (coat made from a blanket) and tells him, "There, now you're dressed like an Indian!"; visitor responds with war whoop (also commonly heard: adults as well as children breaking into war whoops as they approach encampment. Native interpreters call it "that White kid noise")
- child showing fear in response to male Native interpreter in historic clothing
- visitors make comments indicating that they assume that the Native women worked as whores for European traders. At Pine City, I asked a visitor, "What about the women in the strap dresses here? Who are they supposed to be?" and he answered, "(laughs) The wenches! . . . They were basically here to cook and clean and sew . . . (slyly) you know"
- visitor approaches lodge, telling boy that interpreter "would scalp him . . . Indians scalped all the time!"
- questions to Native interpreters: Are you an Indian princess? Are you Pocahontas? Where's your chief?

Aboriginal interpreter Leah Still, in her sixth season at LFG in the summer of 2005, also noted that visitors "think that we just stay in a tipi all the time and are kind of shocked when I say well we have small houses and farms back at our community."

One of the crucial acts in which visitors engage at historic sites (and they do this in a myriad of ways) is to imagine themselves in relation to the people and lifeways depicted. The constant refrain "would you like to have lived back then?," the ordinary domesticity shown, the unfamiliar furnishings of wigwams, conversations with interpreters: all of the stimuli at reconstructions prompt visitors to reflect on how the lives of people "back then" were both like and unlike their own. Visitor responses to the Native encampments suggest that they are certainly making such comparisons in these areas of historic sites between their own lives in the present and the lives of others in the past, but that they also add to this a comparison of cultural worth, bringing into these comparisons the idea of progress (see Bruner 2005:147). One of the most common questions interpreters ask is whether the visitor thinks s/he would have liked to live back then. This is generally asked in the context of some aspect of historic technology that has changed greatly, such as heating or medicine. Despite the longing for utopian aspects of the past that many visitors wish for, the implied answer to this question is "no": there are aspects of these sites that confirm the notion that we have "made progress" since then (see Lutz and Collins 1993:266–67). When such questions are asked in the cross-cultural setting of the Native encampment, one gets an extra spin on this: not only is the Native encampment a place to compare then and now, but it is also a place to compare Us and Them. Abbink (2000:16) feels that one of the attractions of cultural tourism for dominant-society tourists is a sense of superiority over the peoples they view, so that tourism functions as "an act of self-confirmation." Similar responses came from American readers of *National Geographic* magazine surveyed by Lutz and Collins (1993) about what they thought of pictures of non-Western peoples: the images were often "read" as implying an evolutionary continuum with the norm, and pinnacle, of cultural and racial existence as being that of White, middle- and upper-class Western civilization.

[LFG, 1994] LP: Did you stop at the encampment? What did you think?

Female visitor, English accent, fiftyish: Oh, very interesting!—I can't imagine people living like that, but they obviously did.

[Summer 2005, NWCFP] LP: And are there things that you wonder about the lives of people who lived here?

Visitor: Oh, the hard life, you know, like the way they extracted teeth for one thing, and bleeding people to make you well. You think, boy, that's barbaric, but in another hundred, two hundred years from now they're going to be . . . thinking that cutting somebody open is barbaric.

[LFG 2005, interview with American couple in fur loft]

LP: What do you wonder about the lives of the people who lived here? You say you are people who are drawn to this kind of place. What do you wonder about their lives?

Female visitor: What kind of people it took to survive it! I mean, to live through these winters, and the mosquitos, and the heat in the summer.

Male visitor: Just think, the mosquitos, with no DEET!

Visitors are so certain of such evolutionary structures that they are often clearly discomfited to find Native interpreters using European tools in the encampment, and expect them to be using "stone-age" items: they cast Native people in the precontact past, even when looking at them in a recreated past located in a specific historical moment. Intriguingly, visitors also brought into such conversations instances where Native culture compared favorably to settler culture. Rather than comment on the "primitive" nature of Native life, one couple stated that they had "more appreciation" for it after their tour of the NWCFP in 2005, in which the heated floor of the winter lodge had been explained to them:

LP: . . .and from what you know now [after visiting the site], do you feel differently about Native peoples past or present?

Female Visitor: I find I've got more appreciation.

LP: Yeah?

Male Visitor: For me it's more appreciation of the hardship, and some of the ingenuity that went into it [life], like the rocks and the wigwam floor: you know, if we're going to be here, then we gotta figure out how to stay warm, and they got it and some people didn't. I mean, [at the fort] they got through 120 cords of wood a winter.

Female Visitor: And they TOLD them how to do it, and they didn't listen!

Male Visitor: Um hm. So that was interesting to me, the ingenuity that went into it.

During another tour of the NWCFP in summer 2005, a group of older women from Minnesota engaged in intense and appreciative conversation with a female interpreter about women's roles and power in Ojibwa life:

Female Visitor: What was the average number of children that each family had?

Interpreter: Two to three. The reason is that my people know that the more children that you have, the more of a burden it is on the tribe. Everyone in the tribe will take care of each other. We know that if not for the person who makes the best fish nets, as my family does, then we are not going to have the knowledge of the fish net making—

Female Visitor cuts her off: A really personal question, how could they limit their family to three children?

Interpreter: The Ojibwa women are very very good at counting the cycles of the moon—Female Visitor: Ok!

Second Female Visitor: That answered it!

Interpreter: —Of course, the best way is abstinence, [women nodding] if you are not for sure, it is abstinence.

Female Visitor: But then did men respect it?

Interpreter: Yes, they do.

Female Visitor: A disciplined people.

Interpreter: Very disciplined, very very much respect between my people. Now let me tell you ladies something. The women rule the wigwam. What she says, goes. [Female visitors all nodding, hmm.] It is her wigwam; when they move, she will carry everything from it. The men will carry their weapons. They are the hunters, and of course they are the protectors. [Female visitors all very quiet, listening.] Now by saying the lodge belongs to the woman, when the man marries the woman, he will move into the lodge with her family, and become the primary hunter in the family.

This is, of course, a feminist interpretation of Ojibwa women's roles and power that omits facts such as high child mortality, and essentializes gender relations, but it is not out of line with available oral evidence for nineteenth-century Ojibwa culture. I found it fascinating to observe this conversation, which was particularly intense: clearly, some of the older women visitors had had very different experiences in their own lives, and found this alternative vision compelling.

Some visitors, of course, come to these places looking for romantic Noble Savages. They see Native peoples as exotic and interesting, and comment on their dignity and beautiful ceremonial clothing as well as about how Native people "lived in harmony with nature" or were very spiritual, and about how tragic it is that they have been so exploited (see Laxson 1991:374 for similar findings). As with the nostalgic narratives evoked by the sight of spinning wheels and log cabins, Native encampments and staff sometimes cause visitors to remark on what they see as a strong communal nature of Native societies as something "we could stand to learn from." These were often the same visitors who asked non-Native interpreters if they felt safe "living so close to those Indians," and the two sets of narratives seemed to coexist in some visitors. Other visitors seemed to know little about Native peoples, past or present, but were very interested in them. Steve Brisson, Chief Curator for Mackinac State Historic Parks, noted that, "many visitors have questions about Native people today. They are often surprised that a vibrant community still exists; that several of my coworkers are tribal members" (Brisson to Peers, e-mail October 27, 2005).

I am speculating here, but I think that this interest stems both from the allure of the exotic, mysterious Other and from a growing popular desire to understand Native people and to include them as members of North American society. Some of this attitude stems from what one might cynically call "White liberal guilt," but not all: there is, I think, a growing acceptance of Native cultures as distinct elements of society. This was particularly evident in the comments of families, who sometimes come to these sites especially to show the Native encampments to their children, and of young and middle-aged people without children. There were certainly lots of exceptions to these general trends—I met some prejudiced parents and children (including one mother who got her young child to "war-whoop" into the camp at CM and refused to stop when interpreters confronted her) and some enlightened seniors—but these seemed to be the general patterns. Many visitors are fascinated by the Native elements of these sites, and actively construct new meanings as they "move through the village and as they interact with the interpreters" (Bruner 2005:164): the past indeed "comes to life," not always in the way that visitors expect, but many of them enthusiastically accept what they are shown.

CONCLUSION

In some ways, then, these sites can "enact an ideology" (Bruner 2005:167) that continues to reassure visitors that history, however unpleasant for the colonized, was inevitable. In response to a question about the annual enactment of the 1763 capture of CM, in which the Native captors are made to look warlike and "savage," one local couple who had attended the pageant for years said that it was "very meaningful" for them. One thinks of Urry's comment (1990:143) about "whether part of the attraction of heritage for many white visitors is precisely the fact that it is seen as predominantly white. . . ." Nostalgia, as evoked by these reconstructions, can serve the purpose of reinforcing such ideologies, and of expressing a longing for certain elements of life in the past such as relations of power, to be continued in the present.

Other visitors, however, are ready to challenge old narratives:

[LFG 2005, local male Franco-Manitoban visitor]

LP: And from what you know, what can you tell me about why these people would have been here?

Male Visitor: Well, it was trade, it was business like it is today. Like I asked her, how did they work back then, it was, I'll do it for eight bucks an hour, or seven bucks an hour; it was the Northwest company versus the Hudson's Bay Company [this is an anachronism; LFG portrays 1850s, after the end of fur trade competition] . . . plus I watch a lot of TV, you know, documentaries about how things were back then . . . but you know, you hear stories, there's always two stories, right, you don't hear [everything]—oh, the White people used to trade fur for scotch, get all the natives [drunk], you know what I mean? You didn't see that in the history book when I went to school. . . .

And many want to learn new information about Native cultures and histories, and about Native-White relations:

[Summer 2005, NWCFP, interview with interpreters Sandy and Robert in voyageurs' quarters]

Sandy: I had a Girl Scout group here a few weeks ago, it just happened to be my turn for the tour, and I showed them how to make moccasins. And they were in awe that I knew how to make moccasins and that I could start fires with flint and steel. So that was two new things for them. So I showed one of the leaders to make fire with flint and steel, they ended up buying flint and steel and taking it with them. They were heading to the Boundary Waters [to canoe in wilderness park]. A lot of knowledge that we're given and they do not know about, you can see a spark in their eyes—

Robert [exclaims]: Oh, yeah—when they get it— it's just fascinating [to visitors], you can see their eyes get big as saucers [Sandy: um hm] when they get a new piece of information, it's like a kid in a candy store [Sandy: um hm]. You know, once you realize that they've got that sponge quality, you just feed 'em and feed 'em and feed 'em, and they go home just with a big smile on their faces.

Sandy: Our tours are 40–50 minutes long, sometimes we tend to go over! But that's because there is so much knowledge that we are wanting to pass on to people. And people are very interested, they walk in the building and they want to know how the building is made [Robert: yeah], they want to know how the canoes were made [Robert: yeah], they want to know what the voyageurs are doing when it's dark outside and they can't be outside working. They're just full of questions, and that makes my job much easier [Robert: yes] because even before I can get anything out, they're asking questions.

Visitors' fascination with elements of the past, and with aspects of Native life, stems from a range of motivations and backgrounds, which, like the dynamics of family visits, potentially enhances (but can also disrupt) the communication of desired messages by the site. As we will see in the next chapter, visitors' assumptions are often directly challenged by their conversations with Native interpreters: there are real opportunities for learning at these places. If the tourist gaze is by a discourse about the object of the gaze, Native staff refute the discourse, refuse to be the symbols that tourists assume they are, and gaze—and talk—right back.

NOTES

1. While I find the concept of the gaze useful in such touristic situations, I also accept Morgan's (2005:3) caveat: "I use the term *gaze* with a certain caution. Like many scholars of visual culture today, I am drawn to the concept of the gaze because the term signals that the entire visual field that constitutes seeing is the framework of analysis, not just the image itself. Yet with this advantage comes the challenge of a passel of meanings and conceptual entanglements associated with the term. The word has been broadly used in the last three decades and often within a thicket of theoretical interpretations that make one wary of the usefulness of the word . . . for many writers the gaze has meant something almost singularly negative—the power of the voyeur, the coercive power of the privileged classes, or the totalitarian authority of surveillance."

2. Many scholars have explored the links between photography and the colonial control of non-Western peoples (Edwards 1992; Lutz and Collins 1993; Banta and Hinsley 1986; Albers and James 1988; Urry 1990; Lippard 1992; Brown, Peers et al 2006).

Chapter Six

Encounters and Borderlands

"Actually" is our favorite word at Lower Fort Garry. . . .[Aboriginal interpreter, summer 2005]

Much has been made in recent scholarship of liminal spaces between cultures and the importance of people negotiating these during historical encounters. In works on colonial North American history, scholars have examined the different expectations, inevitable misunderstandings, cross-cultural prejudice, and extraordinary attempts to understand each other that marked early Native-White relations.[1] The basic messages of this literature are that although tribal peoples and Europeans in North America misunderstood and manipulated each other, and interrelated within contexts of shifting power, they also—sometimes, to some extent—understood each other's languages, empathized with one another, adopted and adapted each other's religious practices and ways of life, married each other and had children, and formed friendships. In other areas of scholarship, work has also focused on the nature of encounters between peoples. Writing of early travel literature and the encounters represented in it, Mary-Louise Pratt developed the concept of the "contact zone"—"social spaces where disparate cultures meet, clash, and grapple with each other, often in highly asymmetrical relations of domination and subordination" (Pratt 1992:4). The "contact zone" has become a very useful model for a range of analyses, especially for museums and the cross-cultural work now being attempted in them (Clifford 1997, Peers and Brown 2003).

In thinking about tourism and the cross-cultural encounters that are central to so much of cultural and heritage tourism, Edward Bruner has adapted these ideas to write of the "touristic borderzone," which he defines as

a point of conjuncture, a behavioral field that I think of in spatial terms usually as a distinct meeting place between the tourists who come forth from their

141

hotels and the local performers, the "natives," who leave their homes to engage the tourists in structured ways in predetermined localities for defined periods of time. . . . The concept of the borderzone focuses on a localized event,
limited in space and time, as an encounter between foreign visitors and locals
. . . [but] what is performed there takes account of global and international
[contexts]. (Bruner 2005:17)

The living history sites discussed in this book—and many others like them
that represent cross-cultural encounters—are touristic borderzones. Quite
often, at these places, non-Native visitors meet Native people for the first
time in their lives; these are also places where very different historical narratives and experiences meet and clash. As with the historical contact zones
these spaces interpret, interpreters and visitors of different cultural backgrounds bring with them misconceptions, misunderstand each other, challenge each other, and, sometimes, manage to transcend these cultural entanglements to communicate with each other (see Deutschlander and Miller
2003:30). I disagree with literature on cultural tourism which insists that
tourists always remain unenlightened by their encounters, although I recognize that touristic interactions are often limited in depth by overarching national and international relations of power. What I wish to do in this chapter is examine encounters between Native interpreters and visitors at
historic sites, and the implications of these for broader society. What happens when dominant-society visitors talk with Native interpreters? Do visitors accept new information given them? How do they mesh new ideas
with existing assumptions?

Freda McDonald, the petite but forceful former head of the Native encampment at Fort William, used to march up to visitors who made rude comments about "Indians" and demand, "Are you here to learn or to make fun of
people?" And then she would say, "If you're here to make fun of people, you
can go back up that path you came in on. If you're here to learn, sit down and
let me tell you about my culture" (McDonald, personal communication 1994;
Wilkins 1994:70). And she would. This is not the usual smiley hostessing
work, nor the polite but emotionally distanced demonstrations of cultural
skills, reported in the literature on the anthropology of tourism. This kind of
sharp, personally engaged, sometimes confrontational response to misinformed and racist comments, as well as to more positive ones, is a constant
feature of the historic sites examined here. Ruth Christie's response to the
taunting child, which prompted this study, was similar, and I have seen
dozens of Native interpreters across the past decade do very much the same
thing. In every case, they focused on providing accurate information, correcting misconceptions, and challenging stereotypes. In every case, these en-

counters highlighted the contact zone nature of this work. In these places, people of very different backgrounds meet: for visitors who have never met a Native person before, these are first encounters.

ENCOUNTERS

There is, of course, no single tourist gaze: "each individual looks with his or her own personal, cultural, and political background or set of interests" (Lutz and Collins 1993:196). And while visitors to historic sites often draw on stereotyped images of Native people in their responses to Native interpreters, these are also places where such assumptions are challenged and revised.

That these places are contact zones, however, is revealed by the behavior and conversations of visitors with Native staff. I was fascinated to notice that many visitors slowed down as they saw the Native structures or interpreters, or attempted to move past the encampment area itself without entering. (Several encampments have been moved away from the direct path from the site entrance so that visitors will choose whether or not they enter this area). Interpreters work hard to coax visitors into the encampment with smiles and invitations to "come and visit!"; these are necessary given visitors' uncertainties about Native people.

As Deirdre Evans-Pritchard has noted of encounters between tourists and Native people in the American Southwest, "when individuals cross boundaries through face-to-face encounters, they . . . rely on stereotypical conceptions of each other to frame and structure the interactions" (1989:102). Photographing tropes in the encampment, a common visitor activity, constitutes such behavior: when visitors feel uneasy because they are unfamiliar with Native cultures, they take pictures of stereotypes in the process of falling back on what they do know (see Cohen, Nir, and Almagor 1992:217). The content of these stereotypes make them hesitant to enter the encampments, though (what if they really are savages? are they sober? will I offend them?), and visitors are often unsure what to say to Native interpreters. This uncertainty on the part of many visitors is a crucial factor in shaping their interactions with the Native staff: it initially raises assumptions in which visitors presume themselves to be superior, but also creates an opportunity for learning.

This process of challenging existing knowledge works at many levels. As we have seen in the chapter on Visitors, the multisensory nature of these places works to communicate information to a broad range of visitors. The meanings that visitors find in a site are produced by what Bruner (2005:165) calls "dialogic interaction." While Bruner characterizes this as specifically verbal interaction between visitors and interpreters, I would expand the concept to include the processing of physical stimuli and information gleaned from the site itself, the engagement of prior knowledge with new, the practice of photography as a way of engaging with the site, and interactions with family members and companions. There is also a postvisit phase of reevaluating information in light of further stimuli from television programs, museum exhibitions, books, and other media. While at the site, meanings are constructed and revised "as visitors move through the village. . . . Experiencing the site gives rise to meanings that might not have been predicted before the visit, so that the site in this sense is generative" (Bruner 2005:164).

The following conversations that I had with visitors at OFW suggest the ways in which visitors process information they receive at these sites. Note that these visitors have excellent recall and are integrating new information into their existing knowledge:

LP (in visitor center): Did you stop at the Native camp?

Visitors (two teenage girls): Yes.

LP: What did you see there?

Visitor: We saw bannock, and beading, and wigwams, and stuff . . .

Visitor 2: And those baby carriages!

Visitor 1: . . . that they carry on their backs.

LP: *Tikinagans*?

Visitor: Yeah, and they were building a sled and a drum.

LP: Did you learn anything new there?

Visitor: I didn't know how they lived there in winter . . . the woman said that it's not smoky at all and they keep pretty warm in winter. I don't think I would, but . . .

LP: Did you get a sense of why they would have been camped there?

Visitor: I don't know. Well, I know they weren't allowed near [in?] the fort; it was sort of separated from the English. . . .

LP: Were they allowed inside the palisades?

Visitor: Well, they were talking about how after dinner they would invite the Native people in [to Hall].

LP: Did you learn anything about what Native people did in the fur trade, what their jobs were?

Visitor: Well, basically I think they were just the workers . . . you know how now there's the top person in business, and then there's the workers . . . they were the workers!

LP: Wow, I like the analogy! Thank you! [when pressed, the visitors weren't able to elaborate on what work Native people did, though]

LP, on wharf: Did you stop in the Native encampment?

Visitor: (oh yes!)

LP: Was it buggy? (it was!)

LP: What activities were going on, did you talk with anybody?

Female visitor (middle-aged couple): We listened to one [person] explain the winter encampment. It was interesting to hear how they made the tipi and insulated it and how they got the bark off the tree, and the youngsters were trained with different games to become good hunters; that was real interesting.

LP: Did you get a sense of why they would have been camped there?

Male visitor: Yeah, didn't she say it was because . . . well, I don't know.

Female visitor: Well, she talked about the trading they did with the Northwest Fur company and then what goods they got from them, and then how many beavers it would take to trade for them.

Male visitor: It was kind of a rip-off!

Female visitor: (laughs) Yeah, she said it was eight beavers for a blanket.

LP: She was explaining about the point blanket?

Male visitor: Yeah, each line was worth two beavers . . .

Female visitor: And we had stopped at the one [fort] in Grand Portage, so it kinda reinforced some of the things they said, like he had a table [of goods] and he asked what we thought would be most valuable to the Indians, and it was the cloth and the metal pots, so they didn't have to cook in birch pots, and you could see [here] she was dressed in the cloth that they had traded for.

LP: And did you get a sense of what jobs Native people did in the fur trade?

(Both visitors): Well, I don't know—we plan to go back when we leave—

Female visitor: Other than providing furs, I guess I'm not really sure. . . .

These visitors had gone to some effort to learn, to watch, to ask questions, and were beginning to incorporate new information into their existing knowledge about Native people.

Visitors tend to spend longer and to ask more questions in the encampments than in other areas of the sites. This intrigued me, because it goes against their unfamiliarity with Native peoples. Many visitors admitted that it was the first time they had ever spoken with a Native person; many stated that that they did not know any Native people, and did not have Native friends, neighbors, or colleagues. Others, especially school-age children, had encountered Native peoples or culture as part of a school field trip or study unit, and were actively building on information acquired through such routes.

The most important source of new knowledge for visitors is their discussions with interpreters. Bruner (2005:166) has described the process by which visitors learn at these sites:

> Although the main message of the museum professionals . . . has been presented to the tourists in the orientation video and the brochures, the tourists' relationship to the interpreters has a more personal and immediate quality. The interpreters, too, have received the official messages of the site . . . but they frequently depart from the official scripts and move off in their own directions . . . The result is a very open format, more like a discussion than a lecture, one that allows for improvisation and that facilitates the constructivist process.

There is, however, an extra dynamic in these conversations when Native interpreters are involved. Snow notes that at Plimoth and other living history sites, "a well-defined code of etiquette [exists] for the encounter between interpreters and visitors that is essentially based on the polite and willing suspension of disbelief" (Snow 1993:170). The "most fundamental rule" for these encounters is that visitors will accept interpreters at face value: that is, as "real" Pilgrims, voyageurs, fur traders—and Indians. As Snow goes on to say,

> The optimal situation occurs when both performers and spectators recognize the contradictions but agree to maintain the play frame anyway. The audience member signals the actor/historian: "I know you're not really a Pilgrim, but I'm going to play along with you, regardless." The interpreter signals back: "I know you know I'm not really a Pilgrim, but I'm going to perform as if I were, for your education and enjoyment." This kind of interaction ritual can be extremely entertaining. . . . (Snow 1993:181)

While this acceptance of multiple, layered reality works well in the rest of the site, where interpreters "play" characters, it often fails in the Native encampment, where Native interpreters are themselves (although there is a certain amount of joking, as when interpreters ask visitors, "Have you paddled far today?" or "Have you come to sign up to work for the Company?"). Visitors who have entered into a playful frame of mind are often discomfited by the sight of a "real Indian" (as they often say on entering the encampments) who really is an Indian. They may be further discomfited by being face to face with a Native person for the first time in their lives; by feeling uncomfortable because they are unfamiliar with Native culture; and by being afraid that they will say something to offend the Native interpreters. Suddenly, there are a lot of "real" —but also uncertain—things going on in this playful place. This is what Schechner calls "dark play," characterized by "unsteadiness, . . . unreliability and ontological riskiness" (Schechner 1993:39, cited in Edensor 2001:77). It is a situation in which one is no longer certain that what one knows is true.

The combination of visitors' fascination and uncertainty, and interpreters' assertion of Native control over these encounters, combines to produce situations in which visitors are likely to accept the "historical ammunition" that Native interpreters deploy. The fascination helps to create teachable moments; the uncertainty brings visitors' stereotypes to the fore, and also lowers visitors' authority; and the ammunition is designed to refute the stereotypes. It is important to remember that the basic mode of communication is question and answer, and that with the exception of guided site tours, visitor contacts with interpreters are uncontrolled, ranging from walk-pasts with no conversation to twenty-minute discussions. Furthermore, interpreters converse with an audience of visitors that is constantly changing, as the following discussion between Keith Knecht and several visitors in the lodge at CM in 1994 demonstrates:

Female visitor: What's that?

Knecht: It's a drum, it's a small personal drum.

Female visitor: What's it made out of?

Knecht: Hide (Female visitor: From . . .)

Knecht: From a deer . . . the way the rawhide is made is you scrape the inside of the hide . . . then you soak it in wood ash and water, and that causes the hair to slip. And then you take it back out and you scrape all the hair off. And now you have what is called rawhide, unfinished, untanned hide, and when you put it on a frame and you sew it down tightly, it stretches. . . .

Female visitor: As it dries it shrinks?

Knecht: Yes, and then of course it makes it nice and tight. I don't know how tight it is now. (takes the drum down and beats it)

Female visitor: Sounds like it's right.

Knecht: Pretty close! And if you listen, you can actually get different tones depending on where you hit it (taps all around the drum)

Female visitor: Wow! . . . (drum stops) Are you painted for war, or would that be ceremonial?

Knecht: No, this is just decorative paint. (Female visitor: Oh, okay)

New male visitor: How far are you from being chief (laughs)?

Knecht: Oh, actually, quite a ways! Today the tribal chairman is elected. And I try to stay out of politics! Both within the Native community and the White community. (Male visitor still chuckles at own "joke.") Back in the eighteenth century as well, most people are under the impression that it was something that was handed from father to son. And it wasn't; they were elected back then as well.

Female visitor: Oh, really.

Knecht: And there's a neat little thing called a recall election that we have today? It existed, too! (visitors laugh)

New female visitor: Oh, this is your sleeping cot, then?

Knecht: Yeah.

New female visitor: And the storage is underneath.

Knecht: Yup, that's right. I keep some firewood under there so it's dry.

New female visitor: And the smokehole looks like it closes up.

Knecht: Yes, there's a flap that goes over it.

Female visitor: What are these?

During this brief exchange, two new visitors entered the lodge separately and initiated new conversations without joining in the ongoing one. This is a very typical sort of exchange, and shows why interpretation "is a very open format, more like a discussion than a lecture, one that allows for improvisation" (Bruner 2005:166).

This exchange also involves an interpreter challenging a visitor's stereotype: the new male visitor enters the lodge saying, "How far are you from being chief?" The visitor evoked the stereotype of the "Indian Chief," and Keith was reframing things to talk about tribal politics, both historically and in the present. This visitor looked to be in his late sixties, and the way that he continued to laugh at his own "joke" suggests that Keith's response was not sufficiently forceful. When interpreters challenged stereotyped remarks made by younger visitors, however, and especially by women visitors, the majority of those challenged accepted the new information provided them, and thanked interpreters for teaching them. I found this behavior surprising given visitors' general lack of knowledge about Native people, and the strength of the stereotypes that they expressed.

The fact that visitors recognize that the "real Indian" interpreters really are Native people seems to contribute to this willingness to learn. Visitors are clearly taken aback—some very embarrassed—when interpreters tell them that "squaw" is an offensive term, or that "our people never said that" (to a greeting of "How!"). Most visitors immediately apologize, thus affirming the interpreters' position of power in the encounter. In the most dynamic of these exchanges, the interpreter then informs the visitor why the phrase or behavior is offensive; how it came to be in popular usage; and what the correct phrase or actual behavior was.

The following are examples of these confrontations. I seldom had my tape recorder running when such events occurred, so they are pieced together from notes taken during and after the incidents. A few are reconstructed from interpreters' information.

(At CM: composite of several incidents witnessed)

Male Visitor: How! (raises palm)

Knecht: Hello! My people never did that, you know. The word that we used to greet each other with was AHNEEN or BOOZHO.

Male visitor: Oh really! I didn't know that. What was that word again?

Knecht: AHNEEN.

Visitor repeats: Ahneen. What tribe would you be?

Knecht: I'm Ottawa. Historically we had villages near here, and we came here in summer to trade and have councils. . . .

(At CM: single incident, child war-whooping)

Knecht: Well, that's a White person's way of pretending to be Indian, but we never actually did that. If you had done that, all your enemies would know where you were! (Child stopped, looked abashed)

(Knecht went on to tell child what life would have been like for him as an Ottawa child in the eighteenth century.)

(At CM: incident reported by interpreter)

Visitor: I guess you guys came here (to the fort) to get drunk.

Knecht: No. Alcohol did play a role in the fur trade, of course, but we came here to do business. Now, you know, the tribes are going dry—for young Native people, alcohol and drugs are uncool—and at powwows, you're removed if you're under the influence.

(Interpreter did not relate rest of conversation.)

(At LFG: composite of several similar incidents witnessed during fieldwork)

Visitor: Hey look, here's the squaws.

Interpreter: Actually, we don't use that word: it's really rude! We're just women.

Visitor: Oh, I'm so sorry! I didn't know that!

Interpreter: Well, the traders and the early settlers, too, you know, they used that word in a nasty way to call Native women sluts. So we don't like to use it.

Visitor: What is the word for woman in your language?

Interpreter: *Ikwe*. (visitor repeats word) You know, White men used to think that our women were real drudges because they did a lot of the heavy work like pulling sleds when families were moving camp, but actually the men had to be unburdened to defend their families. And unlike your women, ours were proud of being strong! (They go on to discuss gender roles).

Some important discussions ensue from these confrontations. The meanings of "squaw" [*iskwe* or *ikwe*, woman, in several Great Lakes languages] and "how" [*ahao*, yes] are discussed most often, and lead to topics ranging from historic Native gender roles and the relative autonomy Native women had vis-à-vis European women, to the occasions and nature of Native-White interaction around the forts. Other conversations tackle assumptions that Native-White relations were always hostile, or that Native peoples were less "evolved" than Whites. Interpreters used these events as opportunities to address the historical realities behind the stereotypes, and visitors were fascinated by these discussions.

These confrontation-induced discussions frequently end either with questions or information about the interpreter's own life and about Native peoples in the present: as Ann Magiskan, Native Heritage Program Officer at FWHP notes, "we talk about history but bring it forward to today," she says, and also noted that she talks about her own life to illustrate the legacies of the past (interview, November 15, 2005). This is significant, for these conversations, brief as they might be, draw visitors past the rich sensory detail of these reconstructions to explore the impact of the past on the peoples depicted. When Annette Naganashe spoke to visitors about her involvement in traditional cultural activities at home, she communicated pride in her heritage as well as the vitality of contemporary Odawa culture. When Ann Magiskan first started to give the "life in a wigwam" program at FWHP, it was just a basic overview of food, shelter, and clothing. Now she might begin the program with a smudge ceremony, introducing participants to spiritual elements of Aboriginal culture, and she educates the audience about Native values and how such things operate in the lives of Native people today. For a school program involving elders who are also brought in to teach, she might do a pretrip visit to the school to talk about the importance and role of elders, and she would teach the students to offer tobacco to the elder, using the traditional protocol to ask to be taught. In such a setting, the historic world shown at the site is linked to the present, and visitors are jolted out of their initial perception of Native interpreters as symbols, and begin to see them as people. Freeman

Tilden, who pioneered the art of historical and cultural interpretation in the U.S. National Parks Service in the 1950s, would have said that these encounters were good interpretation: "the chief aim of interpretation," he believed, "is not instruction, but provocation" (Tilden 1977[1957]:9). I would argue that these encounters do both.

CAN TOURISTS LEARN?

Other scholars, however, have argued that such encounters change nothing. A remarkable amount of the literature on cultural tourism is extremely pessimistic about whether tourists learn anything: Bruner, for instance, concludes that tourists "accept no moral or political responsibility for the people they visit" (Bruner 1991:239, 1995:238 and n.d.; see also Harrison 2003: 11, 14). Van den Berghe (1994:18–19) describes the characteristics of encounters in cultural tourism as brief, reinforcing asymmetrical relations of status and power, and occurring "within the framework of crude stereotypes." That they often see Native peoples as primitive or as Noble Savages, and enthuse nostalgically about life in the past, suggests that many visitors come to historic sites to reaffirm, unconsciously, their vision of the past and their participation in mythologies that have justified Native disempowerment.

I also believe that other things can and do happen in conversations between visitors and Native interpreters: that such mythologies and assumptions are challenged, and that quite often, visitors accept new information and corrections. In thinking about the question of what visitors to historic reconstructions learn about Native peoples, Native-White relations, and revisionist perspective, I will bring in the findings of other scholars on this debate and explore how, and why, mine may differ from theirs.

In an intriguing analysis of a tourist performance involving music, dance, and spoken interpretation given by First Nations performers near Ottawa, Mason (2004) noted ways in which performers created authority and used this to successfully challenge stereotypes. One performer sang a welcome song with drum accompaniment to begin the event, and later demonstrated "a musical example from Hollywood Westerns," noting its difference from the traditional welcome song. He encouraged the audience to hear the differences between the two pieces, noting that the popularly known beat "was invented by Euro-American imaginations working in the entertainment industry" (Mason 2004:844). Mason argues that while the performer was certainly being processed by the tourist gaze, the performer's authority in this Native-controlled context confounded the gaze: "constituting his position as educator rather than entertainer, Jim was in control of the event and he used his authority to recode stereotypes" (Mason

2004:845–46). Crucially, I think, visitors were assigned an active role in this encounter, being asked to listen to and identify the differences between pieces of music; visitors' input was then incorporated into the Native performer's educational talk. I believe very strongly that at historic reconstructions, leaving Native-looking articles out for visitors to touch and see without Native interpreters there to explain them can simply reinforce stereotypes. It is the interpreters, speaking face to face with visitors, who weave such objects into new narratives and thus challenge older ones.

Mason's optimistic conclusion from this encounter was that it is possible to disrupt stereotypes, using Native-led conversations to communicate new information. FWHP thinks along the same lines, and when there is an individual on the staff in the Native encampment who is comfortable drumming and singing in public, Ann Magiskan sometimes asks them to do so in the main square, which is otherwise a European-looking space. The staff member sings traditional songs and interacts with visitors, answering questions about Native music and culture. This is a way of teaching visitors about Aboriginal culture and history through the fort (Magiskan, interview, November 15, 2005). Here, it is the provocative use of Native sound within a space which does not appear to be Native, and the assertive teaching by the Native interpreter, which opens new ways of thought.

Similar conclusions emerged from a detailed visitor evaluation of a challenging new exhibition at the Australian Museum in Sydney. Called "Indigenous Australians: Australia's First Peoples," the exhibition opened in 1995 and presented revisionist historical information and contemporary Aboriginal voices discussing the legacies of problematic relations with settlers.[2] Visitors surveyed before and after viewing the exhibition "gave many examples of gaining greater understanding through relating what they had seen in the exhibition to their own experiences and knowledge. . . . Participants also talked about thinking differently after seeing the exhibition" (Kelly and Gordon 2002:162). Exit surveys showed striking results:

> The visitor survey showed an increase in understanding as well as engendering a sense of empathy for the way Indigenous people had been treated in the past. Regarding questions about increased knowledge of stolen children and native title, the rate of converting "don't know" answers to correct answers was between 50 and 75 percent. . . . When surveyed on exit, 57 percent of visitors stated that the exhibition made them more interested, 54 percent more understanding, 50 percent more informed, 43 percent sad and 39 percent hopeful. (Kelly and Gordon 2002:161)

Crucially, visitors reported that the prominence of the Aboriginal voices in the exhibition, especially the use of first-person quotes, was important in their learning process (Kelly and Gordon 2002:161). In addition, the multidimensional format of a museum exhibition, like the multisensory experience at historic reconstructions, provides many potential links between content and visitors. In a large-scale study of visitor responses to heritage sites, McIntosh and Prentice (1999:598) noted the importance of the "affective nature of the experiences" in enabling visitors to respond with "empathy and critical engagement in relation to the past." This study concluded that

> a substantial minority (45.8 percent) of all the tourists interviewed during the quantitative research at the three attractions reported that they had gained an understanding of how people lived in the past; and a further, 19.7 percent stated that this understanding was the most important benefit gained from their visit. (McIntosh and Prentice 1999:602)

In other words, visitors can learn at these places. One intriguing interview I had with an adult female visitor at Lower Fort Garry in 2005 suggested some of the ways they do:

> LFG, summer 2005, LP to Female visitor: What did you learn about Aboriginal culture while you were here?
>
> Female visitor: Maybe not more than I knew already, because in Nova Scotia we'd been to Kejimkujik National Park and seen some of this, so it wouldn't be completely new to me.
>
> LP: And from walking through and talking to the ladies, did you get a sense of why this camp would have been here?
>
> Female visitor: No, not yet, but I've only just started, so perhaps as I continue. . . .
>
> LP: What would your guess be?
>
> Female visitor: Well, based on what they have said, it's part of the communication and the trade exchange going on between the traders . . . because I believe this is a spot along the trading route. Now, what one of them did say is that they are here in order to build up credits, doing work of some kind or another. Now, I realize that I'm not too sure what that credit would then be used for, I suppose it was exchange of some kind, I'm not too sure what the aboriginal people would be wanting, but perhaps rifles, gunpowder, beads . . . so yes, putting it all together, ok [I understand].

This visitor initially said she didn't know the answer to my question, but then began reviewing what she had seen and heard in a settler's cabin and the Native encampment. She hadn't been inside the walls yet and so had not yet seen the trading shop. Her thinking incorporated existing knowledge ("perhaps rifles, gunpowder, beads") as well as things she had heard only a few moments ago, and her answer included a fair amount of correct historical information. What she had taken in during her few minutes on site before I encountered her, though, was mediated by the Aboriginal interpreters in the encampment and by an interpreter portraying a Métis woman character in the cabin. Had she only seen furnishings and props, I doubt she would have been able to piece together such an answer. The voice and presence of Native (and, in this case, Métis) people is crucial in visitors' ability to acquire new information and merge it with what they bring to the site.

This meeting of new and old information and perspectives can be difficult, as discussed earlier. When I spoke with visitors after confrontations they had with interpreters, however, the majority were positive rather than embarrassed and negative. They stressed that they had not known what they had been told, and said things like, "I didn't know they actually married" or "Well, why wouldn't they have had tin lamps if they could get them? I just never thought about it before." They were also actively trying to fit the new information into their framework of reference about Native people, and sometimes that framework was being revised pretty drastically. The boy whose earnest questioning of Keith Knecht was described at the beginning of the chapter on visitors was asking such a range of questions and being given such new information that pretty much everything he thought he knew about Native people was being debunked—and yet he kept asking, and asking. A woman I talked to at the NWCFP who read romance novels about the frontier had me explain some things in the wigwam to her, and then commented in a thoughtful tone that the novels she read focused on certain aspects of Native life (the image of the noble, mystic Indian) that were quite different from reality, and that of course, when you stopped and thought about it, these people were human beings like us. At their best, both confrontations and the more ordinary conversations between interpreters and visitors provoke visitors into beginning to rethink their opinions of Native peoples and their roles in history.[3] To me, these conversations involved the most significant work that these sites do: challenging, engaging, teaching. They also illustrated one reason why historic sites are not yet communicating some of the darker aspects of colonial history, for clearly much of the communication which needs to take place in these conversations is teaching visitors about the positive aspects of Native cultures and countering a profound collective ignorance about Native peoples.

I did not get the sense that visitors were going along with or apologizing to interpreters merely to smooth over an awkward encounter: if they just wanted to avoid a scene, they would have left the encampment immediately after being confronted. Instead, they tended to stay around and ask questions, which seemed very much a genuine desire to hear the interpreter's perspective.

A certain number of visitors who are challenged by interpreters do not back down: the gentleman who continued to chuckle at his "joke" to Keith, and the woman who continued to war whoop with her child after being asked to stop, are two such examples. Male visitors tend to be more reluctant to concede authority to interpreters, especially when the interpreters are female. From the way that interpreters described such incidents to me, and from my own observations, though, I would say that these people are very much in the minority. Even European visitors who arrive with expectations of seeing Karl May's characters or the Sioux camp from the movie "Dances with Wolves" seem to accept reality pretty well. In 2005, one LFG interpreter described one such encounter with a European tourist to me:

Interpreter: Well, they came here expecting to see a cowboys and Indians kind of fort where wars had taken place, so I was able to tell them a little bit about the cooperation that took place and how most of the people living here were at least part Native, and set their minds straight!

LP: So they didn't know much about the Hudson's Bay Company.

Interpreter: No, they didn't . . . so I talked about . . . how we had a really good rapport with them [the Native people]. They [tourists] were a little bit disappointed, actually!

LP: And how did they take the information you gave them?

Interpreter: They were really good, they asked a lot of questions, they were quite interested.

Intriguingly, the personal agendas of Native interpreters, linked to the revisionist perspectives that sites wish to communicate about the past, can work very well to provoke visitors to rethink. Handler and Gable (1997) have claimed that Colonial Williamsburg subverted its aim to teach new perspectives on African Americans in the past through fear of offending visitors,[4] and through an emphasis on consumerism across the site that diluted the site's pedagogy. However, I would say that interpreters, Native and non-Native, at the sites discussed here consider it their duty to provoke visitors, and exercise this regularly. None of them, or their managers, shied away from challenging visitors when they express racist perspectives. With the occasional exception during especially sharp confrontations, interpreters try not to be rude, and always try to maintain an educational framework for conversations. Nor do messages about consumerism (including ideas about the "progress" of society from past to present through material change) and transnational economy dominate site messages at the reconstructions I have analyzed, even at the fur trade sites where it might. These places focus on political, social, cross-cultural, and economic relations between

Native and non-Native peoples. Gable and Handler's concern that the messages about consumerism over-rode those about social and political aspects of cross-cultural relations does not seem to translate to the sites I examined:

> Though the unevenness of the playing field was occasionally mentioned, the fact that the game was fundamentally unfair was not stressed . . . [far from using] the museum to "disturb" complacent Americans about the injustices of the past and, indeed, about the relationship of those injustices to present-day social conflicts, . . . social history on the front line tended to comfort visitors' qualms about social injustice or banish a discussion of it altogether. (Handler and Gable 1997:121)

Yes, there are period trade shops which are interpreted, but I have often seen the conversation in these rooms turn to thorny issues of cross-cultural marriage as a factor in the success of the fur trade, or the labor of Native women in processing furs to make the trade work. That trade goods were desired by Native peoples is explained all across the site, but then so is the relative helplessness of Europeans in the wilderness. If anything, the implicit message these sites often tell is the opposite of that which Gable and Handler saw at Colonial Williamsburg: not how far we have come, but how problematic things have become, a sense of loss (especially regarding Native peoples, but also triggered by utopian nostalgia) rather than gain. Interpreters made sure they inserted such critiques into their conversations with visitors, and visitors tended to agree with them and draw out their comments with further questions. Visitors often come to these sites with Hollywood ideas of Native-White relations and the inevitability of progress, but I have seen them provoked out of such assumptions time and again.

In contrast to these more optimistic readings of visitor encounters, other perspectives suggest that visitors neither want nor assimilate new information about Native peoples and Native-White relations in the past. Julia Harrison (2003:18) mentions an evaluation of a First Nations tourism operation analyzed by Butler and Hinch (1996), who concluded that:

> intensive experiences are not what many visitors to the region want. Their interest in Aboriginal culture is shallow, and on their afternoon visit to Shawenequanape Kipichewin they want to see what they understand as the markers of Aboriginality: dancing, drumming, and feathers. They often leave disappointed if they fail to see these things. Such responses threaten the ability of such programs to ameliorate the politically, culturally, and socially marginalized position of Aboriginal people within Canada. (see also Butler and Hinch 1996)

This fits with the conclusions of Joan Laxson (1991) and Deidre Evans-Pritchard (1989:99), who do not believe that face-to-face meetings erode stereotypes. Laxson concluded from her work with Native tourism in the American Southwest that "brief encounters appear to reinforce ethnocentrism and convince tourists of the correctness of their own worldview" (Laxson 1991:365). I would argue that the confrontations I witnessed, and their overtly educational context at historic sites, produce more positive results than the rather different dynamics involved in the jewelry fairs and ceremonies which Laxson and Evans-Pritchard observed.

Some scholars have concluded that photography—one of visitors' major activities at historic sites—is actually a barrier to learning. For some tourists, it is images, selected by their resemblance to preexisting stereotypes, rather than dialogue with local people or interpreters, which underpin their experiences. After leading tourist groups for several years, Edward Bruner wrote despairingly of this use of the camera to avoid real interaction with cultural Others:

> As tourists approach the Other with camera in hand, they "see" the Balinese or the Toradja through their viewfinder. The camera held in front of the face of the tourist serves as a mask, a way of enhancing the distance between subject and object, of hiding oneself from the Other. The tourist can move in for a closeup but this is accomplished without direct eye-to-eye contact. . . . Photography is a way of examining the native, a voyeurism, without being personal or committed to the relationship, without seeming to look. (Bruner n.d.)[5]

While I agree that some visitors engage in taking photographs rather than with interpreters or information, I also think that the contexts in which Bruner observed this behavior—like those in which Evans-Pritchard and Laxson worked—are very different in some ways to those of historic reconstructions examined here. Especially in the guided tours offered by NWCFP, but in all cases where interpreters take a firm hand, visitors tended to take pictures after the tour or conversation ended, often asking permission of the interpreter first. I didn't actually see cameras acting as barriers to conversation at these places, although they may have been used to photograph tropes that interpreters were simultaneously trying to disrupt.

Whether through photography or other mental processes, visitors do to some extent override new information in favor of older perceptions. In a large-scale study at British heritage sites, McIntosh and Prentice noticed a tendency to filter new knowledge through existing perceptions. Although these visitors said they gained new empathy and insight into the past, they did not express this in terms of actual historical themes or specific knowledge about the past. Rather,

> in describing their overall experiences gained, some tourists reported a more "rosy" view of the past in relation to reminiscences of their own histories, memories, or

nostalgia . . . the qualitative research showed that past society was described, potentially "re-defined," by a significant minority of visitors as "the good old days,"
"good times," "better previous days," "the time of our childhood" and "of fond
memories." (McIntosh and Prentice 1999:599)

At heritage sites, then, it is nostalgia, with its accompanying narratives and
assumptions about Natives, Europeans, and their relationships, which may be
the key barrier to communicating new information. That such older assumptions are still prevalent in some visitors was made quite clear by an American
couple interviewed at LFG in the summer of 2005, in which the wife stated:

Female visitor: I was just saying as we came in from the museum, I get tired of
being the bad guy all the time. The White guy is not necessarily the bad guy because progress came through the introduction of the European peoples, and as a
people you have the choice either to adapt, or to succumb, or to join. . . . So
many of these museums make you feel, like, "oh, you're bad because you're
White!"

This visitor gives a clue to one of the most important dynamics of encounters
between visitors and historic reconstructions, which is the role of existing
(mis)information in mediating the reception of new information. In asking
"do visitors learn?" we need also to ask, "how do visitors learn?" If, as I believe, the majority of visitors do accept and even seek new information, does
what they learn stay with them? Or does it fade into more established misinformation and disappear from mental view? While I believe that the confrontations over stereotypes are effective, I am not sure how well such salvos
work against the larger body of beliefs most visitors carry with them about
the superiority of the dominant society. Frustratingly, I have never found a
useful way to evaluate such processes in visitors. I will quote here a large por-
tion of an interview with a retired Baptist minister ("Male visitor") in his late
60s that I conducted in the exhibit area of the NWCFP in summer 2005, as
this visitor was leaving the site after a tour. He clearly states that he has received new information and perspectives, but is also clearly fitting these into
older information and frameworks:

Male visitor: American history is a hobby with me and we've followed the Oregon Trail, and also the Lewis and Clark trail, so we have a sense of it.

LP: So you know a fair amount about relationships between early settlers and
Native people.

Male visitor: Yes.

LP: And from what you know, and from what you heard on site, can you tell me
what was going on at this place?

Male visitor: Well I was interested to know if there was a relationship between the fur trade here in the Mississippi valley and Lewis and Clark who spent the winter with the Mandans on the Missouri, but there wasn't. This was sort of the western border [of the established trade], and that makes Lewis and Clark and their courage, their purpose, extremely more valid and purposeful than we could imagine.

LP: And from what you know, what are the women doing on site? Who are they portraying?

Male visitor: Well, my tour guide brought out very skillfully how the women were the key to the workload. Whereas the men had to provide food and so on. But it was the women who did the detailed work. And the hardship the women went through, and to think they didn't have anyone to speak out like we do to-day for the women, like the feminist movement!

LP: But I think it sort of got reversed, didn't it, that they were proud of doing all that work?

Male visitor: Yeah, they enjoyed it and expected it, there wasn't any challenge to it.

LP: And what were the relationships like with the men here?

Male visitor: Well, apparently in the Indian culture the women depended on the protection of the clan, and they couldn't marry outside their clan [this is wrong, clans were exogamous] and I was interested in the wife of twenty-seven some years of Mr. Sayer here, when he retired and went to Montreal, his wife did not or would not go with him. And I thought that was interesting, that she was queen of the hill, as long as the hill was right here. I assume that he made the decision [to go] and she did not go with him, and he remarried and established another life . . . so I guess it's this way in every civilization, I guess there's some people who have to carry the load and the buck stops there!

LP: And are there things that you wonder about the lives of the people who lived at this place?

Male visitor: I really was curious about the Chippewa, where they came from. They apparently were a peaceful type of Indian as contrasted to, say, the Apache, or the Blackfoot, but nobody seems to know where they came from. . . . I'd like to know where the Chippewa came from, obviously, they defeated the Sioux in 1750 and established themselves here, but they never went further west appar-ently [untrue], this place met all their physical needs. So I'd be interested to know about the origin of the Chippewa. We visited the Wind River Indian Reservation a year ago, and it seems like their language is duplicated [this is not true] in the southern Cheyenne: how could that have been? There's so many mysteries. There had to be a root for both of them. So the American Indian is a fascinating subject. It's a bad chapter in the history of our country—not that they were defeated, because they defeated somebody else, maybe centuries ago, but America didn't keep the treaties, and that's a blemish on our history.

LP: Do you think that understanding this part of the past helps us to understand American Indians in the present?

Male visitor: I don't know. They're a puzzle. As I say, I'm a Baptist minister and I've worked with a number of missionaries who have worked with American Indians, various tribes, and they are very difficult. There's an instability with the American Indian generally—you can have a number of families that accept Christ and become Christians and want the Bible, and next week, the head of the family could go off on a drunken binge, nobody can figure this out. I guess the government is doing the best they can do with the reservation system and trying to integrate them into American society but it really is a tragedy . . .

In this intriguing interview, the visitor indicated that he had received a good deal of new information, and that he was working this new information into existing frameworks of understanding. He also indicated that he had some misinformation, and that his existing perceptions (which include the idea of Native peoples as weak, drunkards, and unwilling to modernize, and an acceptance of the role of government in trying to assimilate Native people) were unchanged after a visit to an historic site that is particularly good at challenging stereotypes through skilled interpretation.

This visitor's responses to new information parallels in some ways the responses found by Lutz and Collins in interviewing readers of *National Geographic* magazine, who sometimes interpreted photographs of non-Western people in several quite different ways within an interview. Lutz and Collins concluded that when asked to describe the meaning of these images, interviewees

> sometimes express(ed) two apparently contradictory ideas with equal conviction. Or they express(ed) contradictions in more experimental or ambivalent ways; they (tried) out sometimes conflicting ideas, with tentative or self-assured tones, hoping for one thing and settling on another, seeing how things sound(ed). (Lutz and Collins 1993:226)

Translated into the context of the sites I am examining, this tendency to produce contradictory ideas may indicate that the visitor is keeping new information and old separate and parallel. This fits with the evaluation by McIntosh and Prentice (1999:602) of visitors to heritage sites in Britain, which concluded that visitors do, in fact, learn new things, although "the new insights gained are not assimilated with personal experience or relevance." Thus, a visitor may speak with a Native interpreter and accept that Native women were crucial workers and translators who made the fur trade possible, but not carry that through to Native-White relations broadly and thus still assume, when viewing the palisade, that such relations were hostile (rather than between kin).

Old knowledge and understandings, then, may twist new perspectives. Judging from visitors' responses to my questions, visitors still tend to interpret the palisades as evidence of hostility between Natives and Whites. If sites are not careful, I think that it is quite possible that visitors not only receive nostalgic messages about utopian pioneer life but add to them the notion "and we were friends with the Indians too, poor things": a patronizing simplification of Native-White relations and Native histories. Sites need to find multiple, multisensory ways of explicitly demonstrating their messages about Native people and Native-White relations, of talking about some of the specifics of culture contact: challenging older perspectives needs to be built in to descriptions of what the site and its staff do, rather than something that happens in order to clear the way for interpreters to deliver official site messages. At present, the aspect of interpreters' work that involves challenging stereotypes is not recognized in their job descriptions, although by my observations it accounts for at least 40 percent of their time with visitors.

It is also possible that the way visitors learn at historic reconstructions may surface not during their visit, but afterwards. Lisa Craig, then Assistant Educator at CM, commented to me in 1995 that "I don't think a lot of visitors realize that they've learned anything while they're here," and that it took the next site they visited, the next TV program they watched, to get them to begin comparing what they knew from having talked with a Native interpreter with what they were later being told. While many of the visitors with whom I spoke were integrating new information right away, Craig's observation is important for the long-term implications of these Native encampments, and deserves further research. In particular, the experience of conversing with a knowledgeable Native interpreter was clearly causing some visitors to reevaluate their preconceptions.

Interviews with experienced Native interpreters at historic sites in 2005 also provided useful perspectives on these questions. Leah Still, in her sixth season as an Aboriginal interpreter at LFG, noted several kinds of responses by visitors to new information:

LP: When you give visitors information that's new to them, do you think that they really accept it?

Still: Some of them do; some of them are like, oh, I didn't know that, and they ask more questions. But some people kind of think that you're pulling their leg, and they're like, oh, sure . . . right, of course, and seem to think that they're going to stick with their idea that they have in their head, even though you've tried to tell them something else. I get mixed reactions.

An interpreter portraying a Métis laborer in the trade shop at LFG felt that visitors tended to have "certain misconceptions about what went on here" and that if it's a big paradigm shift, they might not [accept it], but I think if we keep on reinforcing it, like they might ask in a few different places and we keep saying, like, no, this isn't a military fort, or no, there's no Northwest Company any more [by the time of LFG's interpretation] then, yeah, probably [they will accept the information].

Steve Greyeyes, also an experienced interpreter in the Aboriginal encampment at LFG, had a different take on this:

Most of the public is very willing to receive new information, and they're genuinely interested, and those who aren't, can't be made interested. If they're not interested in learning and they have some very strong preconceptions, then oftentimes there's no way to change that, but they are quite in the minority of visitors that we have here. (Greyeyes, interview, LFG 2005)

I find it important that these interpreters, who spend a considerable part of their time day after day challenging misconceptions, agree that many visitors receive new information well, even if some don't. Having witnessed many encounters between visitors and Native interpreters, I believe that interaction between them does effectively challenge the conventions that surround these places so closely, and jolts many visitors out of "the conspiracy of their own illusions" (Dening 1993:74) that the physical sets of the sites bring into play. If visitors break into war-whoops and make jokes about scalping when they arrive at the encampments, Native interpreters challenge them. If tourists gaze on these interpreters and see "Indians," "braves," and "squaws," the interpreters insist on their own identities, and gaze—and speak—right back to the tourists, refusing to be symbols.

[at CM, talking to family with little girl, 1994]

LP: Have you ever been in an Indian lodge before?

Family: No.

LP: So this is a new thing for you. What kinds of things did you see in there that were interesting to you?

Woman: I just think that the way that they traded, and the different values that they put on furs. . . . I had read about it, but it's neat when you see it all written out, and the value of a blanket . . .

LP to girl: What did you see?

Girl: The baskets, the pot over the fire, . . . and the toys!

LP: Did you get a sense of why the Native people would have camped here?

Woman: I would think they would do it for a sense of security, being friends with them, being protected.

LP: Did they have relationships with people inside [the walls]?

Man: Well some did they traded with them.

Woman: Now, I'm just trying to think . . . they didn't say a whole lot about the Indians that camped on the outside.

LP: Did you get a sense of why the fort was built?

Man: Uh . . . well, it was built as a trading post, right on the lake, stuff was brought here from Canada. . . .

Girl: I like the different kinds of furs.

LP: Do you know any Native people yourself?

Man: No.

LP: No? So this is kind of a new thing for you. . . .

REFLECTIONS, LESSONS, CONCLUSIONS

When I began this study, I expected to find a close fit between the dominant-society perspective on history that historic sites have traditionally communicated, and visitors' perspectives on the past, especially on Native people and Native-White relations in history. Even so, I was startled by the overwhelming numbers of visitors who clearly looked at the Native staff and areas through stereotyped goggles, who had no other way of seeing these people, either in the past or in the present. On the other hand, it was also apparent that from the time that visitors enter these sites, their ideas and knowledge, comparisons and conclusions slip and shift constantly. When they enter the encampment areas at these sites, visitors often talk with Native people for the first time in their lives. And despite the unfamiliarity and stereotypes with which visitors initially approach these parts of historic sites, they often leave statements such as "Show more of the native side of the story. The effects to their existence not the struggle of the Jesuits" (SMAH visitor survey cards August 1–7, 1994) in visitor registers when they leave.

At present, Native interpreters provide the most effective challenge to visitors' preconceptions, although their words and perspectives are reinforced by many of their non-Native colleagues. The Native presence on sites is critical: it is the one thing that can powerfully bring visitors face to face with real lives, real histories, real legacies of the past instead of stereotypes, the one place where visitors can confront their prejudices about both past and present. Freda McDonald's "Are you here to make fun of us or to learn from us?" is an extraordinary challenge—and offer—within the larger context of these sites and of the tourist gaze. These people offer themselves, their knowledge, and their perspectives to foster increased understanding and respect, new understandings of history, and new relationships between Natives and non-Natives in the present. If tourists come to these sites to be entertained, if they expect to gaze upon familiar symbols that affirm their own place in the world, they are often surprised to find other things happening instead, and the "symbols" being people who insist on respect. This has also been the finding of Deutschlander and Miller (2003:42) about other kinds of Aboriginal tourism: "these sites have made openings for new ways of thinking."

As contact zones and touristic borderzones, the historic reconstructions I have studied function very much as "social spaces where disparate cultures meet, clash, and grapple with each other, often in highly asymmetrical relations of domination and subordination" (Pratt 1992:4). The encounters between Native interpreters and visitors are not simply about the past, but about the ways in which members of the dominant society regard Native peoples, past and present. Like the historical contact zones they interpret, visitors and staff at these sites bring their different cultural backgrounds and preconceptions to their interactions. The results are sometimes awkward, even banal:

> Native interpreter, LFG 2005: . . . so you'll see a lot of people around wearing moccasins that we made; and we also do day labor; we get a job from Mr. Lane and we do things like chopping and hauling wood, general labor . . .
>
> Female visitor: Thank you! So you're just hanging out around the campfire?
>
> Interpreter: Yes, we're starting to think about lighting the fire, we'll want to eat shortly.
>
> Female visitor: And what sorts of things do you eat for lunch?
>
> Interpreter: Well hopefully they'll bring some fish that we can eat, and also some bannock, maybe stew.

Sometimes, as I have shown, they are also fraught, full of tension and possibility. Having seen interpreters interacting with the full spectrum of visitors, however, I am left with the image of Keith and the boy who wanted to know, and Keith turning to me at the end of the encounter and saying, "That is why I work here!"

One must also remember, of course, that at these sites, the representation of the past has multiple meanings or interpretations to multiple audiences, and that visitors are a varied group who range from families to university students to new immigrants to groups of plainly dressed Mennonites and Buddhist monks. One cannot entirely control the way visitors will assign meaning to any aspect of these sites, or how meanings they acquire will change once visitors leave the sites. Unlike earlier forms of cultural representation and tourism, however, Native interpreters at these sites are not just "entertaining icons from the past" whose performances "were not ones that would contribute to improved recognition and social standing in the modern world," as Gleach has concluded for one historic display (Gleach 2003:440). The sharpness of many of these encounters, the sense of confrontation, reinforce Kapchan's reminder (1995:482) that cultural performance can either be a means of oppression or a way of resisting authority. Visitors are not locked into predetermined ways of thought. In fact, many of the encounters between Native interpreters and visitors at historic reconstructions are about breaking such scripts, and challenging relations of power in the present. Using their positions of authority as educators and as tribal members, Native interpreters challenge stereotypes and create teachable moments. In so doing, the interactions between them and visitors who represent the dominant society challenge much larger social and political dynamics: contact zones are also places where relations of power are challenged, and where they begin to shift.

NOTES

1. See, for example, *Where Two Worlds Meet* (Gilman 1982), *The Middle Ground* (White 1991), *Strangers in Blood* (Brown 1980), *The Invasion Within* (Axtell 1985), *At the Crossroads* (Merritt 2003).

2. The exhibition is described on the museum's website at www.amonline.net.au/visiting/exhibitions/indigenous.htm (accessed March 4, 2006).

3. Tim Edensor (2001:60) also discusses—in very different contexts—how "touristic conventions can be destabilized by rebellious performances."

4. I should note that in informal observations on several occasions at Colonial Williamsburg, I have not seen this in practice; indeed, I have seen some rather hard-hitting interpretation and conversations between interpreters and visitors regarding slave life.

5. And see Bruner and Kirshenblatt-Gimblett (1994:455) who claim that in photographing Maasai performers, "tourists make the Maasai safe for their own purposes by enclosing them within the white borders of a photograph or within a video frame . . . all by sophisticated Western technology."

Vignette: Angelique

"Angelique" is about eight; her mother is an interpreter at the Northwest Company Fur Post. She wears a miniature version of her mother's costume: Great Lakes cloth strap dress, moccasins, head scarf, suggesting a Métis character. Wisps of reddish-blonde hair escape her head scarf; she has enchanting freckles. She is standing at a rough wooden table under an even rougher canvas awning inside the palisade, mixing bannock, when a visiting girl of her own age approaches. "Angelique" continues to stir as the other child stands beside her and touches the iron baking kettle, the pitcher, the wooden spoon, and "Angelique's" head scarf. "Angelique" keeps up a sweet patter; they sound like two little girls playing house in the woods. "Angelique" finishes the dough and gives it to the older woman who will bake it, washes her hands, and then takes the visiting girl by the hand and says, "Come on! I'll show you the wigwam!" Together they skip hand-in-hand out of the palisade and along the path; the visiting child's mother and I tag along.

When we catch up to them, they are seated in the wigwam. The visitor is holding the *tikinagan*, and "Angelique" is saying to her: this is where my grandma sits; this is where grampa sits; this moss is the baby's diapers; this is what grandma uses to hit the rice with so it falls off; here's a game grampa made for me. . . . Race, which is discussed in the tour within the palisades, ceases to be an issue, as does the fact that the absent "owners" of the wigwam were (are?) Native. We are all playing house; it could be our families; everything is in the present tense, and it all seems perfectly appropriate. The visitors eventually leave, and as she enters the path that goes through the pine grove to the parking lot, the little girl turns and waves to "Angelique," who waves back.

Chapter Seven

The Living and the Dead: Conclusions

Summer 2005, fur loft, LFG, conversation with an American couple:

LP: What do you think, sir, does understanding the past help us to understand the present?

American male visitor: I'm not so sure about the present, but possibly the future. I mean, things you've done wrong, or things you could have done different, those you can't change. It's only the future that you have a chance of changing.

> We hold in common the belief that it is the obligation of historic sites to assist the public in drawing connections between the history of our site and its contemporary implications. We view stimulating dialogue on pressing social issues and promoting humanitarian and democratic values as a primary function. (International Coalition of Historic Site Museums of Conscience, cited in Norkunas 2004:118)

The addition of Native themes to historic sites suggests not only a broader view of the past, but the inclusion of Native people within North American society today. When scholars and interpreters suggest that Native people were partners in the past, competent humans with crucial skills, adaptable people who modernized while retaining core aspects of cultural identity, people who pursued their own goals in the face of considerable change, what does the public make of such messages? In changing our representations of the past, can we actually affect present-day relations within society to any significant degree? What is the future for such programs, and how best can sites work to communicate their messages to their visitors?

Such questions do not align well with the usual academic interests in cultural tourism, which tend to focus on issues of authenticity, the behavior of tourists, and the effects of tourism on indigenous cultures. Nor do they match the pragmatic concerns of site managers about visitor numbers, health and safety guidelines, stretching limited budgets to hire enough summer staff, and replacing rotting palisades. From the perspective of a manager who needs to increase visitor numbers or face the permanent closure of the site in the future, academic analyses may seem irrelevant.

There are good reasons, though, why both scholars and managers should think about the broader implications of revisions to historic reconstructions. Rosenzweig and Thelen's conclusions (1998:197) that not only were many middle-class Americans passionate about the past, but that they actively discussed the ways in which they engaged with the past, and connected national and personal histories "each time they toured a museum or visited a site with family or friends," suggest important possibilities for historic reconstructions. So does the survey's conclusion that multisensory, "creative approaches to presenting the past and connecting with audiences" were strongly desired by public audiences: historic reconstructions can engage far more strongly, and with broader audiences, than traditional taught narratives about the past (1998:179). Historic reconstructions thus have incredible potential to communicate about complex aspects of cross-cultural relations and the experiences of Native peoples.

Despite their carefully researched period features, much of what really goes on at historic sites has very little to do with the past. Historic reconstruction is "a mode of cultural production in the present that has recourse to the past" (Kirshenblatt-Gimblett 1995:370). Visitors' engagements with the past, and their encounters with Native interpreters, take place in the present. We make meanings for the past in the present, selecting bits of the past to string together in narratives that make sense today. The decisions to add Native peoples to the representation of the past at public history sites have been made in the context of present-day realities, which include challenges by Native peoples to structures of power within which historical knowledge is produced. While referring to the past, these encounters have serious implications for the future.

Across this work, I have explored the idea that reconstructions are sites of cultural performance, places where the dominant society, Native and non-Native staff, and diverse audiences enact very different understandings of the past and equally different cultural expectations in the present. Traditionally, historic sites have been places where dominant-society beliefs set in the past which underpinned national identity in the present have been articulated, places where stories of heroic conquest and triumph of Europeans over the wilderness could be told. When Native people were represented on site, it was to enhance these narratives by suggesting primitive "Others," sidekicks to Europeans who were the real makers of history. These stories legitimated the conquest of North America and its indigenous peoples historically, implied that Native peoples were unimportant in the past and inferior to settler groups, and thus justified the continued marginalization of Native peoples in the present.

Like other forms of public spectacle, which solidify "a network of social and cognitive relationships existing in a triangular relationship between performer, spectator, and the world at large" (Beeman 1993:386), then, enacting a revised past, as these sites try to do, involves suggesting new relationships between peoples, both past and present. If we change what we say about the past in such spectacles, we suggest new paths from then to now, and, ultimately, new ways of understanding the present.

The recent assertion by historic sites that Native people played central roles in history, that Europeans were often dependent on Natives, that Native cultures adapted and survived, and that peoples of different groups had complex, sometimes positive relationships with each other, is a dramatic revision of the messages communicated by these places in previous decades. At the NWCFP site, manager Patrick Schifferdecker told me in 1994 that he and his staff want visitors to leave

> with the impression that this was a mutual enterprise between the Europeans who came out here and the Ojibwa . . . we're trying to dispel a lot of the myths of the savage, and [to communicate] that these were living, breathing, thinking, feeling people and [had] hopes, dreams, aspirations. . . .

This is a radical shift in the messages that historic sites communicate, made even more radical by the work of Native interpreters who directly challenge myths and stereotypes. Native interpreters have an agenda of their own which involves educating non-Native people about the important historical roles and human dignity of Native people. This agenda is often different from managers' desire to communicate historical information; it is a response to broader Native-White relations and their histories, as well as to the stereotyped manner in which many site visitors view them. Marie Brunelle, a former interpreter at SMAH, expressed this goal by saying, "If we can just reach one person, teach one person that we are real human beings, then it's all worth it." Between their work and the changed messages given by these places, historic reconstructions have begun to replace, as James Clifford has suggested, "narratives of cultural disappearance and salvage . . . [with] stories of revival, remembrance, and struggle" (1991:214). These new narratives do not justify the marginalization of Native peoples as the old ones did. They relate, instead, to the very contemporary concept of self-determination.

It is no accident that Native peoples have targeted publicly sponsored forms of representation as ripe for challenge. Like museums, historic reconstructions are places associated with the dominant society and its forms of control over colonized peoples: places "for defining who people are and how they should act and as places for challenging those definitions" (Karp 1992:4). Public history sites are important stages for the enactment of widely-held beliefs about cultural worth and accepted forms of cross-cultural relations. One British forum on multiculturalism noted something quite relevant for North America:

> Acts of racism, racial violence, racial prejudice and abuse do not exist in a vacuum. They are not isolated incidents or individual acts, removed from the cultural fabric of our lives. Notions of cultural value, belonging and worth are defined and fixed by the decisions we make about what is or is not our culture, and how we are represented (or not) by cultural institutions. (Commission on the Future of Multi-Ethnic Britain 2000:159, cited in Sandell 2002:10)

That historic representations of Native cultures are related to issues of racism is demonstrated very strongly by visitors' references to squaws, chiefs, braves, princesses, war whoops, and scalping. Visitors' comments in the encampments reveal their assumptions that Native people were "primitive," that Native technology was inferior to that of Europeans, and that the frontier involved hostile race relations.

Despite the certainty of these stereotypes, there is also an element of uncertainty in the encounters between visitors and Native interpreters, for most visitors are meeting Native people for the first time in their lives. Native interpreters make use of this uncertainty as they assert control over the encampment areas and challenge visitors' stereotypes. Virtually all communication in the encampments, from answering visitors' questions about artifacts to confrontations over stereotypes, involves educating visitors. If these sites are arenas for cultural performance, they are also places for cross-cultural encounter and dialogue.

Native interpreters at historic reconstructions are thus very different from performers in other cultural tourism situations. Consider again Bruner and Kirshenblatt-Gimblett's (1994:467) pessimistic conclusions about the Maasai performers at Mayers Ranch in Kenya:

> [They] are merely players in a show written by international tourist discourse. . . . The story line of the show, the colonial drama of the primitive Maasai and the genteel British, of resistance and containment, of the wild and the civilized, was in place long before the Maasai or the Mayers mounted their production. . . . They do not have to perform for tourists. If they choose to do so, however, they must follow the script.

Although Native interpreters wear historic tribal clothing, and appear in settings imbued with colonialism, they refuse to "follow the script": they refuse to appear dominated, they insist that the Europeans were dependent on them, and they critique the standard plot and characters of the "colonial drama."[1] These people are pursuing their own agendas of educating non-Native people and exploring their own histories. Keith Knecht shaved his head, and Native interpreters always ask me about archival sources for tribal clothing and hairstyles, because of their personal investment in research on their tribal identities and histories, not to look like "savages" for tourists. None of these people are powerless pawns, and they challenge tourists' preconceptions forcefully.

Examining the agency, agendas, and impact of Native staff within the context of the revised messages adopted by historic sites, reveals that these have become places where Native and non-Native peoples confront the different stories they have been telling about Native histories: forums for discourse between people who hold different views on the past (Ames 1991:14). Similarly, while the literature on tourism suggests that Western tourists force non-Western "tourees" to conform to their expectations, and that the "tourist gaze" is a controlling one, the behavior of Native interpreters demonstrates that they can return this gaze and speak about tourists' expectations and their own realities.

While it is difficult to measure the success of the work of Native interpreters and historic sites, I believe that the encounters between visitors and Native staff, and the new information and perspectives that Native staff present to visitors, are important in fostering increased respect and understanding between peoples. Native interpreters provide a vivid contradiction to visitors' stereotypes, and can change the way that visitors feel about Native peoples today and in the past. They open doors to reevaluation, and prompt questions of other images of Native people that visitors encounter after these meetings. Lutz and Collins (1993:272) similarly conclude of the photographs in *National Geographic* magazine that "The most we can ask of an image is that it leave us with questions, with an aroused interest in the subject, a desire to know more fully the conditions surrounding the representation." From the behavior of visitors when confronted by interpreters, and their comments afterward, I believe that these encounters provoke such interest. Indeed, I think they do far more. These meetings between Native interpreters and non-Native visitors are one of the few opportunities available in North American society in which these peoples can talk with each other, compare perspectives, and learn from each other. They are extremely important, for face-to-face communication is far more powerful than television dramas, news stories, books, or other forms of media. The conversations that occur every day at these reconstructions begin in a very powerful way to bridge cultural divides by creating a personal sense of connection to Native peoples and a model for alternative ideas about them. I am encouraged by Rosenzweig and Thelen's survey, which showed that over half their interviewees had visited a museum or historic site in the past year, that these visits "invited them to revisit experiences at other times and places, to imagine how they might have felt and acted, to reflect on how the earlier experiences or circumstances might have changed or been changed by those who had originally participated in them" (1998:195). I am even more encouraged by their statement that for such ordinary people, "Understanding the past was a first step toward respecting, engaging, and even embracing unfamiliar people, practices, and faiths" (1998:193). Face-to-face, cross-cultural conversations are a powerful tool in such work.

This is not to say that Native interpreters and historic reconstructions have been entirely successful in communicating revisionist messages or challenging visitors' assumptions. On some days, inexperienced interpreters never get past visitors' materially oriented questions to address tough social history issues, or visitors prove resistant to new ways of thinking about the past. Even with the best interpretation, I am concerned about the effects of the patterned diminution of the roles and presence of Native people expressed through the physical elements of reconstructions, and the general absence of representations of cross-cultural relations. Seeing Native peoples only outside the palisade, only associated with fur rather than food or politics, and shown only as a fraction of real population numbers can negate the new messages that sites are trying to communicate.

The more positive and detailed interpretations of Native culture given now can also avoid the tougher aspects of history, making everyone feel happy about the past rather than delving into such topics as, for instance, alcohol abuse and its effects during fur trade competition, epidemics and their legacies, or the dilemmas facing families who adopted Christianity. I have enormous respect for staff at historic sites who have worked very hard to deepen their teaching about Native culture, and I think this work is crucial. I wonder, though, whether we haven't simply moved from representations of a heroic, celebratory, pioneer past to those of a happy, celebratory multicultural past. SMAH has had a drama in which Christian and traditional members of a Huron family debate whether to baptize a dying child, but this is one of the few suggestions of the darker sides of Native-White relations at any of the sites I studied. Portraying the more painful elements of history has traditionally been avoided by historic sites (Schlereth 1990:347–75), and without careful interpretation, the addition of Native themes to historic reconstructions can simply convey an image of a happy multicultural past with fun cross-cultural markets or exotic religious ceremonies, a colonial version of the frontier where the Natives are certainly exotic, but rather helpful, and thriving under paternal guidance. Valda Blundell has made this point for contemporary tourism featuring Native peoples: "Too often aboriginal forms are employed as mere props in a universal(izing) narrative of Canadian history that obscures the colonial and postcolonial relations that form part of the context within which tourism practices take place" (Blundell 1995–1996:46).

This is the accusation made of Colonial Williamsburg by Handler and Gable, who note (1997:220–21) that despite the addition of African American staff and narratives to the site, Williamsburg "downplayed class conflict, denigrated those who complained about their lot, and celebrated upscale consumerism." In particular, the emphasis on commerce, combined with the addition of a sort of "benign multiculturalism" represented by the presence of African American staff and a policy of uncritical discourse about the past, suggested that people at Williamsburg had simply been

> striving to better themselves, to live the good life, to succeed. Though the unevenness of the playing field was occasionally mentioned, the fact that the game was fundamentally unfair [to African Americans] was not stressed . . . [far from using] the museum to "disturb" complacent Americans about the injustices of the past and, indeed, about the relationship of those injustices to present-day social conflicts, . . . social history on the front line tended to comfort visitors' qualms about social injustice or banish a discussion of it altogether. (Handler and Gable 1997:121)

I do not entirely agree with this assessment of Williamsburg, but can see that it would be entirely possible to represent the fur trade as a happy meeting of consumer interests, rather than as a complex set of relationships, some economic, some social, some political, perceived differently by all parties and in which different peoples pursued their own agendas, not always successfully. Indeed, this is often the effect of even the best-researched revisions to historic sites, which have begun to communicate some of the complexities of the past, but seldom (officially, at least) discuss the legacies of the past for the present: the overall loss of control of their lives by Native people across the historic era, and the effects of this in the present. Without this discussion, new interpretive programs focusing on Native cultures and histories risk glossing over the very different historical experiences of Native peoples and others on site. Yes, these places are supposed to be entertaining: but for places claiming to be "authentic," they leave a great deal out of the stories they tell.

I accept that these sites have other messages to communicate, and that managers have to make difficult choices to cope with budget cuts and the broader political contexts in which they work. (As I write this, Fort William is once more flooded; serious structural repairs will dominate the attention of staff this year.) I am concerned, however, that by continuing to minimize the representation of the numbers and roles of Native peoples, by failing to show real interactions between Native peoples and others, by a relative lack of Native people in managerial positions, and in the absence of strong relations with local Native communities, these sites have not only compromised the implementation of their intended critical histories, but have also compromised the potential impact of such critical histories on the present. I am reminded of James Clifford's critical comments on the heritage industry as it affects Native peoples:

> Heritage can be a form of self-marketing, responding to the demands of a multicultural political economy that contains and manages inequalities. Sustaining local traditions does not guarantee economic and social justice; claiming cultural identity can be a palliative or compensation rather than part of a more systematic shift of power. (Clifford 2004:8)

Neither does adding to the messages that historic reconstructions communicate without changing key aspects of their representations of the past, or structures of power in the present, do much for changing the status quo. Using colonial situations as a hook for tourism without sufficiently exploring the dynamics and legacies of colonialism can simply perpetuate aspects of colonial control. Native interpreters and the addition of Native perspectives may be a way to address the legacies of the past, but these need to be fully embraced by sites as core aspects of their operations.

Historic sites and heritage agencies have not traditionally identified such work as part of their official themes or mandates. This aspect of the addition of Native perspectives to historic sites goes far beyond the communication of information about life in the past. It is closely linked, though, to what sites are trying to do, and the difficulties they have in fulfilling their mandates to portray more balanced views of history.

At present, these sites tend to talk about revisionist historical messages in official documents more often than they actually show them to visitors. I wish to emphasize that every site at which I did research has incredible strengths in its communication of a more complex past. These strengths are not even across sites, though, and there are aspects of representation that remain collectively weak. What I present here is an analysis, a set of ideas to think with; it is not intended to be a critical report card. I would note that across the board, the ideas that are actually communicated by the site, by the physical juxtaposition and relative sizes of the Native and non-Native areas, by brochures and orientation areas, by activities demonstrated and props seen, can be very different from those intended. Traditional historical narratives in which Native histories are incorporated into the non-Native histories of the site, and occupy marginalized positions in the past, are still what many visitors are "getting" from these places. It is unfair to expect interpreters to communicate new messages if what visitors are actually seeing across the site are the old ones. I would also note that there seem to be no formal mechanisms to evaluate the transmission of intended historical messages, or the problems in doing so.

If heritage agencies are serious about communicating certain messages about Native cultures and about alliances, relationships, and interdependence between Native peoples and non-Native peoples, then it is crucial to show these in tangible ways. The trading of food and essential country produce needs to be shown, as does the negotiation of political relations with Native people and the existence of marriages, friendships, and other relationships between Native peoples and Europeans. Creative solutions need to be sought to the pragmatic difficulties of showing the real historic ratio of Native to non-Native peoples. The realities of historic life need to be shown: if wild rice or corn or soldiers were the most important commodities on site, then show these in something like their real quantities, rather than just furs. If Native people came inside the palisade to trade, labor, or live, then show that: make it clear who is Native inside the palisade, who else is there, and who does what on both sides of the walls. This requires creative solutions, but think how powerful it would be to show a mixed-race couple in the fur trade—or a Native father-in-law and his Scottish son-in-law—interacting in a drama. Such interactions were the heart of what revisionist scholarship has explored and historic sites wish to communicate: they need to be shown to visitors more often.

It would assist Native interpreters in communicating desired historical messages if, as A. J. B. Johnston has stated, site and agency "managers and front-line interpreters recognize the false preconceptions many visitors have about First Nations as being peoples of the past" (Johnston 1995:9). All too often, site staff know that visitors bring misinformation with them, and that front-line staff spend a lot of time addressing these, but fail to work with this knowledge as part of official site planning. This recognition needs to happen across the site: in brochure texts, orientation videos, staff training, interpretation, and education programs. Sites need to acknowledge the existence of stereotypes and provide information and images that counteract these. Gateway-area images could include Native people in the present; orientation displays could discuss Native technology and its adoption by Europeans at the site, as well as the dynamics of Native-White relations; brochures could mention that the palisade was to define a European space rather than for defense; interpretation could include conversations between members of different peoples who occupied the site historically. Native staff do an excellent job of attacking stereotypes, but both their work and the site's intentions could be more effectively communicated by acknowledging the assumptions visitors bring with them.

It would also help if managers acknowledged the special nature of the work that Native interpreters do. Staff training should include information about the origins and functions of stereotypes, typical visitor preconceptions, and the need for all interpreters to work together to deal with these. Obviously, Native and non-Native staff need to get to know each other: interpretive positions may be the first time that many non-Native staff members have worked with Native people. Sites also need to reaffirm their commitment to Native themes by maintaining the numbers of Native interpreters and encouraging the development of their programs through the allocation of budgets and by permitting opportunities for research, the development of craft skills, and the acquisition of traditional cultural knowledge. Visitors' comments indicate that interpreters are the most important communicative elements of these sites: the reconstructions act as backdrops for them, and they and their interaction with visitors can never be replaced by other forms of communication. Investment in staff and in staff training pays off at these places.

Site staff, both managers and interpreters, might also give thought to discussing the legacies of the past as part of their work. This happens informally, and is included in some site manuals and planning documents, but tends to be dealt with quite unevenly from site to site. As Michael Wallace has noted for other historic reconstructions across the twentieth century, this

> disconnection of past from present and the separation of culture from politics was itself a political act. History was to be confined to providing entertainment, nostalgia, or interesting insights into vanished ways of life. It was not to be freed to become a powerful agent for understanding—and changing—the present. (Wallace 1991:196)

Wallace's thoughts have been echoed by Abram, who writes specifically of the Tenement Museum in New York City but with the goals of the Coalition of Historic Site Museums of Conscience in mind:

> If the Tenement Museum sets out, as it has, to use history to address prejudice against poor people, we can and should measure the outcome of that programme. It is not enough for us to ask simply whether participation in our programme made children think about the issue, for that was not our objective. Rather, we must ask whether children, who prior to their participation in the Tenement Museum programmes described a poor person with words such as 'mean', 'ugly', 'dishonest' and 'dangerous' actually changed their viewpoint after participating in our programme. If they did not, we must alter the programme so that the outcome meets our stated and explicit objective. (Abram 2002:139)

This is an ambitious and radical approach to public history that aims to engage visitors in dialogue and get them to rethink assumptions about structures of power, past and present. It is not unlike the goals of Native interpreters, and the potential goals of historic reconstructions. Abram and her colleagues take an equally engaged approach to educating their visitors: "the Tenement Museum uses history to teach English and civil rights to immigrants; to generate dialogue on current social issues such as sweatshop labor; to combat class and racial prejudice against immigrants past and present" (2002:136–38). What if historic reconstructions that involve Native peoples took similar approaches? What if in some ways they were able to work with Native communities as a focus for transmitting historical and cultural knowledge within those communities? For revitalizing historical technical and craft skills? For teaching the non-Native community about issues of racism, prejudice? For relationship-building across Native and non-Native communities? As Abram states, "If we are successful, we will not only break new ground in the use of history, but also, because our visitors are diverse, pioneer in establishing a dialogue that crosses the usually divisive line of class, race, religion, national origin and more" (Abram 2002:136). Abram is not alone in such beliefs. In an intriguing overview of the social potential of museums and heritage institutions, Richard Sandell has stated that,

> museums can impact positively on the lives of disadvantaged or marginalised *individuals*, act as a catalyst for social regeneration and as a vehicle for empowerment with specific *communities* and also contribute towards the creation of more equitable *societies* . . . it is through the thoughtful representation of difference and diversity that all museums, regardless of the nature of their collections, the resources available to them, their mission and the context within which they operate, can contribute towards greater social equity. (Sandell 2002:4; emphasis in original)

Clearly, such approaches have tremendous potential for local, regional, and national society. They have special importance for Native peoples, for whom fighting prejudice and regaining control over their lives is necessary for survival:

> Native survival was and remains a contest over life, humanity, land, systems of knowledge, memory, and representations. Native memories and representations are persistently pushed aside to make way for constructed Western myths and their representations of Native people. (Harlan 1995:20)

That these sites have begun to encourage the representation of Native perspectives on the past, to challenge "Western myths and their representations of Native people," signals the beginning of a major change in the "social process, in which competing interests argue for their own interpretation of history" (Bruner 2005:163). These changes are potentially very important for the self-determination of Native communities and the development of increased respect of Native peoples by non-Native society.

I am not making these comments as a neutral observer. Like Gable and Handler (1993:30), I have learned that it is impossible to do so. I write as a curator and ethnohistorian with a materially and archivally based sense of the physical texture and human activities at these sites. I write as someone who believes that what we say about the past is not only shaped by, but can shape, the present. I write as someone who believes in the communicative possibilities of historic interpretation. I also write as someone who works outside public history, who is unaffected by drastic budget cuts and the institutional climate of frustration these cause.

Historic sites will continue to shift directions in the future. Bruner's statement that "to construct, produce, invent, and market are verbs which highlight the processual, active nature of culture, history, tradition, and heritage" (Bruner 1993:14) reminds us that these places will continue to move with the tides of national and local politics, annual budgets, and contemporary Native-White relations. I have hope, though, that as they rebuild after floods, stretch budgets, hire staff every spring, and work with heritage agencies and their politics, they will remember how important parts of their work can be, and how very much the past—and what we say about it—matters in the present.

NOTE

1. Tim Edensor (2001) has also explored how touristic expectations and patterns of tourist behavior are challenged, subverted, and bypassed in a variety of touristic settings.

References Cited

Abbink, Jon. "Tourism and Its discontents: Suri-tourist Encounters in Southern Ethiopia." *Social Anthropology* 8, no. 1 (2000): 1–17.

Abram, Ruth J. "Harnessing the Power of History." Pp. 125–41 in *Museums, Society, Inequality*, edited by Richard Sandell. London and New York: Routledge, 2002.

———. "History is as History Does: the Evolution of a Mission-Driven Museum." Pp. 43–58 in *Looking Reality in the Eye: Museums and Social Responsibility*, edited by Robert R. Janes and Gerald T. Conaty. Calgary: University of Calgary Press, 2005.

Adams, Kathleen. "Cultural Displays and Tourism in Africa and the Americas." *Ethnohistory* 50, no. 3 (2003): 567–74.

Albers, Patricia C., and W. R. James. "Travel Photography; a Methodological Approach." *Annals of Tourism Research* 15, no. 1 (1988): 134–58.

Ames, Michael. "Biculturalism in Museums." *Museum Anthropology* 15, no. 2 (1991): 7–15.

———. *Glass Boxes and Cannibal Tours*. Vancouver: University of British Columbia Press, 1992.

———. "How to Decorate a House: the Renegotiation of Cultural Representations at the UBC Museum of Anthropology." Pp. 171–80 in *Museums and Source Communities: a Routledge Reader*, edited by Laura Peers and Alison K. Brown. London: Routledge. (Reprinted from *Museum Anthropology* 22, no. 3 2003[1999]: 41–51.)

Anderson, Benedict. *Imagined Communities: Reflections on the Origin and Spread of Nationalism* (1983). Rev ed. London: Verso, 2003.

Anderson, Jay, ed. *A Living History Reader: Museums*. Vol. 1. Nashville: American Association for State and Local History, 1984. Rev. ed. 1991.

Andrews, Wesley L. "Appropriate Representation, Cultural Interpretation and Exhibit Policy: A Perspective for Consulting with Native American Indian Communities in Northern Michigan." Unpublished consultant's report prepared for the Mackinac Island State Park Commission, 1995.

Armour, David A., and Keith R. Widder. *At the Crossroads: Michilimackinac during the American Revolution*. Mackinac Island: Mackinac Island State Park Commission, 1978.

———. *Michilimackinac: a Handbook to the Site* (1980). Mackinac Island: Mackinac Island State Park Commission, 1990.

Axtell, James. *The European and the Indian: Essays in the Ethnohistory of Colonial North America*. Oxford: Oxford University Press, 1981.

———. *The Invasion Within: The Contest of Cultures in Colonial North America*. New York and Oxford: Oxford University Press, 1985.

Backhouse, Meghan. "A Material Culture Study of Subversion: Interpreting English Medieval [sic] History." *Journal of the Anthropological Society of Oxford: JASO* 31, no. 3 (2000): 345–51.

———. "Re-enacting the English." Paper given at the Ruskin Public History Conference: People and the Past. Oxford, England, 17 Sept. 2005.

Bakhtin, M. M. "Discourse in the Novel." Pp. 259–422 in *The Dialogic Imagination: Four Essays*, edited by Michael Holquist. Austin: University of Texas Press, 1981.

Banks, Marcus. *Visual Methods in Social Research*. London: Sage Publications, 2001.

Banta, Melissa, and Curtis Hinsley. *From Site to Sight: Anthropology, Photography and the Power of Imagery*. Cambridge, MA: Peabody Museum, 1986.

Barthel, Diane. "Nostalgia for America's Village Past: Staged Symbolic Communities." *International Journal of Politics, Culture, and Society* 4, no. 1 (1990): 79–93.

Baxandall, Michael. "Exhibiting Intention: Some Preconditions of the Visual Display of Culturally Purposeful Objects." Pp. 33–41 in *Exhibiting Cultures: the Poetics and Politics of Museum Display*, edited by Ivan Karp and Steven D. Lavine. Washington, D.C.: Smithsonian Institution, 1991.

Beauvais, Johnny. *Kahnawake: A Mohawk Look at Canada*. Rev. ed. Kahnawake, Quebec: Kanata Industries, 1985.

Beeman, William O. "The Anthropology of Theater and Spectacle." *Annual Review of Anthropology* 22 (1993): 369–93.

Blackstone, Sarah J. *Buckskin, Bullets, and Business: a History of Buffalo Bill's Wild West*. New York: Greenwood Press, 1986.

Blakey, Michael. "American Nationality and Ethnicity in the Depicted Past." In *The Politics of the Past*, edited by P. Gathercole and D. Lowenthal. London: Unwin, 1990.

Blanchard, David. "For Your Entertainment Pleasure—Princess White Deer and Chief Running Deer—Last 'Hereditary' Chief of the Mohawk: Northern Mohawk Rodeos and Showmanship." *Journal of Canadian Studies* 1, no. 2 (1984): 99–116.

Blundell, Valda. "Riding the Polar Bear Express: and Other Encounters between Tourists and First Peoples in Canada." *Journal of Canadian Studies* 30, no. 4 (winter 1995–1996): 28–51.

Bodnar, John. *Remaking America: Public Memory, Commemoration, and Patriotism in the Twentieth Century*. Princeton, N.J.: Princeton University Press, 1992.

Boniface, Priscilla, and Peter J. Fowler. *Heritage and Tourism in 'The Global Village.'* London: Routledge, 1993.

Bronner, Simon J. "Object Lessons: the Work of Ethnological Museums and Collections." Pp. 217–54 in *Consuming Visions: Accumulation and Display of Goods in*

America, 1880–1920, edited by Simon J. Bronner. New York: W. W. Norton and Company for the Winterthur Museum, 1989.

Brown, Alison K., Laura Peers, and members of the Kainai Nation. *Pictures Bring Us Messages/Sinaakssiiksi aohtsimaahpihkookiyaawa: Photographs and Histories from the Kainai Nation*. Toronto: University of Toronto Press, 2006.

Brown, Jennifer S. H. *Strangers in Blood: Fur Trade Company Families in Indian Country*. Vancouver: University of British Columbia, 1980.

Bruner, Edward M. "Transformation of Self in Tourism." *Annals of Tourism Research* 18 (1991): 238–50.

———. "Introduction: Museums and Tourism." *Museum Anthropology* 17, no. 3 (1993): 6.

———. "The Ethnographer/Tourist in Indonesia." Pp. 224–42 in *International Tourism, Identity and Change,* edited by Marie-Francoise Lanfant, et al., London: Sage Publications, 1995.

———. "The Ethnographer/Tourist in Indonesia." N.d. (Undated and different earlier draft of 1995 paper available at www.nyu.edu/classes/tourist/brun-ind.dos, accessed July 11, 2006.)

———. "Tourism in Ghana: the Representation of Slavery and the Return of the Black Diaspora." *American Anthropologist* 98, no. 2 (1996): 290–304.

———. *Cultures on Tour: Ethnographies of Travel*. Chicago: University of Chicago Press, 2005.

Bruner, Edward M., and Barbara Kirschenblatt-Gimblett. "Maasai on the Lawn: Tourist Realism in East Africa." *Cultural Anthropology* 9, no. 4 (1994): 435–70.

Burns, Georgette Leah. "Anthropology and Tourism: Past Contributions and Future Theoretical Challenges." *Anthropological forum* 14, no. 1 (2004): 5–22.

Butler, Judith. *Excitable Speech: a politics of the performative*. London: Routledge, 1997.

Butler, Richard, and Thomas Hinch, eds. *Tourism and Indigenous People*. London: International Thomson Business Press, 1996.

Cannizzo, Jeanne. "Living in the Past." *Ideas*. Canada Broadcasting Corporation Radio. Toronto, ON. Transcript. 1987.

Carlson, Keith Thor, and Albert "Sonny" McHalsie. "The Sto:lo Nation and the Fort Langley National Historic Site: Overcoming Pan-Indianism and Defining Sto:lo Culture and Tradition." Paper presented to the Second Columbia Department Fur Trade Conference, Vancouver, WA, 1995.

Clifford, James. "Introduction: Partial Truths." Pp. 1–26 in *Writing Culture: the Poetics and Politics of Ethnography*, edited by James Clifford and George Marcus. Berkeley: University of California Press, 1986.

———. *The Predicament of Culture: Twentieth-Century Ethnography, Literature, and Art*. Cambridge: Harvard University Press, 1988.

———. "Four Northwest Coast Museums: Travel Reflections." Pp. 212–54 in *Exhibiting Cultures: the Poetics and Politics of Museum Display,* edited by Ivan Karp and Steven D. Lavine. Washington: Smithsonian Institution Press, 1991.

———. "Museums as Contact Zones." *Routes*: *Travel and Translation in the Late Twentieth Century*. London; Cambridge, MA: Harvard University Press, 1997.

———. "Looking Several Ways: Anthropology and Native Heritage in Alaska," *Current Anthropology* 45, no. 1 (2004): 5–30.

Cohen, E., Y. Nir, and U. Almagor. "Stranger-Local Interaction in Photography." *Annals of Tourism Research* 19, no. 2 (1992): 213–33.

Commission on the Future of Multi-Ethnic Britain. *The Future of Multi-Ethnic Britain*. London: Profile Books Ltd., 2000.

Connerton, Paul. *How Societies Remember*. Cambridge, Cambridge University Press, 1989.

Coombes, Annie E. *Reinventing Africa: Museums, Material Culture and Popular Imagination in Late Victorian and Edwardian England*. London and New Haven: Yale University Press, 1994.

Coutts, Robert. *Lower Fort Garry: An Operational History, 1911–1992*. Ottawa, ON: Parks Canada, 1993. (Microfiche Report Series 495).

———. *The Road to the Rapids: Nineteenth-Century Church and Society at St. Andrew's Parish, Red River*. Calgary: University of Calgary Press, 2000.

Darby, Wendy Joy. *Landscape and Identity: Geographies of nation and class in England*. Oxford: Berg Publishers, 2000.

de Azeredo Grünewald, Rodrigo. "Tourism and Cultural Revival." *Annals of Tourism Research* 29, no. 4 (2002): 1004–1021.

Deloria, Phillip J. *Playing Indian*. Yale: Yale University Press, 1998.

DeMallie, Raymond. *The Sixth Grandfather: Black Elk's Teachings as Given to John G. Neihardt*. Lincoln: University of Nebraska Press, 1984.

Dening, Greg. "The Theatricality of History Making and the Paradoxes of Acting." *Cultural Anthropology* 8, no. 1 (1993): 73–95.

———. *Performances*. Chicago: University of Chicago Press, 1996.

Deutschlander, Sigrid, and Leslie J. Miller. "Politicizing Aboriginal Cultural Tourism: The Discourse of Primitivism in the Tourist Encounter." *Canadian Review of Sociology and Anthropology* 40, no. 1 (2003): 27–44.

Dickason, Olive. *The Myth of the Savage*. Edmonton: University of Alberta Press, 1984.

Duncan, Carol. *Civilizing Rituals: Inside Public Art Museums* (1989). London: Routledge, 1995.

Edensor, Tim. "Performing Tourism, Staging Tourism: (Re)producing Tourist Space and Practice." *Tourist Studies* 1, no.1 (2001): 58–81.

Edwards, Elizabeth, ed. *Anthropology and Photography*. New Haven: Yale, 1992.

Ettawageshik, Frank. "My Father's Business." Pp. 20–29 in *Unpacking Culture: Art and Commodity in Colonial and Postcolonial Worlds*, eds. Ruth B. Phillips and Christopher B. Steiner. Berkeley: University of California Press, 1999.

Evans-Pritchard, Deirdre. "How 'They' See 'Us': Native American Images of Tourists." *Annals of Tourism Research* 16 (1989): 89–105.

Fabian, Johannes. *Time and the Other: How Anthropology Makes its Object*. New York: Columbia University Press, 1983.

Fife, Wayne. "Semantic Slippage as a New Aspect of Authenticity: Viking Tourism on the Northern Peninsula of Newfoundland." *Journal of Folklore Research* 41, no. 1 (2004): 61–84.

Francis, Daniel. *The Imaginary Indian: the Image of the Indian in Canadian Culture*. Vancouver: Arsenal Pulp Press, 1992.

Friedman, Jonathan. "The Past in the Future: History and the Politics of Identity." *American Anthropologist* 94, no. 4, 1992: 837–59.

Friesen, Jean. "Heritage: The Manitoba Experience." *Prairie Forum* 15, no. 2 (1990): 199–220.

Fort William Historical Park Interpretive Manual. Unpublished document. n.d.

Fort William Historical Park Indian Encampment Manual. Internal site document, 1986.

Gable, Eric. "Maintaining Boundaries, or 'Mainstreaming' Black History in a White Museum." Pp. 177–202 in *Theorizing Museums: Representing Identity and Diversity in a Changing World*, edited by Sharon Macdonald and Gordon Fyfe. Oxford: Blackwell Publishers/The Sociological Review, 1996.

Gable, Eric, and Richard Handler. "Colonialist Anthropology at Colonial Williamsburg." *Museum Anthropology* 17, no. 3 (1993): 26–31.

———. "The Authority of Documents at Some American History Museums." *The Journal of American History*, 81, no.1 (1994): 119–36.

———. "Public History, Private Memory: Notes from the Ethnography of Colonial Williamsburg, Virginia, USA." *Ethnos* 65, no. 2 (2000): 237–52.

Gable, Eric, Richard Handler, and Anna Lawson. "On the Uses of Relativism: Fact, Conjecture, and Black and White Histories at Colonial Williamsburg." *American Ethnologist* 19, no. 4 (1992): 791–805.

Gamper, Josef. "Reconstructed Ethnicity: Comments on MacCannell." *Annals of Tourism Research* 12, no. 2 (1985): 250–53.

Garner, Andrew. "Living History: Trees and Metaphors of Identity in an English Forest." *Journal of Material Culture* 9, no. 1 (2004): 87–100.

Gell, Alfred. *Art and Agency: an Anthropological Theory*. Oxford: OUP, 1998.

Gilman, Carolyn. *Where Two Worlds Meet: the Great Lakes Fur Trade*. St. Paul: Minnesota Historical Society, 1982.

Gleach, Frederic W. "Pocahontas at the Fair: Crafting Identities at the 1907 Jamestown Exposition." *Ethnohistory* 50, no. 3 (2003): 419–46.

Goodacre, Beth, and Gavin Baldwin. *Living the Past: Reconstruction, Recreation, Reenactment and Education at Museums and Historical Sites*. London: Middlesex University Press, 2002.

Goodsky, Sandra L. (O-zhaa-wazsh-ko-ge-zhi-go-quay). "Angwaamass—It's About Time: A Research Report on the Ojibwa-European Fur Trade Relations from an Ojibwa Perspective." Report prepared for the Minnesota Historical Society's North West Company Fur Post. Ms. copy courtesy of Minnesota Historical Society. 1993.

Gosden, Chris, and Chantal Knowles. *Collecting Colonialism: Material Culture and Colonial Change*. Oxford: Berg, 2001.

Grant, John Webster. *Moon of Wintertime: Missionaries and the Indians of Canada in Enounters Since 1534*. Toronto: University of Toronto Press, 1984.

Greenspan, Anders. *Creating Colonial Williamsburg*. Washington: Smithsonian Institution Press, 2002.

Hammond, Joyce D. "Photography, Tourism and the Kodak Hula Show." *Visual Anthropology* 14 (2001): 1–32.

Handler, Richard. "Authenticity." *Anthropology Today* 2, no.1 (Feb. 1986): 2–4.

Handler, Richard, and Eric Gable. *The New History in an Old Museum: Creating the Past at Colonial Williamsburg*. Durham, NJ: Duke University Press, 1997.

Handler, Richard, and W. Saxton. "Dyssimulation: Reflexivity, Narrative, and the Quest for Authenticity in 'Living History'." *Cultural Anthropology* 3, no. 3 (1988): 242–60.

Hanna, Margaret G. "A time to choose: 'Us' versus 'them' or 'all of us together.'" *Plains Anthropologist* 17(1):33–36, 1999.

Harlan, Theresa. "Creating a Visual History: A Question of Ownership." *Aperture,* no. 139 (Spring 1995): 20–34.

Harris, Neil. *Cultural Excursions: Marketing Appetites and Cultural Tastes in Modern America.* Chicago: University of Chicago Press, 1990.

Harrison, Julia. *Being a Tourist: Finding Meaning in Pleasure Travel.* Vancouver: University of British Columbia Press, 2003.

Hastrup, Kirsten, and Peter Elsass. "Anthropological Advocacy: A Contradiction in Terms?" *Current Anthropology* 31, no. 3 (1990): 301–12.

Hawkes, Christopher. *Sainte-Marie among the Hurons.* Toronto: Ginn and Company, 1974.

Hendry, Joy. *The Orient Strikes Back: A Global View of Cultural Display.* Oxford: Berg, 2000.

———. *Reclaiming Culture: Indigenous People and Self-Representation.* New York: Palgrave MacMillan, 2003.

Heth, Charlotte. *Native American Dance: Ceremonies and Social Traditions.* Washington: National Museum of the American Indian, Smithsonian Institution, 1992.

Hewison, Robert. "Heritage: An Interpretation." Pp. 15–23 in *Heritage Interpretation, Vol. 1, Natural and Built Environment,* edited by David L. Uzzell. London; New York: Belhaven Press, 1989.

Hickerson, Harold. *The Chippewa and Their Neighbours: A Study in Ethnohistory.* Rev. ed. Jennifer S. H. Brown and Laura L. Peers, eds. Prospect Heights, IL: Waveland, 1988.

Hill, Jonathan D. "Contested Pasts and the Practice of Anthropology." *American Anthropologist* 94, no. 4 (1992): 809–15.

Hill, Tom. "The History of Performance at Six Nations." *Wadrihwa* 14, no. 4 (1999): 4–9.

Hitchcock, R. K. "Cultural, Economic and Environmental Impacts of Tourism Among Kalahari Bushman." In E. Chambers ed., *Tourism and Culture: An Applied Perspective.* Albany: State University of New York Press, pp. 93–128, 1997.

Hobsbawm, Eric, and Terence Ranger. *The Invention of Tradition.* 1983. Cambridge: Cambridge University Press, 1992.

Horne, Donald. *The Great Museum: the Re-Presentation of History.* London: Pluto Press, 1984.

Horton, James Oliver, and Spencer R. Crew. "Afro-Americans and Museums: Toward a Policy of Museums." Pp. 215–36 in *History Museums in the United States,* edited by Warren Leon and Roy Rosenzweig. Urbana: University of Illinois Press, 1989.

Huhndorf, Shari M. *Going Native: Indians in the American Cultural Imagination.* Ithaca: Cornell University Press, 2001.

Innis, Harold. *The Fur Trade in Canada: An Introduction to Canadian Economic History* (1930). Toronto: University of Toronto Press, 1999.

Janes, Robert R., and Gerald T. Conaty, eds. *Looking Reality in the Eye: Museums and Social Responsibility.* Calgary: University of Calgary Press, 2005.

Jasen, Patricia. "Imagining: Romanticism, Tourism, and the Old Fort, 1821 to 1971." Thunder Bay Historical Museum Society. *Papers and Records* 18 (1990): 2–19.

———. *Wild Things: Nature, Culture, and Tourism in Ontario, 1790–1914.* Toronto: University of Toronto Press, 1995.

Johnston, A. J. B. "Toward a New Past: Reflections on the Interpretation of Native History Within Parks Canada." Unpublished manuscript, copy from author, 1994. Rev. draft circulated as internal report for Historical Services Branch, National Historic Sites Directorate, Parks Canada, 1995.

Johnstone, Barbara A. "Lower Fort Garry Complete Conversion to National Historic Site Plan # 1." 1960. Barbara Johnstone Papers. Hudson's Bay Company Archives, Provincial Archives of Manitoba, Winnipeg, Manitoba (E.97/53).

———. "A Broad Outline of Exhibit Stories for Lower Fort Garry National History Park." 1962. Barbara Johnstone Papers, Hudson's Bay Company Archives, Provincial Archives of Manitoba, Winnipeg, Manitoba (E.97/53).

Jonaitis, Aldona. "Franz Boas, John Swanton, and the New Haida Sculpture at the American Museum of Natural History." Pp. 22–61 in *The Early Years of Native American Art History*, edited by Janet Catherine Berlo. Seattle and London: University of Washington Press, 1992.

Kapchan, Deborah A. "Performance." *Journal of American Folklore* 108, no. 430 (1995): 479–509.

Karp, Ivan. "Introduction: Museums and Communities: the Politics of Public Culture." Karp et. al., *Museums and Communities*, (1992): 1–18.

Karp, Ivan, Christine Mullen Kreamer, and Steven D. Lavine, eds. *Museums and Communities: the Politics of Public Culture.* Washington: Smithsonian Institution Press, 1992.

Kelleher, Michael. "Images of the Past: Historical Authenticity and Inauthenticity from Disney to Times Square." *CRM: the Journal of Heritage Stewardship* 1, no. 2 (2004): 6–19.

Kelly, Lynda, and Phil Gordon. "Developing a Community of Practice: Museums and Reconciliation in Australia." Pp. 153–74 in *Museums, Society, Inequality*, edited by Richard Sandell. London: Routledge, 2002.

King, Anthony. "Cultural Hegemony and Capital Cities." Pp. 251–70 in *Capital Cities, Les Capitales: Perspectives Internationales, International Perspectives*, edited by J. Taylor, J. Lengelle, and C. Andrew. Ottawa: Carleton University Press, 1993.

———. "A Century of Indian Shows: Canadian and United States Exhibitions in London 1825–1925." *Native American Studies* 5, no. 1 (1991): 35–42.

Kirshenblatt-Gimblett, Barbara. "Theorizing Heritage." *Ethnomusicology* 39, no. 3 (1995): 367–80.

Korn, Randi and Associates. "Enemies to Allies: Cultural Accommodations in the Western Great Lakes, 1760–1783. A Front-End Evaluation: Part II." Unpublished consultant's report for Colonial Michilimackinac, 1995.

Kreamer, Christine Mullen. "Defining Communities through Exhibiting and Collecting." Pp. 367–81 in *Museums and Communities: the Politics of Public Culture*, edited by

Ivan Karp, Christine Kreamer, and Steven Lavine. Washington, D.C.: Smithsonian, 1992.

———. *The Ecological Indian: Myth and History*. New York: W. W. Norton and Company, 1999.

Laxson, Joan D. "How "We" See "Them": Tourism and Native Americans." *Annals of Tourism Research* 18 (1991): 365–91.

Leon, Warren, and Margaret Piatt. "Living-History Museums." Pp. 64–97 in *History Museums in the United States: A Critical Assessment*, edited by Warren Leon and Roy Rosenzweig. Chicago: University of Illinois Press, 1989.

Lidchi, Henrietta. "The Poetics and Politics of Exhibiting Other Cultures." Pp. 151–222 in *Representation: Cultural Representations and Signifying Practices*, edited by Stuart Hall. London: Sage Publications, 1997.

Limerick, Patricia Nelson. "The Adventures of the Frontier in the Twentieth Century." Pp. 67–102 in *The Frontier in American Culture*, edited by James Grossman. Berkeley: University of California Press, 1994.

Lippard, Lucy. *Partial Recall: Photographs of Native North Americans*. New York: The New Press, 1992.

Long, John. "Manitu, Power, Books, and Wihtikow." *Native Studies Review* 3, no. 1 (1987), 1–30.

Lowenthal, David. *The Past is a Foreign Country*. Cambridge: Cambridge University Press, 1985.

———. "Pioneer Museums." Pp. 115–27 in *History Museums in the United States: A Critical Assessment*, edited by Warren Leon and Roy Rosenzweig. Chicago: University of Illinois Press, 1989.

Lunman, John. "From Motion Picture to Audio-Visual Presentation as an Orientation Technique at Sainte-Marie among the Hurons." *Annual Relations from Sainte-Marie: the Magazine of Sainte-Marie among the Hurons* no. 1.1, 1995.

Lutz, Catherine A., and Jane L. Collins. *Reading National Geographic*. Chicago: University of Chicago Press, 1993.

MacAloon, John, ed. *Rite, Drama, Festival, Spectacle: Rehearsals Toward a Theory of Cultural Performance*. Philadelphia: University of Pennsylvania Press, 1984.

MacCannell, Dean. *The Tourist: a New Theory of the Leisure Class*. New York: Schocken Books, 1976.

———. "Reconstructed Ethnicity: Tourism in Third World Communities." *Annals of Tourism Research* 11, no. 3 (1984): 375–91.

Maddra, Sam. *Hostiles? The Lakota Ghost Dance and Buffalo Bill's Wild West*. Norman, Oklahoma: University of Oklahoma Press, 2006.

Manning, F. E., ed. *The Celebration of Society: Perspectives on Contemporary Cultural Performance*. Bowling Green, OH: Bowling Green University Press, 1983.

Mason, Kaley. "Sound and Meaning in Aboriginal Tourism." *Annals of Tourism Research* 31, no. 4 (2004): 837–55.

McClurken, James M. *Gah-Baeh-Jhagway-Buk: A Visual Culture History of the Little Traverse Bay Bands of Odawa*. East Lansing: Michigan State University, 1991.

McConnell, Michael N. *A Country Between: the Upper Ohio Valley and Its Peoples, 1724–1774*. Nebraska: University of Nebraska Press, 1992.

McGuire, Randall H. "Archaeology and the First Americans." *American Anthropologist* 94, no. 4 (1992): 816–36.

McIntosh, Alison J., and Richard C. Prentice. "Affirming Authenticity: Consuming Cultural Heritage." *Annals of Tourism Research* 26, no. 3 (1999): 589–612.

Medina, Laurie Kroshus. "Commoditizing Culture: Tourism and Maya Identity." *Annals of Tourism Research* 30, no. 2 (2003): 353–368.

Meeker, Joseph W. "Red, White, and Black in National Parks." Pp. 127–37 in *On Interpretation: Sociology for Interpreters of Natural and Cultural History*, edited by Gary E. Machlis and Donald R. Field. Corvallis, OR: Oregon State University, 1984. Reprinted from *The North American Review*, 1973.

Merritt, Jane. *At the Crossroads: Indians and Empires on a Mid-Atlantic Frontier, 1700–1763*. Chapel Hill: University of North Carolina Press, for the Omohundro Institute of Early American History and Culture, Williamsburg, VA, 2003.

Meyn, Susan Labry. "Who's Who: the 1896 Sicangu Sioux Visit to the Cincinnati Zoological Gardens." *Museum Anthropology* 16, no. 2 (1992): 21–26.

Mirzoeff, Nicholas, ed. *The Visual Culture Reader*, 2nd ed. London and New York: Routledge, 2002.

Mitchell, W. J. T. "Representation." Pp. 11–22 in *Critical Terms for Literary Study*, edited by Frank Lentricchia and Thomas McLaughlin. Chicago, London: University of Chicago Press, 1990.

Morgan, David. *The Sacred Gaze: Religious Visual Culture in Theory and Practice*. Berkeley: University of California Press, 2005.

Moscardo, Gianna, and Philip L. Pearce. "Understanding Ethnic Tourists." *Annals of Tourism Research* 26, no. 2 (1999): 416–34.

Moses, Lester George. *Wild West Shows and the Images of American Indians, 1883–1933*. Albuquerque, NM: University of New Mexico Press, 1996.

Myers, Fred R. "Culture-making: Performing Aboriginality at the Asia Art Gallery." *American Ethnologist* 21, no. 4 (1994): 681–97.

Nash, Dennison. "Tourism as a Form of Imperialism." In *Hosts and Guests: the Anthropology of Tourism*, edited by Valene L. Smith. Oxford: Blackwell, 1978, 33–47.

Nesper, Larry. "Native Peoples and Tourism: an Introduction." *Ethnohistory* 50, no. 3 (2003a): 415–17.

———. "Simulating Culture: Being Indian for Tourists in Lac du Flambeau's Wa-Swa-Gon Indian Bowl." *Ethnohistory* 50, no. 3 (2003b): 447–88.

Neufeld, David. "The Commemoration of Northern Aboriginal Peoples by the Canadian Government." *The George Wright Forum* 19, no. 3 (2002): 22–33.

———. "Parks Canada, the Commemoration of Canada and Northern Aboriginal Oral History." Draft submitted October 28, 2004 for *Oral History and Public Memories*, edited by Paula Hamilton and Linda Shopes, in press.

Nicks, Trudy. "Indian Villages and Entertainments: Setting the Stage for Tourist Souvenir Sales." Paper presented at American Ethnological Society 115th Annual Meeting, Santa Fe, New Mexico, 1993.

———. "Indian Villages and Entertainments: Setting the Stage for Tourist Souvenir Sales." Pp. 301–15 in *Unpacking Culture: Art and Commodity in Colonial and Postcolonial Worlds*, edited by Ruth Phillips and Christopher Steiner. Berkeley: University of California Press, 1999.

Nora, Pierre. "Between Memory and History: Les Lieux de Memoire." *Representations* 26 (Spring 1989): 7–24.

Norkunas, Martha K. *The Politics of Public Memory*. Albany, NY: SUNY Press, 1993.

――. "Narratives of Resistance and the Consequences of Resistance." *Journal of Folklore Research* 41, nos. 2 and 3 (2004): 105–23.

Parks Canada. "National Historic Sites Systems Plan Review, 1992–1994." Unpublished discussion paper. Hull, Quebec, 1992.

Parks Canada. "Parks Canada Response to Request for Update on Task Force on Museums and First Peoples by Canadian Museums Association." Unpublished paper. Hull, Quebec, 1995.

Peers, Laura. *The Ojibwa of Western Canada, 1780–1870*. Winnipeg, Manitoba: University of Winnipeg Press, 1994.

――. *The Aboriginal Presence at Lower Fort Garry*. Report submitted to Heritage Canada [Parks Canada], Lower Fort Garry, 1995.

――. "Fur Trade History, Native History, Public History: Communication and Miscommunication." Pp. 101–20 in *New Faces of the Fur Trade: Selected Papers of the 7th North American Fur Trade Conference*, edited by Jo-Anne Fiske, Susan Sleeper Smith, and William Wicken. East Lansing: Michigan State University Press, 1998.

――. "Playing Ourselves: Native Peoples and Public History Sites." *The Public Historian* 21, no. 4 (1999a): 39–59.

――. "'Playing Ourselves': First Nations Interpreters and Historic Sites." Keynote plenary address, Ontario Museum Association Meetings, Burlington, Ontario, 1999b.

――. "Interpreting First Nations Histories at Public History Sites." Lecture given at The International Workshop on History, Interpretation, and Management of Fur Trade History Sites. Sponsored by the National Council on Public History, U.S. National Parks Service, and Parks Canada. Grand Portage, Minnesota, 2000.

――. "Revising the Past: the Heritage Elite and Native Peoples in North America." Pp.173–88 in *Elite Cultures: Anthropological Perspectives*, edited by Chris Shore and Stephen Nugent. Association of Social Anthropology Monographs, no. 38. London: Routledge, 2002.

Peers, Laura, and Jennifer S. H. Brown. "The Chippewa and Their Neighbors: A Critical Review." Pp. 135–46 in *The Chippewa and Their Neighbors: A Study in Ethnohistory*, edited by Harold Hickerson. Rev. ed. Prospect Heights, IL: Waveland Press, 1988.

Peers, Laura, and Robert Coutts. "Aboriginal History and Historic Sites: The Shifting Ground." In *Essays in Honour of Jennifer S. H. Brown*, edited by Carolyn Podruchny and Laura Peers, forthcoming.

Peterson, Jacqueline. "Many Roads to Red River: Métis Genesis in the Great Lakes Region, 1680–1715." Pp. 185–93 in *The New Peoples: Being and Becoming Métis in North America*, edited by Jacqueline Peterson and Jennifer S. H. Brown. Winnipeg: University of Manitoba Press, 1985.

Peterson, Jacqueline, and Laura Peers. *Sacred Encounters: Father De Smet and the Indians of the Rocky Mountain West*. Norman: University of Oklahoma Press, 1993.

Phillips, Ruth. "Why Not Tourist Art?: Significant Silences in Native American Museum Representations." Pp. 98–125 in *After Colonialism: Imperial Histories and Postcolonial Displacements*, edited by Gyan Prakash. Princeton: Princeton University Press, 1995.

———. *Trading Identities: the souvenir in Native North American art from the Northeast, 1700–1900*. Seattle and Montreal: University of Washington Press and McGill-Queen's University Press, 1998.

Pink, Sarah. *Doing Visual Ethnography: Images, Media and Representation in Research*. London: Sage Publications, 2001.

Pitchford, S. R. "Ethnic Tourism and Nationalism in Wales." *Annals of Tourism Research* 22, no. 1 (1995): 35–52.

Porter, Philip. Interpreters' manual, Indian Encampment, Colonial Michilimackinac. Internal document for site use, 1992.

Pratt, Mary Louise. *Imperial Eyes: Travel Writing and Transculturation*. London: Routledge, 1992.

Prendergast, Christopher. *The Triangle of Representation*. New York: Columbia, 2000.

Prentice, Richard. *Tourism and Heritage Attractions*. London/New York: Routledge, 1993.

Price, Sally. *Primitive Art in Civilized Places*. Chicago: University of Chicago Press, 1989.

Prösler, Martin. "Museums and Globalisation." Pp. 21–44 in *Theorising Museums*, edited by Sharon Macdonald and Gordon Fife. Oxford: Blackwell, 1996.

Rodman, Margaret C. "Empowering Place: Multilocality and Multivocality." *American Anthropologist* 94, no. 3 (1992): 640–55.

Rosaldo, Renato. *Culture and Truth: the Remaking of Social Analysis*. Boston: Beacon Press, 1989.

Rosenzweig, Roy, and David Thelen. *The Presence of the Past: Popular Uses of History in American Life*. New York: Columbia University Press, 1998.

Rossel, Pierre. "Tourism and Cultural Minorities: Double Marginalisation and Survival Strategies." Pp. 1–20 in *Tourism: Manufacturing the Exotic*, edited by Pierre Rossel. Copenhagen, Denmark: International Working Group for Indigenous Affairs, 1988.

Said, Edward. *Orientalism*. London: Vintage Books (Random House), 1978.

———. "Representing the Colonized: Anthropology's Interlocutors." *Critical Inquiry* 15, no. 2 (1989): 217–24.

Sandell, Richard, ed. *Museums, Society, Inequality*. London and New York: Routledge, 2002.

Schechner, Richard. *Between Theater and Anthropology*. Philadelphia: University of Pennsylvania Press, 1985.

———. *The Future of Ritual*. London: Routledge, 1993.

Schlereth, Thomas. *Cultural History and Material Culture: Everyday Life, Landscapes, Museums*. Ann Arbor: UMI Research Press, 1990.

Schmidt, Peter R., and Thomas C. Patterson, eds. *Making Alternative Histories: the Practice of Archaeology and History in Non-Western Settings*. Santa Fe, NM: School of American Research, 1995.

Slotkin, Richard. "The 'Wild West'." Pp. 27–44 in *Buffalo Bill and the Wild West*. Exhibition catalogue: no ed. given; The Brooklyn Museum and Buffalo Bill Historical Center, 1981.

Smith, Valene L. *Hosts and Guests: The Anthropology of Tourism*. Oxford: Basil Blackwell Ltd., 1977.

Smolenski, John. Review of *At the Crossroads: Indians and Empires on a Mid-Atlantic Frontier* by Jane Merritt. In *William & Mary Quarterly* 60, no.4 (2003); www.wm.edu/oieahc/wmq/Oct03/smolenski_Oct03.pdf, accessed March 6, 2006.

Snow, Stephen E. *Performing the Pilgrims: Ethnohistorical Role-Playing at Plimoth Plantation.* Jackson: University of Mississippi Press, 1993.

Stanley, Nick. *Being Ourselves for You: the Global Display of Cultures.* London: Middlesex University Press, 1998.

Stocking, George, ed., *Objects and Others: Essays on Museums and Material Culture.* Madison: University of Wisconsin Press, 1985.

Stronza, Amanda. "Anthropology of Tourism: Forging New Ground for Ecotourism and Other Alternatives." *Annals of Tourism Research* 30 (2001): 261–83.

Swain, Margaret Byrne. "Cuna Women and Ethnic Tourism: a Way to Persist and an Avenue to Change." Pp. 71–82 in *Hosts and Guests: the Anthropology of Tourism,* edited by Valene L. Smith. Oxford: Blackwells, 1977.

Task Force on Museums and First Peoples. *Turning the Page: Forging New Partnerships Between Museums and First Peoples.* Ottawa: Assembly of First Nations and Canadian Museums Association, 1992.

Taylor, C. J. "Some Early Problems of the Historic Sites and Monuments Board of Canada." *Canadian Historical Review* 44, no. 1 (1983): 3–24.

———. *Negotiating the Past: the Making of Canada's National Historic Parks and Sites.* Montreal: McGill-Queen's, 1990.

Taylor, C. J., and Michael Payne. "Animated Adventures in the Skin Trade: Interpreting the Fur Trade at Historic Sites." Paper presented at the Rupert's Land Research Centre Colloquium, Winnipeg, Manitoba, 1992.

Thompson, Judy, and Ingrid Kritsch. *Long Ago Sewing We Will Remember: the Story of the Gwich'in Traditional Caribou Skin Clothing Project.* Gatineau, Quebec: Canadian Museum of Civilization, 2005.

Tilden, Freeman. *Interpreting Our Heritage* (1957), 3rd ed. Chapel Hill: University of North Carolina Press, 1977.

Trask, Haunani-Kay. "Lovely Hula Hands: Corporate Tourism and the Prostitution of Hawaiian Culture." Pp. 136–47 in *From a Native Daughter: Colonialism and Sovereignty in Hawai'i,* by Haunani-Kay Trask. Honolulu: University of Hawai'i Press, 1999.

Trigger, Bruce A. "The Past as Power: Anthropology and the North American Indian." Pp. 49–74 in *Who Owns the Past?* edited by Isabel McBryde. Oxford: Oxford University Press, 1985.

———. *Children of Aataentsic: a History of the Huron People to 1660* (1976), 1st ed. Montreal: McGill-Queen's University Press, 1987.

Truettner, William H. "For Museum Audiences: the Morning of a New Day?" Pp. 28–46 in *Exhibiting Dilemmas: Issues of Representation at the Smithsonian,* edited by Amy Henderson and Adrienne L. Kaeppler. Washington, D.C.: Smithsonian Institution Press, 1997.

Tummon, Jeanie, and Sandra Saddy. *Sainte-Marie among the Hurons: Guidebook.* Toronto: Ministry of Culture, Tourism and Recreation, 1993.

Ulrich, Laurel Thatcher. *The Age of Homespun: Objects and Stories in the Creation of an American Myth*. New York: A. A. Knopf, 2001.

Urry, John. *The Tourist Gaze: Leisure and Travel in Contemporary Societies* (1990), 2nd ed. London: SAGE Publications, 2002.

van den Berghe, Pierre L. *The Quest for the Other: Ethnic Tourism in San Cristobal, Mexico*. Seattle: University of Washington Press, 1994.

van den Berghe, Pierre L., and Charles F. Keyes. "Introduction: Tourism and Recreated Ethnicity." *Annals of Tourism Research* 11 (1984): 343–52.

van den Berghe, Pierre L., and Georges Ochoa. "Tourism and Nativistic Ideology in Cuzco, Peru." *Annals of Tourism Research* 27, no. 1 (2000): 7–26.

Van Kirk, Sylvia. *Many Tender Ties: Women in Fur-Trade Society, 1670–1870*. Winnipeg: Watson & Dwyer, 1980.

Wallace, Michael. "Visiting the Past: History Museums in the USA." Pp. 184–99 in *Living History Reader Volume 1*, edited by Jay Anderson. Nashville: The American Association for State and Local History, 1991. Reprinted from *Radical History Review* 25 (1981): 63–96.

West, Patsy. *The Enduring Seminoles: from Alligator Wrestling to Ecotourism*. Gainesville: University Press of Florida, 1998.

White, Bruce. "Give Us a Little Milk: The Social and Cultural Meanings of Gift-Giving in the Lake Superior Fur Trade." *Minnesota History* 48, no. 2 (1982): 60–71.

———. "A Skilled Game of Exchange: Ojibway Fur Trade Protocol." *Minnesota History* 50, no. 6 (1987): 229–40.

White, Richard. *The Middle Ground: Indians, Empires and Republics in the Great Lakes Region, 1650–1815*. Cambridge University Press, 1991.

———. "Frederick Jackson Turner and Buffalo Bill." Pp. 7–66 in *The Frontier in American Culture*, edited by James Grossman. Berkeley: University of California Press, 1994.

Wilkins, Charles. "From the Hands of a Master: Freda McDonald Reaffirms Her Roots by Teaching Crafts in the Ojibwa Tradition." *Canadian Geographic* 114, no. 3 (May/June 1994): 64.

Wilson, Alexander. *The Culture of Nature: North American Landscape from Disney to the Exxon Valdez*. Cambridge: Blackwell, 1992.

Index

Aboriginal. *See* Native, Métis, "Indian"
Abram, Ruth, xxxii–xxxiii, 43, 178–79
acculturation, 64, 66, 103, 106
administration, xxiv, xxviii
advisory boards, site/museum, 50
agency: within historical accounts,
    xxxii, 50,131; of Native interpreters,
    64, 173; of Native people xx, xxi, 3,
    37, 45, 84, 102; and objects, 90–91
alcohol. *See* fur trade, and alcohol
American Revolution, 20, 99
Anishinaabeg (Anishinawbek). *See*
    Ojibwa
archaeology: archaeological resources,
    5, 9; archaeologists, 42; excavations,
    11, 21; historic reconstruction based
    on archaeological evidence, 21, 95;
    archival materials: and discrepancies
    with historic site reconstructions,
    xiii, xxi, xxvi, 107, 108; documents,
    6, 14; used by interpreters, xxv, 58,
    104, 173; photographs, 6; used for
    reconstruction, 9, 14, 36, 90;
    research program, 21
artifacts. *See* material culture
authenticity: 57, 65, 79, 86n24, 92–93,
    100, 109, 111n1; "authentic
    untruths", 104; and authority, 91, 92,
    104, 106, 109, 110. *See also*
    authority; and myth, 36, 38, 109,

130; of objects and reconstructions,
xxx, 3, 83, 89, 90, 91, 92–93, 100,
103, 107, 110; of representations,
xviii, xxi, xxxi, 31, 34, 64, 79, 82,
92, 99, 107, 110, 130, 175; and
tourism, xviii, xxxi, 54, 64–65, 77,
82, 109, 111n1, 119, 128, 130,
169–70; authority, xvii, xviii, xix,
xxi, xxx, xxxi, 44, 45, 48, 57, 65, 72,
91–92, 104, 110, 112n6, 139n1, 147,
151, 155, 165

Barnum, P. T., 62
Beeman, William O., 130
Binekwe (Mary Vanderpoel), 19
Blundell, Valda, 174
borderland, xxxi, 141; borderzone, 2,
    141–42, 164
Boyle, Peter, 15, 16
Brisson, Steve, ix, 23, 24, 137
British: as allies, 23, 73; British-
    Canadian, 10, 40; culture, 5, 40, 172;
    heritage industry, 111, 120, 157; law,
    13, 41; presence in North America,
    5, 20, 21, 23, 115; representations of,
    36, 172; soldiers/officers, 24, 69
Bruchac, Margaret, 85–86n17
Brunelle, Marie, 69, 71, 72, 86n18, 171
Bruner, Edward, xviii, xxx, 32, 53, 73,
    85n14, 91, 92, 93, 97, 106, 107, 110,

Wendat. *See* Huron

Wild West shows, 61, 62, 63. See *also* Buffalo Bill's Wild West Show and myths, of the frontier

Women, xv, 15, 32, 132, 159; interpreters, 7, 12, 14, 27, 72, 78, 93, 136, 159; Métis, 11, 14, 106; Native, xi, xxii, xxv, 2, 11–12, 14, 24, 33, 55, 59, 72, 73, 77, 78, 106, 115, 122, 132, 134, 136–37, 149–50, 156, 159, 160; settlers, 56, 59, 72, 78, 79, 91, 114,150; visitors, 136–37, 148

World's Fairs, xvi, xvii, 37–38, 60

Wyman, Audrey, 18, 55, 68, 72

About the Author

Laura Peers is a lecturer in the School of Anthropology and Museum Ethnography, curator at the Pitt Rivers Museum, and fellow of Linacre College, at the University of Oxford.